Just a Little

Just a Little

The Life of an Early Settler

Bert O'Flannnagan

***

Copyright © 2016 Bert O'Flannagan

The moral right of the author has been asserted.

All rights reserved.
No part of this publication may be reproduced, stored in a retrieval system, or transmitted, in any form or by any means, without the prior permission in writing of the publisher, nor be otherwise circulated in any form of binding or cover other than that in which it is published and without a similar condition including this condition being imposed on the subsequent purchaser.

Book Design and print management: Pickawoowoo Publishing Group

National Library of Australia Cataloguing-in-Publication entry
Creator: O'Flannagan, Bert, author.

Title: Just a little : the life of an early settler / Bert O'Flannagan.
ISBN: 9780994282729 (paperback)
Subjects: Immigrants–Western Australia.
Emigration and immigration.
Pioneers–Western Australia.
Agricultural colonies–Western Australia.
Western Australia–History–20th century.
Dewey Number: 305.906912

I have dedicated this book to my father's mother, my Granny. She was typical of those fearless and hardworking early settlers of those times. The hardships that all these settlers had to endure must have been horrendous, but the womenfolk had to put up with these hardships, and still raise a family. Remember they had no mod cons to make life comfortable, but these frontier ladies did what they had to do with no complaints. I salute my Granny and all the early settlers, especially the womenfolk.

To my wonderful wife, I thank you for putting up with the endless hours of my being in another world. A world where us writers are guided to release part of our inner self. This cannot happen without the support of our loved ones.

To our granddaughter Ashlee, thank you for all those hours of editing. If I have made any mistakes in naming the person or persons concerned in any of the incidents in this novel, then I humbly and sincerely apologize. I wrote from memory and it may be possible that I have gotten some names wrong. I have though, chosen to deliberately change some names, in some circumstances, for political reasons.

Foreword

Most of us as kids have probably had our parents tell us stories. A few lucky kids may have been told by one, or both their parents, how they came to this big country as early settlers. I consider myself to be one of these lucky few. Both my parents arrived as "ten pound poms," way back in the early nineteen hundreds, and my father, no doubt at my constant pleading, used to tell me stories almost every night, right up until I was a teenager, when it was then considered uncool to have stories told to you. These stories have somehow stayed in my memory bank, and now something is telling me to put pen to paper, and to try to live out what my mind is wanting me to release.

So with this book I have tried to do justice to, not only my parents, but to all of the early settlers who had to do it tough, and in so doing, helped make this country of ours what it is today. I know that all I have written is the truth, as told to me as a child.

Acknowledgments

To the first people to live in this place Australia, the Aborigines, I humbly acknowledge their part in history. They, the traditional owners of this great land, deserve this acknowledgement. So if in my writings I have offended their customs, or their spiritual ways, I humbly apologize. It has been with the deepest respect that I have tried to convey what my ancestors have passed onto me, and I believe what they have told me, is the truth as it happened to them.

I must acknowledge all the early settlers who's willingness to come to this country and have a go, inspired me to put pen to paper. These hard times, as told to me by my father, were indicative of the way things were them days.

I cannot name all of these pioneers, but a couple I must thank, are a wonderful happy pair of true Aussies. These two early settlers, who came out in the year nineteen twenty five, helped make our country what it is today. They are Mr and Mrs Kevin Flanagan of Northcliffe, where they still live happily today. My wife and I have visited them and had a good old fashioned cuppa with them. They told us many stories of those early days. When I asked Kevin if times were really tough back then, he simply said, 'yes, I suppose they were. But we didn't know any difference.' This is a typical answer from a man brought up in those days. They had to be tough to survive. Kevin Flanagan is pushing ninety, but he can still be seen most mornings jogging to the Northcliffe store to get his newspaper. As the pioneers of the early days were, the Flanagan's still are, wonderful hosts, and they make a good cup of tea. So thank you and bless you both. Their good nature and friendliness is carried on through their son Ray, who made himself known to my wife and myself, whilst we were holidaying and book writing, in a beautiful spot on the south coast of Western Australia. This quiet little holiday village is aptly named Peaceful Bay.

I acknowledge and respectfully mention the current day relatives of the late Charlie Burns. My father and the highly respected Mr Burns were good friends, and they shared many good times together. This man was lucky enough to be born with the rare, but amazing ability to be able to use what nature intended us to be able to use to its fullest. The human mind is the most amazing thing in the world. The average human brain has more electrical impulses in one day, than all the telephones in the world put together. Charlie Burns was obviously gifted, and my father learnt a lot from him. As a boy, I was fortunate enough to meet this wonderful Indigenous Australian. I salute your memory Charlie.

When looking for characters to acknowledge, it would be unjust and unkind not to give special accolades to the wonderful Schoolteacher Mrs Bunn. This lady was respected and loved by all the hundreds of children she taught. There are many relatives of this special lady, and I acknowledge them for me being able to mention her in this book.

The overall acknowledgement, I feel must go to my late father, who passed on to me the happenings in this book. I hope I have done justice to him, and all mentioned in this novel.

Contents

Prelude	1
Chapter One To Australia	2
Chapter Two Northcliffe	12
Chapter Three Becoming An Aussie	24
Chapter Four Hard Times	30
Chapter Five The Call of The Wild	40
Chapter Six Too Many Spirits	51
Chapter Seven Testing Times	65
Chapter Eight Gold Fever	72
Chapter Nine Not So Easy	81
Chapter Ten Sunshine	87
Chapter Eleven Peggy's Wedding	92
Chapter Twelve Gold In Your Veins	98
Chapter Thirteen Annie Gets A Gun	112
Chapter Fourteen There's Life In The Kimberley	127
Chapter Fifteen Wrong Chemistry?	147
Chapter Sixteen Never Again	155
Chapter Seventeen Go Blackie Go	159
Chapter Eighteen Not Again	165
Chapter Nineteen "Take Me"	171
Chapter Twenty Riots	178
Chapter Twenty One Beatrice	182
Chapter Twenty Two Life Is Good	186

Chapter Twenty Three What War Brings	189
Chapter Twenty Four Goodbye Farm	196
Chapter Twenty Five Life Goes On	202
Song Reference	225
Epilogue	226
Other Titles by Bert O'Flannagan	228
The Spirit of Ned	228

Prelude

WHO are we that have big comfortable houses, new motor cars, televisions, modern schools with computers, money in our pockets, and plenty of food? Who are we?

We are the prodigy of our forefathers and mothers who paved the way for us to be able to live as we do today. We do not know the feeling of having to leave families behind, as they had to, knowing that they would probably never see them again.

Not long after the end of the great-war, it was decided that Australia should be settled more, and the south west of Western Australia appealed as a good area for farming, and needed populating. So in conjunction with the Western Australian Government, and in particular, Premier James Mitchell, a new immigrant idea was formed. This idea was named the "Land Settlement Scheme." As a result, in the year nineteen twenty four, some three hundred and fifteen families left the mother country and were shipped to a tiny town named Northcliffe. The journey took about seven weeks, with a stop at the Canary Islands, where vendors boated fresh fruit and vegetables to the eager passengers. The ships also stopped at Cape Town for two days, and the passengers were allowed to disembark to explore this famous landmark.

Chapter One
To Australia

THE adventurous lad took one last look at the amazing view from the top of Table Top Mountain, then he slid down to where his friend Dave was waiting. Dave had just called out to Bill to hurry, because their ship sails at four o'clock. 'Don't worry old chap, we'll make it,' replied Bill, as he started running.

The two sixteen year old friends had taken a short cut to the top of this mountain, via a goat track, on the advice of a local stallholder. It had been Bill's idea to climb this famous landmark, but they had not told their parents of their plan. Now they not only looked likely to miss, or hold up their ship, but would be in trouble from their fathers.

It had been several weeks since their ship the "Ballarat" had left port with Bill and Dave's, and many other families. All these families were leaving the old country to start a new life in Australia under a new venture called "The Land Settlement Scheme." Each family that had signed up to this new venture had done so with the knowledge that they were leaving behind everything that they had ever known. Their whole lives, they knew was about to change. The emotions and sadness that they went through, when they had to say their last goodbyes to brothers and sisters, parents and grandparents, as well as friends and even pets, still played heavily on their minds. They knew they were never to again see these loved ones. Never would they again see the country of their birth.

These things though, were not on the minds of young Bill Evans and Dave Thomas as they raced down the track to try to board their ship. Bill could see that his friend was having trouble keeping up, so he slowed a little, to let Dave catch his breath. Then he said, 'you must keep up Dave. Just slowly increase your pace and lengthen your stride. That's it Dave, keep going.'

At last Bill could see the wharfs of Cape Town. Then the Ballarat came into view. 'Quick Dave, I can see them starting to raise the gangplanks.' Bill sprinted towards the ship, yelling at the top of his voice. Luck was with them, because the first mate noticed them running towards the waiting ship.

Both boys were relieved to hear this officer's voice. 'Lower the gangplank,' he ordered, and Bill knew that they had made it.

The officer of the day was waiting for them, and Bill knew he was in trouble. 'Get below you two. The Captain will deal with you later,' snarled the officer.

The two worried boys hurried down to deck three, where Dave waved to Bill as he headed to his parents cabin. Bill readied himself for the trouble he was in, and sure enough, as soon as he opened the cabin door of number 147, his father said loudly, 'where in the blazes have you been boy? Your mother has been worried clean out of her mind, and your sister is no better for the worry you have caused us.'

Before Bill could get a chance to explain, his mother rushed to him and said, 'thank God you're safe son. Come and sit with Peggy now, she's not doing too well.'

Thankful to be out of his father's reach for at least a while, Bill hurried to his sister's bedside. He caught his breath when he got close, as the smell of stale vomit was so strong. Peggy, Bill's younger sister, had been seasick for almost the whole journey since leaving England. Now, as the ship started to pull away from the wharf of Cape Town, South Africa, Bill looked at his sister, and he was shocked to see her condition had worsened badly in the last few hours.

Peggy must have sensed Bill was near, and she opened her eyes a little and forced a smile to her brother, to whom she was very close. Peggy tried to talk, but nothing came out. Bill hugged his pale lifeless sister, then turned to his parents Joe and Mary Evans, and asked if the ship's doctor had been to attend Peggy. When his father told him that the doctor had not been, Bill felt his blood begin to rise, then he said, 'I'll get the doctor one way or another,' as he pushed past his father and out the door.

Worried that his sister might die, he headed up through deck two, and was going to go up the steps into deck one, but barring his way was a big sailor who blocked his path. 'Where do you think you are going boy?'

Bill was in no mood to answer this man mountain, so he feinted to his left then ducked under the man's guard to the right then rushed up into deck one, where he immediately bumped into an important looking officer. 'Hang on young man, why are you in such a big hurry?'

Sensing that this officer might be a bit more helpful, Bill explained that his sister was near death, and that even though his family had asked several times to have the ships doctor attend her, no one had been near her. 'If my sister dies Sir, then I will not be responsible for my actions,' said Bill.

Luck was on the side of the young man, because this officer was one of the better and more experienced ones on the ship. 'Follow me lad, and we'll see what we can do.'

Bill was led towards a larger than normal cabin with a sign above the door saying, ''Captain Bronson". The polite officer told Bill to wait, then he went in and spoke to the Captain. After a few moments he was called inside, where an obviously important man, introduced himself, then asked him his name. 'Well, Bill Evans is it? I have a note here explaining that you and your friend were responsible for my ship being delayed today. But I will get to that later young man. Now my first mate has just informed me that your sister is very ill. Is this true?'

Before Bill could speak, the first mate came back with the doctor, and Captain Bronson turned his attention to him. 'Is it true Doctor Johnson that you have been notified of a Miss Evans being ill in deck three, yet you have not attended her?'

Bill was surprised at the tone in the captain's voice, and even more so when Doctor Johnson lowered his head and mumbled something like he was very busy with the upper deck passengers.

Captain Bronson stood up from behind his desk and glared at the ships doctor, then ordered him to take his assistant with him and go immediately to cabin 147 and tend to Miss Evans, and to make positive he continued to treat her until she was well. Bill watched as the doctor saluted the captain, then left to do as he was ordered.

Bill then started to leave also, but stopped when he heard the captain say, 'not so fast young man, I have not finished with you yet.'

So, when Captain Bronson pointed to a chair in front of his desk, Bill sat down, even though he wanted badly to get back to see his sister. Sensing this, Captain Bronson said, 'don't worry lad, the good doctor will look after your sister. Now Bill, about you're holding up my ship today?'

Bill quickly answered, 'I'm truly very sorry Sir. We just wanted to climb the famous Table Top Mountain, and time slipped away. I really am sorry Sir.'

The captain tried to hide his smile as he remembered how, when he was a lad of similar age to Bill, he held up a ship in much the same way in New Zealand. He did smile now as he told Bill not to do it again. 'I hope your sister is well again soon,' he said.

As Bill started to leave he said, 'thank you Sir, for your kind words, and thank you for allowing your doctor to help my sister.'

Captain Bronson then said to Bill, 'you know something young man, you reminded me of someone the minute I saw you. Now I remember. You're that young middleweight boxer who didn't show up for the final of the golden gloves contest in London. Picture in the paper and all. First time ever someone won the golden gloves without throwing a punch, the story said. Tell me Bill why did you not fight in that final? Everybody that knows anything about the game could see you were going to win. I mean, the golden gloves boy. Next step would have been a shot at the middle weight title of Great Britain. Why Bill?'

Bill's mind raced back to when he should have been getting ready to fight in that final. The final that his father did not know that he was in. Bill's father, for reasons not known, was against boxing, and did not know that his son was entered into the golden gloves championship. Joe Evans only found out that Bill was fighting on the very day of the final, in fact only three hours before the event was due to start. There had been no time to rearrange the fight, so Bill's opponent, who had duly shown up, was declared the winner by forfeit.

Bill at the time was at home, under the watchful eye of his father, who had refused to let him fight that night, and told him he was never to fight again. Now, looking directly at the Captain, a man who seemed to really want to help, Bill said, 'I am sorry I had to let down you, and the boxing game that I truly love, that night Sir.' He then asked to be excused, and headed back to his family's cabin.

The ship's doctor was still attending Peggy when Bill arrived back. All was quiet, until the doctor gave Peggy an injection, then he called Bill's parents aside and told them that he thought their daughter would be alright. He explained that he had given her fluid replacements, and the necessary medication to replace lost vitamins. 'I will call each morning,' he said.

After the doctor had left, Joe Evans turned to his son and said, 'I don't know what you done Bill, but your mother and I are proud of you.'

Bill was not used to getting praise from his father, so not sure of what to say, he just grinned and said playfully, 'does this mean I'm off the hook for holding up our ship then?'

Joe Evans then took a playful swipe at his son and told him that he hoped that he had learnt his lesson.

Peggy got better each day and it was not long before she was up and about. Her colour improved, and she was getting her appetite back, which made Mary Evans happy, because before she got sick from the ship's rolling, Peggy was a big eater, and Mary loved cooking for her family.

Time went fast for the Evans family, but they were all longing to get to Australia and their new life. Doctor Johnson did not need to call to attend to Peggy so much anymore, but on his last visit he told Bill that the Captain wished to see him, and was going to send for him soon. This caused some worrying times for the family, because they didn't want any trouble, especially now that Peggy was getting well.

It was only a few days later that the first mate came to number 147 and asked Bill to accompany him to see the Captain. Bill was shown into Captain Bronson's cabin, and was surprised when he got up and shook his hand. 'If you agree Bill, there's someone I'd like you to meet.'

So Bill followed the Captain and the first mate up through to the ship's deck, where a boxing ring was being used by someone that looked amazingly fit.

This man moved gracefully around the ring, throwing punches at shadows at such a speed it was hard to see his hands move. At the captain's invitation, Bill sat down and watched this master of boxing for several minutes, until Captain Bronson waved to the boxer to come over.

When the Captain introduced Bill, then said this man dressed in green silks and green singlet, was the former world champion, "The Real McCoy", Bill was not really surprised. He knew that this was no ordinary boxer. The two shook hands, and Bill said it was an honour to meet him. 'So Bill, the captain tells me you can box a bit?'

Bill was not sure how to answer this man he was in awe of, so he mumbled, 'just a little Sir.'

McCoy nodded then invited him to spar a few rounds. Eagerly Bill accepted the invitation, and in no time had put on a set of gloves that McCoy had there ready. The next twenty minutes were some of the best that this youngster from Buckinghamshire had ever enjoyed. Bill found that he could almost match the former world champion for speed, and even though he thought the older man was probably pulling his punches a bit, he was able ride the blows that McCoy landed. Afterwards they shared an orange drink, then talked for a few minutes, during which time Bill learnt that this boxer's name used to be "Kid McCoy", but after he had won the title in eighteen ninety six, when he fought as a welterweight, another boxer from Ireland started to call himself "Al McCoy". 'So that's when I changed my handle to "The Real McCoy", he explained to Bill.

Bill then asked him if he was an American. 'So you picked up on my accent did you lad?' asked McCoy.

They chatted for a little longer, then McCoy asked Bill if he would like to train each morning with him. Bill quickly accepted, then asked the Captain if would be alright, and if so, could he be allowed to bring his sister up on deck also, as the sunlight would be good for her health.

Captain Bronson gave his permission, and each morning after that, Bill and Peggy were escorted to the ship's deck for about an hour. Bill, knowing his father would probably not allow him to train for boxing, told his sister to support him when he told their parents that the reason they were going up to the deck was so Peggy could enjoy some sunshine. Mary Evans said she thought it was a very good idea. So it was decided, and the happy brother and sister both got healthier each day, and they were ready to go long before their escort arrived each morning.

As Bill got fitter, he found that he could in fact almost match it with McCoy, but each time he jabbed with his left, then followed up with his favourite right cross, which was aimed at McCoy's chin, a punch that had served him well in all his bouts in England, he found that McCoy would beat him to the punch, then would hit him with a right to the jaw. After a couple of weeks of this, Bill decided to ask McCoy what he was doing wrong. 'I would have told you earlier Bill,' the former champion said, 'but I was waiting for you to be humble enough to ask me.' He then explained to Bill that a humble learner is a good learner, and to reach the top in this game you must want to learn.

He went on to explain to Bill that his left hand lead was very good, with lots of power, which is also good if you only want it to be a one punch challenge. 'But,' he said, 'if you intend to follow up with your right cross, then I would suggest that you not put your full power into your left lead, but pull it a fraction short, and throw your right much quicker and with more power, and aim to hit your opponent on the point of his jaw. Also lad, as you withdraw your left, don't keep it so low, but bring it quickly up and across to cover your right jaw.' Bill thanked his mentor, and at McCoy's suggestion they finished training for the day.

That night, when Bill felt sure his parents were asleep, he practised what McCoy had told him. After about an hour he could do this two punch attack at top speed, and he could feel the power in his right cross because of the extra time and balance he had by pulling back a little on his left lead. That night Bill dreamt he was back in London fighting in the final of the "Golden Gloves" as he was meant to do a couple of months previous.

The next morning Bill was a little more tired than usual, 'probably because of the extra practice I did last night,' he thought.

Anyway, with Peggy alongside him, he followed the first mate up to the deck where he was surprised to see about fifty people seated around the ring. Captain Bronson met Bill and his sister, and after showing Peggy to a ring side seat, he helped Bill into the ring and as he started to help him put his gloves on, he explained that McCoy thought that it was about time to have a practise bout, and if it was alright, then he, Captain Bronson would act as Bill's second. 'Just five rounds Bill,' he said. 'Don't worry son, McCoy told me it will only be a demonstration bout and he won't go all out.'

Bill was a bit caught out and not sure of what to say, but before he really worked out that he was about to fight the best opponent he had ever had the opportunity of even seeing, the crowd which had increased as he was putting his gloves on, started clapping, then cheering loudly. Then along the ship's deck came a figure jogging and throwing air punches in all directions.

Unbeknown to Bill, the Captain had spread the word amongst the deck one passengers that there was to be a boxing match on this morning, and that the former world welter weight champion was the main attraction. As there was not a lot of entertainment on board the ship, most of the deck one passengers had come to watch this bout.

As Bill watched McCoy enter the ring, dressed in a sparkling hooded yellow gown, which he threw off to reveal green boxing shorts, and snow white sandshoes, he realised he was set up, and this was going to be a real fight. Bill glanced to where his sister was sitting, and he saw the worried look on her face, but before he could try to yell for her not to worry, McCoy was now dancing right in Bill's face, smiling as he said, 'sorry lad, but I have to earn my keep.'

Bill did not know that "The Real McCoy" was on the ship's payroll, and did this at least once on every trip that Captain Bronson's ship did.

From out of the crowd came a man dressed all in whites, who Bill thought was the referee, and he did not have to wait long to find out he was right. The man in white called the two boxers to the middle of the ring. Bill felt like he was in a sort of trance, still finding it hard to believe that he now had to fight the man who had been seemingly trying to help and train him. Then as the referee told the two boxers to go back to their corners, then come out fighting at the bell, McCoy out of the corner of his mouth said to Bill, 'I'm going to have to belt you lad.'

Still not sure that this was real, Bill was slow out of his corner. But not so McCoy, the more experienced man of over two hundred fights, charged straight at Bill and hit him at will with both hands.

Bill took plenty of punishment over the next two rounds, but it was not until the third round that McCoy's punches started to take its toll, and the crowd were now roaring encouragement to the former world champ. Until now Bill had hardly thrown a punch, such was the onslaught that McCoy had set upon him, and he knew that if he didn't do something soon he would be belted senseless.

Then he heard a voice bellowing louder than all the crowd noise, 'hang in there son. Cover up.' Bill thought he must be dreaming, but no, it was his father's voice he heard. He glanced over to where the voice came from, and he saw his father, standing on the outside of the ring, in the position where his second was meant to be. Bill's attention was only distracted for a brief second, but it was enough for McCoy to throw a knockout punch, which Bill somehow sensed was coming, and just in time he moved his head to the side. But it was not far enough, and he felt his legs turn to rubber, and his head turn black.

From somewhere far away, Bill could hear his father's voice telling him to get up. 'Come on son, you must get up.'

Bill shook his head, and staggered to his feet just as the referee counted to eight. 'Box on,' he heard the man in white say, and though his vision had not returned fully, he could see McCoy dancing his way across the ring. The much older man should have known from all his experience, not to get over confident, because this can make you drop your defence a bit, which he did.

The now forty two year old, was so enthralled in the crowd's encouragement that he actually gave a little victory wave as he moved in to finish off this brash young middleweight from mother England. McCoy had always thought that his American boxers were the best, and he held English boxers with a view of contempt. The small delay that McCoy caused by showing off to the crowd, was enough for Bill to regather himself, and he was ready. After hearing his father's voice, Bill was more confident, and instead of delivering what he thought was going to be the fight ending blow, McCoy walked straight into a left hook that Bill had put all his strength into.

The silence was deafening as they watched in disbelief as their hero fell face first into the canvas. The referee seemed to take a long time to start counting the former title holder out, but out he was. When the count got to seven, the timekeeper rang the bell to end the round. Joe Evans, upon hearing this bell, which was the only thing that had saved McCoy, jumped into the ring and told the referee that there was still thirty seconds left on the clock. 'End of round three,' the referee yelled as McCoy's second helped him to his corner.

Bill was hoping that the fight was over, but to his surprise, his father, who ushered him to his corner and sat him down on his stool, was acting as if he was enjoying himself immensely.

A bemused Bill, who by now had got his second wind, asked his father how he knew that there was a fight on. 'Don't worry about that now son,' said Joe Evans. 'Now listen.' Bills father quickly told him how he was not asleep the previous night when he was practising, and was impressed with his two punch attack. 'Don't forget to hold back your left lead and throw your right cross quickly, and keep your left up when you pull it back,' Joe told his son.

'Is that all Dad?' Bill was surprised that his father let him continue fighting on.

'No, that's not all. Don't use your double attack straight away, throw a couple of straight lefts first son, and don't hang back when the bell goes, get straight into him. You can do this Son.'

The break between rounds was obviously longer than usual, and the crowd started booing and calling out to McCoy to get on with the fight. Bill, who was on his feet and ready to start, was surprised to hear some of the crowd now barracking for him, instead of McCoy, as they all were before. Finally the bell was rung, and at his father's urging, Bill danced straight across the ring, and as he reached the middle, he could hear his sister Peggy's voice yelling him on, so his confidence grew, and he quickly jabbed out a left which McCoy took on his gloves.

Bill was feeling good and his head was clear, so he danced a little as if he was backing away from McCoy, then immediately went forward as fast as he could and threw another left jab which landed on the nose of the older boxer. Bill danced away again, then he feigned as if to throw another left, but stopped his punch and danced back a bit, but halfway through his backward movement he double stepped, then moved forward close to McCoy and led with his left, remembering to pull it a fraction short.

All Bill's practise came to fruition, because like he could in all the training sessions, McCoy thought he could easily hit this young lad with his right, because Bill always was slow with his right, and kept his left glove too low to protect himself.

But this did not happen today. Bill was very fast with his right cross, so fast in fact, that it would not have mattered if he didn't get his left glove up, because the right cross that Bill hit McCoy plumb on the point of his jaw with, contained all his body weight behind it. This time McCoy did not get up from the canvas, and the disgruntled home chosen referee had no choice but to raise Bill's glove, acknowledging him the winner.

The silence which had been on the ship's deck, because of the surprise turn around in the fight, was broken by firstly Peggy Evans. 'Good on you Bill,' she yelled.

Then the roar was deafening, as the whole crowd rose to their feet and applauded the young Boxer who had beaten the odds. Odds that were deliberately stacked in favour of McCoy, by Captain Bronson.

Joe Evans walked to his son, who was trying to help the still groggy McCoy to his feet, and said 'leave him son, we're going.'

Bill, as he had be taught, wanted to shake hands with his opponent. Even though he did feel he had been used, and tricked, into giving the richer top deck passengers some entertainment, Bill still tried to shake McCoy's hand, but did not succeed as the ship's Captain got in the way in his hurry to see if his boxer was alright. Captain Bronson did not even acknowledge Bill, or his father, who after going to Peggy to escort her, headed through the still applauding crowd, and back to their cabin.

Mary Evans was waiting patiently, not yet knowing what had happened, and as soon as she saw that Bill was alright, she smiled and said, 'good boy.' Joe Evans hugged his wife of eighteen years, and smiled at her, knowing very well that she did not really care whether her son won or lost, as long as he was unhurt. Joe Evans did not mention the fight or say anything about that day again, but he did say to his son, 'there will be no more top deck going for you from now on Bill.'

So after that, Bill never did see either "The Real McCoy," or Captain Bronson for the rest of the journey. He and Peggy missed the sunlight that they had grown to enjoy up on top deck, and Bill missed his training, but each morning he would do about an hour of stretches and push ups in the family cabin.

There was not much excitement for the rest of the journey. The weather remained calm, and their ship, the "Ballarat" made good time, and in fact arrived nearly two days earlier than expected at Fremantle, Western Australia. The Evans family were packed and ready to disembark, and as soon as the gangplank was let down, they were amongst the first group to leave the ship.

Chapter Two
Northcliffe

As they put foot on Australian soil for the first time, the Evans family were directed to a section marked Northcliffe Settlers. Bill spied his friend Dave Thomas heading off with his family to their section, so he ran over and wished him well, and said goodbye. Bill felt a little strange knowing that he may never see his childhood friend again. The Thomas family were heading to the wheat belt town of Corrigin, to start their new lives as farmers under the "Land Settlement Scheme." Bill then had to run to catch up with his family, who were signing the necessary customs papers.

Some families were to stay overnight in accommodation provided at Fremantle, but Joe Evans decided to take the choice of boarding the first train heading south to their new adventure. Bill enjoyed the trip to Perth in a motor charabanc, which delivered them to the Wellington street station where a steam train was waiting. Peggy loved trains, and was excited all the journey, passing through many towns on the way.

When the train made its customary stop at Pinjarra, which was a small town on a river called the Murray, Bill's father gave him some coins to buy a pie for each of them. 'I would like tomato sauce with my pie,' Peggy told Bill.

As Bill was walking to the station canteen, he noticed several dark skinned people sitting in a group around a small fire. Bill had read about the Australian Aborigines at school, but this was his first sighting of them. Being inquisitive by nature, he walked closer to the group, who did not seem to take any notice of him, so he said hello, but no one spoke back to him. 'Better you leave them alone,' came the voice of the train's guard, who had been watching.

Bill said, 'I didn't mean them any harm,' as he walked back to buy four pies with tomato sauce, and some tea for his mother and father.

The rest of the trip to this timber mill town of Pemberton, was uneventful, though Bill was, as were all the settlers on the train, amazed at the size of the huge Karri trees, which grew to seemingly hundreds of feet high. The bark on these massive tree was almost white, and Peggy Evans in particular, was so impressed that she ran to the nearest tree and rubbed her hands over it. 'My, what a magnificent thing you are. I am going to name you Kenneth, after my uncle in England,' she said.

Bill knew he should not, but he was so taken with his sister's apparent liking for this tree, that he got out his pocket knife and carved this name into the thick bark. When he had finished, and was admiring his handiwork, his father, who unbeknown to Bill, had been watching, said to his son, 'let that be the last time you harm such a wonderful specimen of nature my boy.'

The young man was humbled and sorry that he had cut into the tree, and he made a silent promise that he would take his father's advice from now on. Little did Bill know that both he and his father would one day have to really harm many of these magnificent trees?

Pemberton, which was a small timber milling town, was the end of the rail line. So the group of eager families, had to be taken the last nearly twenty miles to Northcliffe by good old horse and carriage. These carriages were pulled by what Australians called draft horses. There were two of these very large, but quiet and placid animals to each carriage. Bill sat up next to the driver, a middle aged man who constantly chewed tobacco. 'Helps keep the horses calm,' he told Bill.

At first Bill did not know how to take this driver, but after a short time he got used to his dry humour, a humour that included the occasional equally dry joke. After introducing himself as Sean, and learning that the young man's name, the driver said, 'well Evans, I suppose you like this game of cricket that everyone seems to be playing?'

Bill explained that he did enjoy playing cricket at school, and he was going to say more, but Sean quickly said, 'did you hear about the first cricket match played in Ireland that they had to abandon?' Bill shook his head, so Sean went on, 'they had to abandon the match alright, because both teams turned up wearing the same colours.'

This brought some laughter from a few people in the carriage, which inspired the driver on. 'Here Evans, you drive for a bit,' he said handing the reins to Bill. 'Just hold the reins loose lad, the horses know the way.'

Sean laughed as he turned to face the several families that were jammed into his carriage. First he asked if anyone knew the words to Waltzing Matilda, and as everyone shook their head, he told them about the swagman, who is what the English call a tramp. 'This swagman,' he said, 'for reasons unknown, had been camping next to a billabong, or waterhole, when this here jumbuck, or sheep, comes down for a drink.' Sean, who had taken no notice of how Bill was doing at driving his horses, continued, telling the now avid settlers how this swagman, being a bit hungry, grabs this jumbuck and is stuffing it into his tuckerbag, when along comes some troopers and catches him in the act.

Everyone is now keenly listening to this storyteller, who goes on to explain that the punishment for stealing livestock here in Australia is very severe, 'been known to be hung for this you know,' Sean says as he is enjoying the attention. 'So what does this poor hungry swaggie do? Why he jumps fair into the billabong and drowns.'

By now even Bill was listening intently as Sean, who has pulled his old army hat even tighter on his head, carries on to explain that a chap by the name of Banjo Patterson had written a poem about this happening, which took place in outback Queensland, near a town named Winton. He then explained that this poem has been turned into a song and is recognised by many Australians as their national anthem. 'So,' said Sean, 'would any of you like me to have a go at singing this song then?'

Most of the people either nodded or said they would, so from under his seat this happy story teller, who Bill sensed had done this very thing many times before, produced a battered old guitar and sang his rendition of Waltzing Matilda. Hands soon started clapping, and as Sean got to the chorus the second time, a few people started singing along. Then as the time went on, and this happy group of settlers got closer to their future farms, everyone on the wagon sang this song with the driver that they only ever got to know as Sean. They never tired of this new to them, Aussie ballad that had been a saviour to so many Australian soldiers during the Great War.

Bill felt a strange feeling take hold of his very soul. A feeling of sort of belonging. 'Yes,' that was it he thought, 'a feeling of belonging.'

Bill had read how Australians, or Aussies, as they liked to be called, had developed this rich feeling that had built up with time and happenings over the years since colonisation of this relatively new country in the year seventeen eighty eight. When Bill's father had first discussed with his family about going to Australia, Bill had gone out of his way to learn as much as he could about this country and its history. He remembered reading about a man named Peter Lalor and the Eureka stockade. He learnt how this young country had come to England's aid during the Boer war, and then again in the terrible war of nineteen fourteen to eighteen. Many stories of bravery by Australian Soldiers have been told and re-told, especially about the Anzacs at Gallipoli. Also a Soldier named Simpson, who with his donkey, saved hundreds of wounded men.

He had also been enthralled by the story of Ned Kelly and the Kelly gang, who had been on the run for nearly three years before they had a shootout with Police at a town named Glenrowan in Victoria. The gang had been dressed in bullet proof armour when they faced the police. He also remembered reading how Ned Kelly had been captured and hung, and that there was some speculation that his brother may have escaped. History shows that many thousands of Kelly sympathisers signed a petition asking for Ned's death sentence to be overturned.

Bill was snapped out of his daydreaming or remembering's by the sudden stop in the group's singing, and hearing the driver Sean yelling, 'we have arrived in Northcliffe good people.' Bill, realizing that he was still holding the reins to the horses, passed them to Sean, who nodded to him and said, 'thanks Evans, nice driving lad.'

Northcliffe was such a small place that it prompted Bill's mother to say to her family, 'it could hardly be called a town. Why it's hardly a village, but I like it.'

A few houses lined a single road with a general store as the main, in fact only shop in the quaint little place. This shop had a big sign across the front saying, "NORTH-CLIFFE STORES LTD."

The storekeeper was obviously also some sort of government agent, because he guided all the settlers into a front room of his store, where they were served hot tea and some delicious fruit cake. He asked each of the settlers to sign a form, then informed them that their luggage was being transferred to a different set of wagons which would take them to their blocks. He then suggested that they probably should purchase enough food and supplies now, while they had the chance. Bill's mother, and his sister Peggy, really enjoyed the opportunity, and after buying a tea chest from the storekeeper, they almost filled it with what they reckoned that the family would need to see them through for about a week.

They did not have to wait long in Northcliffe before they were taken to their respective future farms, or blocks, as the "Land Settlement Scheme" officially called them. There were still plenty of Peggy's favourite karri trees in and around the small town, but as they headed along a road, or more like a track, which did have a small sign saying that it was Richardson road, Bill noticed that there were not quite as many of these giant trees. By the time they had reached their "block", the trees had given way to mostly scrub, with the occasional jarrah or peppermint tree. Bill felt disappointed, because he had learnt at school that where no big trees grew, the soil was not all that good.

Joe Evans jumped down from the wagon, and after helping his tired wife down, and seeing that his son had helped Peggy down also, walked to where a sign showed that this was their block. It seemed to Bill a very long time before his usually mild tempered father, who was obviously the leader of this family said, 'how does anyone expect us to make a living or to even survive out here. Look at this soil, just hungry sand. Good for growing nothing,' he yelled.

The driver of the wagon, a little nervous of this obviously irate Joe Evans, quickly started unloading the meagre luggage belonging to the Evans family. Then as he quietly picked up the last bundle to be stacked, he said, 'Mr Evans, there is a tent, some blankets, cooking utensils and some farm equipment here. If you would kindly sign the acceptance form I'll be on my way. I'll be back tomorrow with more gear for you mate.'

Bill watched as his father did sign the form, and the driver, who had called his father ''mate'', left them standing on this nearly two hundred acre farm, which as his father had correctly described it, was hungry sand. Bill walked over to look at the farm tools that the driver had unloaded and saw there was an axe, a crowbar, a shovel, and a set of wire strainers. Bill then looked more closely at their new farm and said, 'mind if I take a walk around Dad?'

His father, who had calmed down a bit by now, told Bill that as it was going to be dark soon that they should be setting up their camp. 'You can have a good look around in the morning Son,' he said. Joe Evans organized his family so that they could get some sort of comfort for the first night here on the place that they had been dreaming was going to be their new and successful life. Bill was given the job of helping his father erect the tent while Peggy was to collect some firewood, then help her mother prepare a meal.

All was going according to Joe's plan, until the three Evans at the designated home site, heard a frightened scream from the scrub where they knew young Peggy had headed.

Peggy was standing dead still, when the three ran to where they had heard her screams were coming from, and there she was pointing to the ground. 'Snake,' she managed to get out.

Bill, who had looked at pictures of Australian wildlife, broke in to uncontrollable laughter, saying to his sister, 'it's only a small goanna Peggy.'

Joe Evans, who was about to strike this reptile a killing blow with a long stick, asked Bill if he was sure it was not a snake. Bill explained that there were actually many deadly snakes here in Australia, but he assured them that this was definitely a goanna. 'A blue tonged lizard, or bobtail, so I learnt at school,' he said, still smiling.

Then they all got another fright. Someone was laughing at them, but the laughter was coming from a tree top. This time it was Peggy's fathers turn to be embarrassed, because he truly believed that the laughing came from a person. Then when more laughter came from another direction, he called out to these people who he thought were laughing at them, 'what are you laughing at?'

Bill was deceived for a moment, but then he said, 'they're Kookaburras Dad. It's only a group of laughing birds.' He had seen pictures of these Kookaburras, but until now, like his family had never heard their almost human sounding laugh.

All went well after that, and the Evans family did have a meal, and did spend their first night in a tent. They had first chatted around the nice warm fire that Bill had helped the still frightened Peggy build, then after a bit of a sing song, which was often their custom back in the old country, sleep came easy to them all after such a tiring few days.

Bill was the first to be woken by a terrible howling just outside their tent in the middle of the night. Shaking his father awake, Bill said in a worried voice, 'quick Dad, someone's getting murdered outside our tent.'

Joe Evans jumped up and sure enough there was a horrible howling outside. So grabbing a torch, and a tent pole that had somehow been left over when the tent was erected, he ventured slowly out into the dark night. Shining his torch around, he saw about a dozen sets of eyes reflecting the torch light. Joe was dumbfounded. 'Aborigines,' he thought, 'who else could they be?' Surely not in the year of nineteen twenty four could there still be conflict between the original land owners and settlers. Joe Evans had had discussions with his son about this. Bill had learnt at school of the early fighting between the early settlers and the Aboriginals, but that was long ago. 'No,' thought Joe, 'it must be animals.'

Then just as he was going to venture closer, there came an almighty bashing and clanging of metal on metal, which was then followed by Bill's loud yelling. 'What are you doing?' asked Bill's father.

Bill said, 'just scaring away the dingoes.' He had remembered reading about them, and how they scavenged around homes and camp sites looking for food. Bill's noise trick worked to some extent, but the dingoes, even though they were frightened away from the Evans campsite by Bill's banging together of two saucepans, kept up their awful howling through the rest of the night.

Early the next morning, when he heard his father get up, Bill followed him outside, and they looked around their tent and campfire area. Sure enough, there were lots of dog size tracks all around in the sand. 'They have been here alright,' Joe Evans told his son.

Bill's father suggested that they look over their new farm before breakfast. They did, and were happily surprised to find that a hundred yards or so from where they had set up camp, there was about five acres of low, almost swampy country. Bill agreed with his father when he suggested that this low ground might be good country to sow some strawberry or white clover for summer feed for their livestock. The father and son were a bit more pleased with the prospects of making some sort of living now that some of the soil looked better. 'We should be able to grow potatoes here,' said Joe.

Mary Evans smiled to herself when she heard them chatting away to each other about fencing and cattle and stuff she didn't know a lot about. She was pleased to hear them a bit happier than last evening when they first saw their new farm. 'Breakfast is nearly ready men,' she called to them as they got closer.

A few of the other group settlers, some of them actually adjoining the Evans block, called to see them that morning. They also were awoken by dingoes, and were not too sure what to do about them as they did not get a lot of sleep. One chap, who introduced himself as David Pitt, said that he thought they were going to be battling to make a go of it here in this sand.

The same driver that brought them to their farm the previous day, arrived that afternoon with some more supplies and some galvanised iron, timber, and nails, fencing wire and staples. Then to Mary Evans delight, they unloaded a wood stove with an oven. Bill then ran to the back of the wagon, and there was a beautiful Jersey milking cow, with a calf at foot. Bill had been hoping they would get a Jersey, because they were well known to produce plenty of cream, which he loved on bread and plum jam. 'Daisy, that's what we'll name you,' said Bill as he untied her from the wagon.

Joe Evans smiled with farmers pride as Bill led Daisy to some scrub to tie her up. 'Better use some of this new material and build a shed for her son,' he told Bill.

The rest of Bill's day was taken with building Daisy and her small calf a home. Peggy, who had fallen in love with the calf, helped her brother build this timber and galvanised iron shed, which they made a separate bay in for hand milking Daisy and the future cows that their farm was allocated.

Joe Evans had earlier discussed with the driver, the problem of the dingoes, and on his advice had gone back to the Northcliffe store to purchase what this driver, who had finally introduced himself as Neil Brooks, had advised him that should solve their dingo problem. So on the second evening that they settled down in their tents, it was not long before the howling of dingoes was again heard.

Bill, his mother and Peggy, stood back to allow Joe Evans out of the tent to where the dingoes were in a pack only about twenty yards from their tent. 'Quick son, bring the torch,' Joe whispered to Bill.

Torch in hand, Bill ventured out and shone the light directly at the noisy animals, and as soon as he seen them, Bill was taken aback with their splendour and the proud way that they seemed to be howling, as if saying 'this is our land.' Bill's mood was soon broken though by the loudest bang he had ever heard, then followed another equally as loud blast that seemed so close to the first one that Bill was not real sure whether there were two shots or one. The shock of these shots from the double barrelled twelve gauge shotgun that his father had gone to Northcliffe to buy yesterday, made Bill drop his torch. 'Hurry up lad,' his surprisingly calm father called to Bill, who reacted quickly to his father's instructions and re-shone the torch to where the dingoes were last seen.

There was no sign of the pack anymore, but lying dead were two of them. Bill gave light while his father roughly tied the two shot dingoes to a small tree not far from their tent. 'I don't think we'll see the pack again,' said Joe Evans.

The storekeeper had advised Joe to string up a dingo or two, as this usually scared other wild dogs away. He was right, and the family had a good sleep that night, and for several more nights, and when the dingoes did start their howling again, it only took one shot into the air to scare them away.

The next week or so went fast for the family, as there was plenty for them to do. Each morning before breakfast, Bill would lead Daisy and her calf out of the shed and into the adjoining milking bay, where he milked her into a bucket. This milk was plenty enough for the family each day, and there was usually enough left for Bill to leave to set overnight. Then the next morning there would be about an inch of cream on the top. Bill would then scoop this cream off and into another dish so the family could spread some onto bread and jam, or onto an apple pie that Bill's mother cooked in her stove. When he had finished milking his cow, Bill would tether her to a stake in the ground in a grassy area so she could feed. Daisy never let all her milk down, saving enough for her calf to suckle.

After breakfast Bill would help his father with the task of fencing their block. Bill's father discussed the fencing plan with him, and they decided to firstly fence off an area of about twenty acres where their house was to be built, then they would fence the entire farm and divide the place up into six paddocks later. Each day the two men would cease fencing about two or three o'clock, then move to the task of building their home from the materials delivered by Neil Brooks. Bill's father had planned to only build a three roomed house, but gave in to his wife's wishes of three bedrooms, and a kitchen. There was no thought given to including a lounge room as materials and money were a bit in short supply.

The first thing that was built though, was an outhouse, or toilet, then a wash-house along next to it. This was hard tiring work, and the men were exhausted by nightfall. So after a wash and their evening meal that Mary and Peggy had prepared, the only thing they wanted to do was go to sleep.

Peggy would often come and help Bill and his father with the house building, and she soon started getting up earlier so she could help Bill with the milking. After a few days Peggy could milk Daisy on her own.

After a week or so, Joe Evans decided to take his wife and daughter to town to replenish their food supplies. Also he wanted find out when the rest of their cattle, and the two horses he had asked for, would be delivered. Bill's father had asked him to stay back and look after the place, to which he was happy to do, as he was nearly finished fencing off the twenty acres around the house site. Bill knew that when this paddock was finished, he could let Daisy roam around during the day, and he would no longer have to tether his cow up. Bill did make sure that he locked both Daisy and her calf in the shed each night, because he was worried that the dingos might attack them.

With the rest of the family gone, Bill got busy with his fencing right away. 'Don't know if I'll be able to finish this fence today,' he said out loud to himself.

Bill got a heck of a fright when from right behind him came a voice saying, 'well then, maybe I better help you finish it brother.' Bill dropped the shovel he was using, and as he spun around there smiling at him was the blackest man that he had ever seen.

More surprised than frightened, Bill was a little slow in talking, so the stranger, who Bill realized was an Aborigine, said, 'well do you want a hand to finish this fence or not? Or are you just going to stand there and wonder who this blackfella is, and what is he doing on a white man's property?'

Bill saw that this very fit looking man, who he reckoned was about ten years older than himself, was smiling and obviously meaning no harm. So he said back with his best smile, 'I reckon I could use a bit of a hand mate.'

The friendly local then said, 'you call me mate? White fellas don't call us people mate you know. Mostly we don't get spoken to, or if we do, we usually just get yelled at. How come you're different?'

Bill then told him how he had heard the driver of the wagon call his father mate, and he thought it meant friend or something like that. Now this stranger went quiet for a moment, then asked Bill that if he knew that mate meant friend, and he could see that this here man is as black as the ace of spades, why did he accept him as a friend?

Sensing that the mood was changing, and that this proud man was serious, Bill put out his hand and said, 'my name is Bill. Bill Evans, and I would be more than pleased if you will join me in a cup of tea and some bread and jam, with cream as thick as hell on top.'

The invitation was accepted, and the two men headed towards the Evans family's campsite where Bill made ready the offered food and drink for them. 'I suppose you don't want to know my name do you Bill,' asked the young man. Bill told him that he would like to hear his name, but it was up to him to offer it. 'Mostly the people don't care enough about us blackfellas to want to call us by our name, but you sure seem not too bad. So I'll tell you my name that has been used in this now white man's world.' Putting out his hand for Bill to shake if he wanted to, he told the confused young man from England that his name was Charlie Burns.

Bill said that he was pleased to meet him, and accepted Charlie's handshake, which started in the normal fashion, but as Bill was about to withdraw his hand, Charlie moved his hand a little higher, and still clasping Bill's hand, he sort of interlocked their hands with mainly their thumbs making the grip or shake. Bill was a bit surprised at this new handshake, but was even more surprised when his new friend said, 'Gooday mate. Let's go and do this fencing, and thanks for the tucker mate.'

So with a new friend as an offsider, Bill finished the house paddock before his family returned back from Northcliffe. Charlie left as soon as the fence was finished, saying to Bill as he went, 'your folks are nearly home, so I'll see you later.' Then he was gone, as silently as he had arrived several hours before.

Bill then went to the corner of their farm to greet his family, but could not see them, so he started walking along Richardson road towards town. He was sure that Charlie had told him that his family was nearly home, but he knew his new friend could not have possibly seen them, so how did he know?

After walking about half a mile, Bill then saw his father and mother, and Peggy trudging towards him, so he met them, and helped carry some of the supplies home. After unpacking the food and more nails and staples, Bills father informed him that their cattle and horses would be arriving in two weeks, and the next day should see more fencing wire and posts delivered.

So the family worked hard from daylight till dark, and just as well, because no sooner had they completed erecting the boundary fence, when Bill was pleased to see Sean, the driver who had delivered the group from Pemberton to Northcliffe a few weeks earlier, driving not a wagon this time, but twenty six milking cows and two horses. Sean who was riding a chestnut gelding, pulled his hat back and said to Bill, 'Gooday Evans. Where do you want this here livestock then?'

Bill's father, who had seen his livestock coming, had already opened the main gate into the newly fenced farm, yelled to Sean to drive them through. Sean had driven these cattle and horses single handed from Pemberton, a distance of twenty odd mile, in just two days, and was now completely exhausted, but had been determined to finish the delivery for the Evans family.

As soon as the livestock were safely inside the big paddock, and the gate shut, Sean asked Bill's father if he could put his bedroll under a tree and have a nap.

Apparently the poor man had not slept for over two days. Normally a drive like the one that Sean had done by himself, was a two or three man job, as one drover had to be alert, even at night to keep the livestock together and to look out for dingoes. This would then allow sleeping shifts so some rest could be taken. Joe Evans, who, like his son, had taken a liking to Sean, agreed immediately to Sean's request, telling him to lay his bedroll anywhere he liked, suggesting that closer to their camp might be better, as it was near nightfall and the nights were starting to get cold. The exhausted drover slept close to the Evans family's fire that night, and did not wake up until he smelt Bill's mother cooking bacon and eggs the next morning.

After a hearty breakfast, Sean asked the family if they knew anyone who might be interested in a job for the next couple of months, helping him drive the livestock from Pemberton to all the group settlers here in Northcliffe.

Bill pricked his ears at this, and spoke with his father earnestly for several minutes. Bill's father then quizzed Sean, asking him about supplies, wages and who was to make the payments. Sean explained that he had been given the contract to deliver all the livestock, and he would pay whoever worked for him after every drive. 'Two shillings a day, cash in hand when the livestock are in the settler's paddocks, all tucker supplied,' he said. 'If you can start today Evans,' he said to Bill, 'then all you will need is a horse, and that black stallion that I brought you today looks a good one. Plus of course a bedroll, and a rifle to keep the dingoes away. Jobs yours if you want it Evans.'

Bill was excited and really wanted the job, so he looked at his father, who smiled and said, 'we're going to miss you boy.'

The next hour was a mad rush at the Evans farm. Firstly Bill took the saddle and bridle that they had delivered before, and went to the stallion to saddle him up. Sean came with Bill and said that he doesn't know if anyone had ridden this horse yet, 'so you had better watch him Evans,' he said.

Bill had done a lot of riding and horse handling back home, and was confident he could handle this big black stallion. He did have some trouble catching him though, until Peggy brought over a carrot, which turned out to be this fine animal's favourite treat. 'There you are Blackie,' Peggy said softly to him. She continued to talk softly to Blackie, as she called him, and stroked his head while Bill put firstly the bridle, then the saddle on him.

Everyone held their breath as Bill mounted Blackie, and it looked as though it was going to be easy, but as soon as Peggy stopped talking to him, he turned into a crazy thing. 'No way was anyone going to ride me,' he must have thought, because he bucked and weaved all over the place, and it was not long before Bill was lying face down in the dust.

Joe Evans laughed out loud and said, 'better I break him in for you son.' Now Bill's father had ridden many horses, and was considered to be an elite horseman, but as soon as he sat in the saddle, Blackie threw him straight out again.

Bill had to control himself so he would not laugh at his father, who picked himself up from the dirt and said to all the smiling onlookers, 'I reckon that saddle is a bit too small for me son.'

Then Bill walked over to his horse, and grabbing the reins said, 'yes Dad, you could be right. But I think it's just about the right size for me.' Then he realized that the horse seemed to like carrots, so he promptly said, 'Peggy, more carrot please.' He was right, for as soon as Peggy fed this wild animal some carrot, Bill slowly got into the saddle. He sat quietly while his sister stroked and fed Blackie.

Bill asked Peggy to keep up the good work, but to slowly start leading the horse around. This worked, and after several minutes of Peggy's leading, Bill said, 'good work Peggy. Now slowly walk away please.' Sure enough Blackie had calmed down, and never again did this big horse attempt to throw Bill out of the saddle.

So with a packed a bedroll, a stockwhip, and a sugar bag of food that his mother packed for him, Bill said goodbye to his mother and sister, then turned to his father, who looked his son square in the eye and told him to take care. Joe Evans then gave his son a hug, something he rarely did, then passed Bill a five pound note, saying it was for him to buy the Lithgow single shot rifle that he had seen in the Northcliffe store. He told Bill to buy a hundred rounds of ammunition and a bullet belt, and to get the storekeeper to show him how to use the rifle safely. Bill thanked his father and told him that he would pay him back from the money he was going to earn.

He then went to join Sean, who was waiting at the gate, but was stopped by his sister, who ran over and gave him a few carrots, saying that they were for his horse. 'Please name him Blackie will you Bill, and take care my brother.' Bill leaned down from his saddle and kissed his young sister goodbye.

Then with a final wave, Bill Evans rode off on his first away from family adventure in this, his new country.

Chapter Three
Becoming An Aussie

By the time Bill, who was riding his Blackie very carefully, and his new boss reached the Northcliffe store, the two drovers were talking like long lost brothers. Sean, at Bill's request, came into the store and helped check over the rifle that Bill's father told him to buy. 'Best rifle you can buy,' said the storekeeper. He then took Bill out the back and showed him how to load and shoot correctly.

Sean then fired a few shots at a target, then adjusted the sights a bit. 'Shoots a little to the left and a little high,' he told Bill.

After about a dozen or so shots, Bill had just about mastered the task of shooting his new rifle. Most of his last six shots hit the target near the middle, and Sean told him he was a natural.

Sean had left his pack horse at the storekeeper's stockyards while he had delivered the cattle and horses to the Evans farm, and now they loaded this spare horse with enough supplies for the job of droving the next group settler's stock from Pemberton to Northcliffe.

When Sean was satisfied that they had everything they needed, the two of them rode off towards Pemberton. Bill had found that he had enough money to buy a saddle scabbard for his rifle, plus a bullet bandolier and three hundred bullets, and as there was still some money left, he bought an eight inch Bowie knife complete with pouch and belt.

Sean told Bill that the small felt cap that he was wearing, was not good enough for the job at hand, so he bought him a second hand "diggers" hat as a present. Now as they cantered their horses along the track, Sean said to his new drover, 'now you are starting to look like an Aussie, Evans.'

They had not gone more than a couple of miles, when Sean quickly pulled his mount off the track and into some thick scrub, and motioned for Bill to do the same. Sean pulled his rifle from its scabbard, and waited behind the scrub, looking intently back along the track that they had just ridden.

It was not long before a man came into view, so Sean urged his horse out from behind the scrub, and pointing his rifle at the man, who Bill could see was running at an easy loping jog that seemed to eat up the ground so that he was going at a similar pace that the horses had been cantering. Bill was worried that his boss was about to shoot this man, so he yelled, 'don't shoot. It's my friend Charlie Burns.'

Sure enough, it was the dark skinned Charlie, who had befriended Bill and had helped with some fencing. 'Well then young Burns, why are you tailing us?,' asked Sean, still with his rifle at the ready.

Charlie Burns gave one of his best smiles, and said that he did not have much to do, so he thought that he might offer his services as a number three drover. 'Well that's mighty kind of you Burns, but how do you think you are going to get to Pemberton and back? I can't see any horse under you lad,' said Sean as he re-holstered his rifle.

Bill told his boss that Charlie could ride on Blackie behind him, but Charlie laughed and said to both of the horse riders that there hasn't been a horse born that he could not outlast. 'You telling us that you can run to Pemberton, then drive stock back to Northcliffe?' Sean quizzed Charlie.

The young Aborigine said, 'don't reckon it boss, I know it, Mr Sean.'

It was obvious that Charlie was very fit, so Sean said, 'well you know what Burns? I think you just might be able to at that, but don't call me Mr, or boss again, okay?'

Charlie, sensing that he may have a job with his friend Bill, said, 'well what I going to call you then?'

Sean pushed his hat back, and said, 'I reckon you can call me anything you like Burns, but don't call me late for breakfast.'

Both Bill and Charlie laughed along with this jovial drover, and then Bills estimate of his boss went up a notch when Sean leant over, and shaking Charlie by the hand, he told him that his god given name was Sean, and that's what he expected his friends to call him. Bill noticed that Charlie had not given Sean the reverse handshake that he had given him the other day, and later when he quizzed Charlie about it he was told that it was a special handshake given to people that he felt he could trust, and he was not yet certain if he could trust Mr Sean. 'Don't call him Mr Sean,' Bill advised Charlie, 'he won't like it if you do.'

Charlie had little trouble keeping up with the two horsemen, but Bill noticed he kept a fair distance from them. Bill decided to slow down and ride next to this obviously natural bushman, but was told that he must ride up ahead with the boss. 'It is our custom Bill,' he said. Bill nodded to his friend and re-joined Sean.

About mid-afternoon, the trio reached the outskirts of Pemberton, so Sean said they would make camp off the track a bit. Bill and Charlie were given the job of collecting firewood and cooking a meal, while Sean would clear a site for the three of them to sleep. When the fire was burning well, Charlie picked up the stick that he always carried, then told Bill that he would be back soon, and he sort of disappeared before Bill realized he was going.

Bill rummaged through the supplies and got out some sausages and eggs, then some potatoes to cook. Before he had started cooking, Charlie was back carrying a small Kangaroo over his shoulder. Bill was fascinated as he watched Charlie skin and cut up this Kangaroo in no time at all. Into the hot coals went half a dozen chunks of "Roo Meat", as Charlie called it.

Sean, who unbeknown to Bill, had been watching as Charlie had taken over as cook, said, 'don't need those sausages Bill. Once you get a taste of this meat you won't want any other.' Sean then suggested that Bill could throw a few spuds into the hot coals, then maybe fry a couple of eggs each.

When the food was announced as cooked, Bill tasted it, then ate with relish. 'Best meal I've had in ages,' he said as he grabbed another piece.

Charlie Burns was pleased that his friend liked the roo meat, 'maybe we can turn you into a fair dinkum Aussie mate,' he said.

The three drovers slept that night near their fire, then after breakfast Sean led them into Pemberton. There, waiting for them were twenty seven cows, plus a chestnut horse. They took two days to deliver these animals to Northcliffe. Under Sean's guidance, they had no problems, and each of them got some sleep overnight. Bill was just turning in, for his sleep on the first night, when he heard Charlie singing. Bill had read how the American cowboys would sing to their cattle herds to keep them calm, but he never thought he would have the chance of ever hearing it happen in Australia. Charlie was singing his own songs, and Bill would try to make out the words. Finally he nodded off, but when Charlie woke him up to take his turn at looking after the herd, he started singing one of Charlie's songs.

This made Charlie laugh and laugh, 'you sound just like me,' he said. After that, Bill would also sing to the cattle, and he found it helped to pass the time away.

When the drive was ended, they delivered the herd to a family named Sparrow. Sean paid both Bill and Charlie eight shillings each for their work.

Bill then went home to his family to spend the night, while Sean and Charlie headed off to Northcliffe together. 'Be ready to start back for the next herd early tomorrow morning Evans,' Sean had told Bill.

The Evans family celebrated with a roast leg of mutton that night, and bright and early the next morning, Bill headed off for the next droving trip.

This pattern of cattle and horse droving went on until all the settlers received their stock. Mostly they all got the same amount of animals, though some had paid the extra money to purchase a bull. Occasionally a bull would play up and be difficult to handle, but Sean taught Bill and Charlie how to use a stockwhip properly to persuade the bull to do as the drovers wanted. Both of these men learnt a lot from Sean, but he had to stop the pair from using their whips as a plaything. He caught them whipping a branch out of each other's mouth. But they soon stopped when told them how his cousin had lost an eye doing just as they were.

During this time a friendship, or more like a sort of a bond, grew amongst the three drovers. This bond grew even stronger on one of the trips back from Pemberton.

Bill had practiced shooting as often as he could with his Lithgow rifle and had become a very good shot. Sean also was a crack shot with his rifle, and would sometimes set up a target for himself and Bill to practice at. This went well until Bill improved to the extent that he could mostly score more target hits than his boss. Charlie Burns would usually sit down and watch while these two shooters would have their contests. But one day he stood up and said loudly, 'why are you silly buggers wasting bullets and our time?'

Sean then asked Charlie if he thought he could do better.

Charlie just shrugged his shoulders and started to walk away, but Sean stopped him and told him to put some money where his mouth was. Bill started to step between the pair, but Charlie told him that it was alright. Charlie then moved the target another twenty paces further away and challenged Sean to hit it. Sean gave a smile and aimed his trusty rifle and squeezed the trigger.

The three of them walked up to the target only to see that Sean had missed. 'Think you can do better?' he asked Charlie.

The now grinning Charlie asked Bill if he could borrow his rifle, and as soon as Bill nodded his consent, Charlie walked to the mark that Sean had fired and missed from. First he stepped back another ten yards, then casually aimed and fired in what seemed like one movement. Charlie didn't bother to check the target, but Sean and Bill both ran to look. 'Good shot mate. You scored a bullseye,' yelled Bill.

Expecting Sean to fire up at getting beaten, Bill was pleased to see the big man walk over to Charlie and shake his hand. 'Well done Burns,' he said. 'Where in the blazes did you learn to shoot like that?'

Charlie was serious now as he said, 'in the bloody stinking rotten war, that's where Sean. That's why I don't like to see you two shooting at nothing.'

A silence came over the three drovers now. Bill was the first to break this silence. 'We're sorry mate. We didn't know you went to war. Crickey Charlie you don't look old enough to be a war veteran.'

The air was clear now, and Charlie thanked Bill for his apology, then said, 'when you have to shoot a fellow man, otherwise he is going to shoot you, then you quickly learn that there is no fun in rifles, or bombs or war.'

Both Bill and Sean shook hands with their fellow man, and quietly packed away their rifles. That night after tea, Charlie told them more about his war experiences. 'I was too young to enlist in the Army, so I did what a lot of other young silly buggers did, and lied about my age. We all thought that we were going on a great exciting adventure, but we soon found out that hell is no adventure. To watch your mates die is not what any man should have to go through. For what, I asked then, and I still ask now. For what? A bunch of politicians who, knowing that they don't have to lie in the mud to dodge bullets, that's why there are wars. No my good friends, I only hope you don't have to go to war. Now if it's alright with you, we'll not again talk of war, and I would appreciate it if we don't shoot for no reason. Now Bill and Sean, I'm going to make us a coffee, then I'll go and sing to the cattle.'

This friendship was increased, or more so proven, one evening when a group of four strangers called at the campfire of these three drovers. After drinking the offered coffee, and eating some of Charlie's cooking, one of the four strangers, a big burley fellow, yelled at Charlie, 'hey you there boy, get me another coffee.'

Charlie, who was sitting a little away from the group, started to get up, but Sean told him to sit down again.

The big stranger got a shock when Sean snarled at him, 'this man not only works for me, he is also my friend, and his name is not boy, it's Charlie. Now Mister, if you want a cup of our coffee, then get it yourself.'

A silence came over the camp, then the big stranger said, 'well I'll be damned, we got ourselves a lover of blackfellas.'

With that Sean jumped up and was obviously about to have a go at the loudmouth, but stopped short when as quick as a flash Bill beat him to the task. 'I'll have to ask you to apologize to my friend,' Bill said.

Now the other three strangers stood up, and were keen to be amongst what was going to be a fight. Then before anyone could move, up jumped Charlie. 'It's my fight Bill, not yours, but thanks anyway mate,' he said.

The big stranger laughed and told Charlie that he was going to knock his head off his black shoulders, and he did try to carry out his threat. The haymaker that he threw at Charlie's head hit nothing but air, because Charlie easily dodged, then as quick as lightning hit the big man in first the solar plexus, then three times on the jaw. With eyes rolled back in his head, this big man fell like a big Karri tree.

Charlie turned to the other three strangers and asked them if they had anything to say. Not one of them spoke as they carried their friend to his horse and left in a hurry. 'Well I'll be a monkey's uncle,' laughed Sean.

Bill joined in the laughter, and patting Charlie on the back, said through tears of merriment, 'I think I'll make the coffee from now on.' This was too much for any of them, and they laughed for what seemed like hours.

Finally, Sean said, 'one of you laughing Kookaburras had better go and sing to the cattle, before our laughing scares them all the way back to Pemberton.'

When the last of the droving had finished, and the three good mates had parted, Bill settled back into helping his father try to make a living on their farm. Bill had saved all of his wages from his droving job with Sean, and like Charlie he had earned nearly thirteen pound. Bill had grown and matured a lot in those two months, and was as proud as punch when the job was over and Sean had thanked him, telling him that he had a job any time he wanted it.

But Bill's biggest thrill came when Sean told him that he was now a "True Blue Aussie". Charlie Burns did not say goodbye to Bill, but instead told him that he would see him around.

The first night that Bill was back on the farm, his mother cooked his favourite meal of tripe and onions with carrots and cabbage, followed by a steam pudding and custard. After the evening meal, which was now in the kitchen of their partly built house, a family sing song was held.

Peggy started the singalong with her rendition of "Keep the Home Fires Burning." Bill then sang "I'll Take You Home Kathleen." Then the proud brother and sister sat and listened to their parents harmonise beautifully together, as they sang "You Are My Sunshine." The night dragged on until finally Mary Evans told them that it was late enough.

Before going to bed, Bill thanked his father for letting him go droving, then paid him back the five pounds that he had given Bill to buy his rifle. Mary Evans then could not hold back her tears as her son gave her two pounds, telling her to buy something for herself. Bill then turned to his sister and gave her the same, then thanked her for helping with all the farm jobs while he was away. Bill figured that the four pounds that he had left might come in handy on a rainy day. Little did he know how right he was?

Chapter Four
Hard Times

Both Father and Son, like all the other settlers, expected tough times on the land. But none of these groups that were given blocks out on this hungry sand, dreamt that things could be as tough as they became over the next couple of years.

The soil unbeknown to them lacked trace elements, and badly needed lime to improve the acidity levels and help release the fertilizers into the soil. Because of these problems, the grass and clovers that were sown, were poor and stunted with no nutriments in them. Therefore the amount, and quality of milk, suffered so much that none of these farmers could make enough money to survive.

Mary Evans was grateful that her son had given her some of the four pounds that he had saved, otherwise, she said many times, 'we probably would have starved.' Also a small part of this money she used to buy a wind up gramophone and several records from one of the neighbours. Mary was hesitant to part with the six shillings that this neighbour, Mrs Cooper wanted for the old gramophone, but she knew that her friend would never sell it unless her family desperately needed the money. Six shillings didn't seem like a lot of money, but it would help feed a family for a few weeks.

The Cooper family were invited to come and listen to the music machine, and they did this on several occasions. Other families would often come over, and a singalong usually started and often went well into the night, or until someone would say, 'well, I don't know about you, but I gotta milk cows in the morning,' and there would be kero lanterns heading in all directions.

Bill made friends with Alan Cooper and one time he and Alan joined a search party to help look for two brothers who had gone marron catching, and had got lost. A Mr Gilmore used an old bugle to attract these lost Blanco brothers, and it was this that helped them to find the boys, or more so the boys were attracted to the bugle.

The storekeeper had a fishing boat and he sometimes took it to Windy Harbour. One of these times he asked Bill and Allan Cooper if they would like to go fishing with him, because his normal crew couldn't make it that weekend. The two boys checked with their parents, who told them to go and have some fun, but to bring back some fish. The plan was to tow the boat to Windy Harbour with a tractor, then weather permitting, they would fish for two days then come home. The storekeeper had done this several times before with no trouble. So with enough food and water for a few days, they put the boat into a nice calm ocean and headed out to sea.

The first day they had a great time and caught several nice fish. The boys thought that this was enough fish for several families, but they were told that they would catch even more the next day. The boat owner decided to go out a bit further that day, as he knew of a spot where he had caught some good snapper. 'Are you lads happy with this idea?' He asked.

Not knowing much about the ocean, both Bill and Allan simply agreed. 'It's your boat, and we have done well so far,' said Allan.

Bill then added, 'our folks will be happy to have some snapper. Mum loves them.' So as the three of them were in agreeance, they went Snapper hunting.

All went well until about midday, when the wind came up fast, and within ten minutes there was a chop on the water. 'Just a couple more snapper and we'll go,' said the skipper. Well they did catch several more nice fish, but when it was time to pull in the anchor the waves were huge, and it was impossible to pull the anchor up. 'Quick Bill, cut the anchor rope,' called the skipper.

Bill had trouble hanging on, but managed to cut through the thick rope just as a wave washed over the boats bow. The sky was now black, and the waves were huge and breaking, causing the boat to roll and surge. 'Hang on boys, were going to make for that island over there,' said the now obviously worried boat owner.

Allan and Bill hung on for dear life as the boat smashed its way through the huge waves. Bill had never really been scared before, at least not this scared, so he was happy when they reached the other side of the island, where it was almost calm. The island protected them from the wind so the skipper carefully anchored the boat in a beautiful bay. 'Lucky I remembered to bring the spare anchor,' he said. 'Righto boys, we may as well set up a camp. We could be here for a couple of days.'

They collected firewood and some rocks and made a fireplace. Then, with a sheet of canvas for the roof, they built a shelter, which was quite waterproof and protected them from the wind and rain. The first night it rained and blew all night, and the next morning, which is when they should have been home, the skipper said that everyone would be worried about them. Allan Cooper suggested that they put green bushes on the fire so people might work out that they must be alright. They did this, and Allan even sent smoke signals in Morse code. Even though the three on the island didn't know it, their signals were seen by a group of rescuers back at Windy Harbour, and the word was sent to Northcliffe that they were alright.

The second day, then the next two after that, were the same as the first on the island. It was way too rough to consider trying to head back, so they ate fish and rationed out the water. Then on the fifth day the fish was starting to go rotten, and try as they might they couldn't catch any fish in this calm bay.

The skipper showed the boys how to follow a mutton bird back to its nest, which was always a hole in the sand, then as soon as the bird left the hole one of them would dash over, and after satisfying himself that there were no tiger snakes in the hole, then he would reach in and grab an egg that the bird had laid. The place was called Mutton Bird Island for obvious reasons. There were thousands of these fat birds, and as Bill was to find out, they were good eating. It was another two days before they could safely go back to Windy Harbour, and when they reached there, about twenty rescuers were waiting for them. Allan Cooper was congratulated for his idea of smoke signalling the people, and the next week he got his photo, and their story in the newspaper.

Needless to say, that was the last time that Bill or Allan chose to go out in a boat for a while. Bill went with Allan to his parent's house and helped explain what had happened. The storekeeper never asked Allan to go fishing again, but whenever he did go, he took a fish to the Coopers house.

During these first years, Bill saw Northcliffe grow, mainly because the "Land Settlement Scheme" did not only include those settlers that were given blocks out on the hungry sand. Many were allocated blocks on better country, closer to, and on the other side of town.

Including the foreman, Mr Lintott, there were twenty six settlers farms out on this poor country, and they nearly all failed, through no fault of their own. Some survived, or managed to somehow exist. Mostly meals consisted of game that they hunted and vegetables that they grew, and home- made bread. Butter was churned regularly from their milk, and some of them even made cheese.

No family would ever starve as such, because the spirit amongst these settlers, who were all in the same predicament, was so strong that if any family was on the border line of starving, then the neighbours, or a friend, would spread the word, and supplies and help would come from all directions. Bill could really feel the Aussie Spirit grow. He knew that without this spirit that bound together all of these battlers, who had taken on this challenge given to them by both England and Australia, they would not have survived.

Bill helped build the first school at Northcliffe, about a year after his family had settled. This school they erected on the opposite corner to the Evans' farm, on the corner of Richardson road and Tattenham road. Then when the school was finished, Bill watched with pride as his sister Peggy, who was now thirteen, walked across the road each morning to continue her schooling.

Peggy was excited after the first day at school, telling her family that she liked her teacher, and that her name was Mrs Radcliffe. Bill watched as Peggy's teacher drove herself to school in a small trap, pulled by a pony. Other schools were built around the district, because over the next three years, some six hundred more settlers were to take up blocks around Northcliffe.

Every morning Bill helped his father milk the cows and feed the calves, then worked on their farm. Bill's father had been allocated a bull, so the size of their herd was increasing, but still they were not producing enough milk or cream to get ahead. To make things worse, the development assistance, that the Agricultural Bank had been paying each settler, was starting to be reduced, and the rumour was that it would soon cease. This bank also charged interest on the initial loan that the "Land Settlement Scheme" had signed each settler up to. After running costs and food money, there was barely enough left each month to pay back the interest, let alone the actual loan?

Finally Joe Evans, and most of the other farmers out on this hungry sand, called a meeting with the Government representative to discuss the possibility of moving to another settlement area, where the soil was much better. This meeting was attended by not only all the farmers from their area, but by many other farmers from the good farming areas.

Bill went to this meeting, which was run by their area foreman, Mr Lintott. After much discussion it was decided that any farmer who wanted to leave the area out on the hungry sand, would be given a block of similar size in a more suitable area. When the meeting was over, many farmers came over to Bill's father and thanked him for suggesting this idea.

The farmers mostly all shook hands with Bill as well, which made him feel grown up. He remembered most of these men from the trip out from England, but that seemed a long while ago. Now he spoke with Luther Cornford, William Crouch, Cecil Fuller, James Knight, Alex Sorley, George Towns, and he was surprised when a Mr William Edmund Gardener patted him on the back and told him that his father had done the right thing wanting to get away from that hungry country. Another friendly farmer, John Jay, who had been talking with George Rudd, also made himself known, saying that his family had also come out in nineteen twenty four and his group was number one hundred and six. George Rudd told Bill his family arrived in nineteen twenty five, and were part of group number one hundred and twenty.

Bill then met a fine gentleman by the name of James Flanagan. 'Pleased to meet you Mr Flanagan,' said Bill.

'Likewise young man,' said this very fit looking farmer, who went on to tell Bill that he and his family had come out from Ireland in nineteen twenty five. Mr Flanagan then introduced Bill to his three sons. Bill shook hands with, Vince, Des and Kevin Flanagan, then turned back to their father.

Bill asked this friendly farmer where his block was, and learnt that the Flanagan family had been lucky enough to have been given some wonderful farming country out along Middleton road. 'Lots of flaming big Karri trees there though,' he said. James Flanagan, who insisted that Bill call him by his God given Irish Christian name, went on to say how they were paid eight shillings an acre to ringbark these big trees.

Later Bill introduced his father to this fine Irish gentleman, and they talked for ages, mostly about farming. Bill thought that it must have been fate meeting James Flanagan, because Joe Evans soon applied for, and got a new block out on Middleton road.

So the Evans family moved, house and all, to much better farming country. The groups that decided to shift farms, all pitched in and helped each other, in turns to make this big move. They worked as a team, firstly cutting the houses down the middle, then loading one section at a time onto a Reo truck, which was supplied by the Government. Then when whosever turn it was to be shifted, their house was put together on their new farm. Their dairy, then their cattle and horses, and in some cases even their chooks were taken as well. This was a long tedious project, but Bill enjoyed it, mainly because he got to meet and talk to many other young settlers.

Bill remembered what James Flanagan had told him about having to ringbark hundreds of big Karri trees, so he rode Blackie over to the Flanagan's farm one day and asked for advice as to the best method to do this mammoth task. James showed Bill around his farm, then how to ringbark trees properly. 'Seems such a shame to kill these beautiful trees doesn't it lad,' he said.

Bill stayed and talked to the Flanagan boys for a while that day, and Mrs Flanagan served them all a huge plate of hot freshly baked scones, followed by a glass of homemade ginger beer. Vince said, 'I reckon you're a bit lucky to have some of this drink Bill. A lot of the bottles blew up yesterday.'

Bill knew that home- made ginger beer had a nasty habit of exploding, mainly because of the build-up of pressure inside the bottle, caused by the fermentation process.

The Flanagan's were doing well out on Middleton road, so Mrs Flanagan gave Bill some home produce to take for his mother. There were bottles of fruit, some pickled onions, and a loaf of freshly cooked bread. This sharing of produce was a common happening amongst the early settlers. Some families may have extra vegetables, so they would pass some on to others, who in return may have just killed a beef steer, so they would pass on some of this meat. This method of sharing, which not only helped each other, but prevented waste, was called the "Barter System", and it worked well.

When Bill and his father started ringbarking these trees, they didn't want to kill them, but kill them they had to. Bill knew that to be able to farm the land, they simply had to clear these trees away, but it took him and his father a long time to get used to doing it. In between milking's, father and son, each armed with a sharp axe, found that they could, on a good day, ringbark nearly an acre. Then when the trees died off they had to fall them with crosscut saws, and then burn them. The smaller trees and scrub they had to dig around the base of, then snig them out with flicker, their draught horse. Any jarrah trees they cut up and stored for firewood, as dry jarrah burnt really well and did not leave too much ash.

The Evans family were lucky enough to get a block that had been started by another family a year or so earlier, so about twenty acres was already cleared and under pasture. This meant that there was enough feed for their cows and horses for a start. As soon as Bill and his father had cleared a few acres, they would plough up this ground then seed it with clover. The farmers in this new area worked in together, sharing equipment, and helping each other, especially at haymaking time.

Time went fast, and before Bill realized it another year or more had flown by. During this time, Charlie Burns would occasionally call to visit, and Bill would only have to suggest fishing or marron catching, and the two of them would be off for a few hours. Then his friend would be gone again, and it could be months before he was seen again, but when he did visit, he was always made welcome. Charlie was a well-liked and respected man all through the district.

Bill, because he worked hard from daylight till dark, did not attend the monthly dances held in Northcliffe. That is until Vince Flanagan came over for a visit one Saturday. After looking around the Evan's farm, Vince complimented Bill for a good job. Then he said that he was going to the dance that night. 'Do you want to come along then?' Bill was not sure whether to go or not, but Vince, who was James and Mrs Flanagan's eldest son, talked him into going, saying that was always a good supper served there. This could have been the telling factor that swayed Bill's mind about going.

So that night Bill went along to his first dance in Northcliffe. He could hear a piano accordion and drums playing loudly, about a half a mile before he reached the dance hall. Bill paid his sixpence entry fee, then went in and joined Vince and a group of other young men who were standing together.

Most of the young men were a bit hesitant asking a girl to dance, but Bill had learnt to dance a bit back in England, and it was not long before a waltz was announced, so he asked a girl to accompany him to the dance floor. Bill had nearly every dance that night, and was in a good mood on the way home. Such was his mood that he burst into song, only to be joined by a pack of howling dingoes. Bill laughed and yelled to them to be quiet. Then he told them they were out of tune anyway.

The next month seemed to fly past, and when dance night came around, Bill went along, sixpence in his hip pocket. He paid the doorman, who he recognized as Mr Knight, then he went in and looked around the hall, but could not see Vince anywhere.

Then from behind him he heard a sweet voice say, 'may I have this dance sir?' Bill turned around to see a pretty young girl who he thought he knew, but could not put a name to, so he nodded, and they danced. 'You don't remember me, do you Bill Evans?'

Bill was, for once in his life unable to talk. He felt all tongue tied and nervous. He could not take his eyes off this pretty girls face. Finally he stammered, 'no, I'm sorry pretty girl, I don't think I know you.' His partner stopped dancing and said, 'did you just call me pretty?'

Bill was having trouble talking again, then he said, 'no, I mean, I don't know. I mean yes, you are pretty, but I did not mean to be rude.' The girl smiled, then held Bill a little tighter and started dancing again.

When the dance ended, Bill started escorting her back to a seat, but she told him that it was supper time and she would get them a plate. Bill then sat down but did not have to wait long for her to come back with a huge plate of cakes. 'I made most of these Bill,' she said shyly. Then she suggested they take their supper outside where there were some seats and tables.

As they were leaving the hall, Bill saw Vince heading towards them. Vince nodded to Bill, but gave his attention to the pretty girl, who was now holding Bill's arm. 'May I have the first dance after supper please Beatrice?'

Vince was a little taken aback when his reply came in a sweet voice, 'sorry Vince, but I have promised the rest of the dances to Bill.'

As Vince walked away, Bill suddenly remembered this girl's name. 'Beatrice Sparrow. That's who you are. But you have grown up since I remember you on the ship,' he said.

The young lady squeezed Bill's arm and said, 'I'm sixteen now Bill, and I can remember you. I hope I was not too forward when I said I had promised all the dances to you.'

After supper, which Bill had no trouble finishing off, the young couple danced and chatted away the evening. Bill could not remember ever having such a good time, and his heart skipped a beat when Beatrice said, 'would you take me home please sir?'

Bill attended every dance for the next several months, and danced nearly every one with Beatrice, then escorted her home each night. Mostly there would be people on horseback, or in horse drawn sulkies, but many would simply walk home from these dances. Everyone though, would either carry a torch or a lantern, and it was quite a sight to see all these lights twinkling away at about midnight. Bill would usually ride Blackie to the dances, then leave him there afterwards while he walked Beatrice home.

The young man was happy and reckoned everything was perfect in his life. 'Here I am he thought,' nearly twenty years old, got myself a pretty girl, the farms starting to pay its way, things are just about perfect.

Then fate stepped in and changed Bill Evans' life, and the life of his family. It happened one morning when Bill was milking the cows. Bill's father had been getting up to help with the milking every morning, but just the last few mornings he was a bit late starting. Bill was not worried about this, thinking that his dad was probably a little tired. But this morning Bill was half way through the milking and started to worry a bit. Then just as he thought that he better go and check on his father, from the house came his sister's screams.

Bill stopped milking and ran to the house to find his mother and sister huddled over his father, who was laying prostrate on the kitchen floor. Bill's mother said, 'quick son, ride and get the new doctor.' As fast as he could, Bill rode Blackie bareback to town. He was lucky because he found Mr Leitch the storekeeper out the front of his shop. Bill told Mr Leitch about how his father was very ill. Then as quick as a flash, Mr Leitch ran to his "T" model Ford and drove to the doctor's house.

He banged loudly on the door until Doctor West answered it. 'Come quick doctor, it's Joe Evans,' said the store keeper.

The news was not good for the Evans family that day. Joe Evans was found to be suffering from Sugar Diabetes. This in turn had caused the overworked farmer to have a slight stroke. Doctor West informed the Evans family that he should be taken to Perth, where he could obtain ongoing specialist treatment, or he could have a major stroke, or die.

The next week was a blur for Bill. He had helped his mother and sister pack their belongings, then watched as the good Mr Leitch drove his parents and sister to Pemberton. From Pemberton they were taken by train to Perth. They stayed at a hostel, while they waited for a house to become available in Perth.

Meanwhile, Bill stayed on the farm to milk the cows and to try to sell their property. Luck was with him as a Mr Brown came and made an offer, which Bill readily accepted. Mr Brown bought the Evans farm lock stock and barrel, which meant Bill had only his own belongings. Of course he would not sell Blackie, and he kept his rifle, a few blankets, two rabbit traps, and his favourite oilskin coat.

The move all happened fast, and before Bill realized that he was no longer a Northcliffe farmer, he was on the train and on his way to Perth and his parents. Bill had ridden Blackie to Pemberton, where he left him with his friend Charlie Burns, who was now living there. Charlie also looked after Bill's rifle and gear, knowing that he would be back for them soon. 'See you soon,' said Charlie as he waved Bill off at the train station. Bill tried to tell his friend not to try to ride Blackie, but the train moved away before he got the words out.

When Bill got to Perth, his father had improved a bit, and could now talk and walk a little. Then after a few days Bill took his mother to look at a house in Oxford Street Leederville West Perth, with the intention of buying it. Mary Evans loved this small dainty house, but they did not have enough money to buy the place, so the agent offered them a rental deal, with the option of purchase. This meant that the house could not be sold to anyone else for a period of two years, but if the Evans family could come up with the money, then they could buy it for the agreed price.

In the meantime, rent of ten shillings per week must be paid. Bill had handed all the meagre profits from the sale of their farm, to his parents. After paying a month's rent in advance, there was enough left for the future rent of the house for the balance of the agreement, plus enough for the family to live on for a few years.

This was better than most of the Northcliffe settlers, that had either gone broke, or been forced off their farms through sickness or hardship, had been lucky enough to have been dealt. Many of them had walked away with nothing, and some with a debt hanging over their heads.

Things seemed to be falling into place, Peggy applied for, and got a good job as a secretary at the West Perth Markets. Joe's health improved to the extent that he only had to see the specialist once a month, though he had to have insulin daily. Mary was happy in her new home. She liked the kitchen, as it had a big "Meters" stove, where she could do plenty of her home cooking. Bill could see that his family would survive. They had a nice place to live, Peggy had a job, and his parents had a little money in the bank.

Bill knew he probably should stay here in the city, but something was telling him to move back to the country that he had grown to love. He got a job in a factory, but only lasted a few weeks. Bill knew that he was not suited to this city life, and his family could sense what was coming. Again he started another job, this time at the markets unloading supplies. Again this young man only lasted a few weeks before he got the call of the wild.

Bill's father was doing well on his medication, so one day Bill said, 'Dad, I think I will go back to Northcliffe for a while, if you give me your blessing.'

Joe Evans was now not the same man he was when he and his family had arrived here in this young country some four years ago, but a spark came back to his eyes as he said to his son, 'Bill, I am so proud of you my boy. You have been as good a son to your mother and me, as any son could ever be. No Bill, don't waste your life here,' he said. 'Go out and follow your dreams, for they are the hopes of the future. Live your life, and go where your heart takes you. But remember this my son, you will always have a home here.'

Both father and son were a bit overcome, but Joe Evans had not finished, and he quietly told Bill to write to his mother, and to visit her whenever he could. Bill gave his word to his father, and the next morning there were many tears and hugs. Then Bill packed to set out on a new venture in his life.

Peggy walked part of the way to the train station with Bill that morning, and when it was time for them to part, she looked long and hard at her brother. 'Please come back to us my brother. It was you that saved me on that ship, and I don't think I ever thanked you. So I want you to always carry this to remember me.'

With that she gave Bill a silver chain, which he put round his neck. The brother and sister then parted, and Bill looked back after he had walked about a hundred yards, and there was Peggy still standing and waving to him. With a final wave Bill headed for his train that would take him to Pemberton, and who knows what he wondered?

Chapter Five
The Call of The Wild

CHARLIE Burns was waiting at the station when Bill arrived in Pemberton. Bill smiled to himself, he wasn't really surprised that his friend was waiting for him. He had gotten used to this man's ways of somehow "knowing" what would happened even before it did.

Charlie had stayed in contact with Bill and his family over the past years, and he was genuinely interested in Joe Evan's health. 'How's your dad mate?'

Bill explained about his father's improvement, and how Peggy has a good job, and his mother loved their house. 'Where are you gonna go now?' This time Bill did not have a ready answer for his friend, and before he could think of one, Charlie said with his usual smile, 'fish are biting at the mouth of the Warren.'

Bill knew this spot, which as Charlie put it, was where the Warren River flowed into the ocean. Charlie then went on to explain that the swollen river, which had been filled by more than usual winter rains, had broken through the sandbar, and was flowing into the sea.

Then Bill asked this man of vision if he had been to this place recently, and Charlie just smiled and shook his head, then said, 'not really, but it'll be open.'

They took enough supplies for a few weeks, which they bundled up into packs that fitted behind the saddles on their horses. Blackie had been well looked after by Charlie while Bill was away, but he was happy to have his master back.

Charlie told Bill that he had tried to ride Blackie to give him some exercise, 'only exercise he got was throwing me out of the saddle,' he laughed, which started Bill laughing. Then he smiled widely as he remembered how his sister had helped him be the only person to be able to ride Blackie.

He smiled even more as he looked over at the ugly, bony animal that Charlie was riding. 'Where did you find that half-starved nag?'

Charlie's answer was to dig his heels into the ribs of his beloved horse, and yell to Bill, 'catch this nag if you can mate.'

Bill was a little slow in reacting to this challenge and before he could say "Jack Robinson", Charlie and his nag were some hundred yards ahead of him and Blackie. So he shook the reins at his horse who he thought could easily catch this runt of an animal that his friend was on. It was still about two miles to the spot where they had planned to camp, so Bill did not push Blackie. Then with about a half a mile to go, he urged his mount into a full gallop, and Blackie responded immediately. With giant strides that seemed to eat up the ground, Bill's big black stallion had almost caught Charlie and his chestnut gelding, but there was one sand hill to go. This was where Charlie's "nag", as Bill had called him, came into his own. Charlie had not yet asked his gelding for an effort, but he did so now. Blackie almost drew level with the other horse, but could not pass him, and Charlie gave a loud cheer as he pulled up his horse at the camp site. Bill dismounted and patted both horses, then asked his friend where he got this fine gelding from. Charlie explained that he had bought him at a settler's clearance sale, for the bargain price of three shillings and sixpence.

After setting up their camp, and gathering a supply of firewood, Charlie said that there was time to catch a few fish for tea. 'You light the fire,' he told Bill, 'and I'll catch tea.'

Bill did light the fire, but just as he stood back to admire the way the dry peppermint branches had sparkled into life, there came a big explosion from the beach where Charlie had headed to. Bill ran to where he reckoned the bomb like noise had come from, and there wading in the river mouth was Charlie.

Expecting to find his friend dead or something, Bill was amazed to see him picking up floating fish of all sorts and sizes. Finally Charlie came out of the water with half a sugar bag of fish. 'Don't need a line here,' he smiled at Bill.

Apparently Charlie had set off a small stick of gelignite to stun the fish, allowing him to just pick them up. Bill was not happy with this idea and promptly told his friend so. This was the first time that the two friends had argued. Bill refused to eat the fish when Charlie cooked them, saying it was a cruel way to catch them. They didn't speak much that night and both men went to their beds early.

The next morning Bill arose at daybreak and took a handline to catch some fish. He had just landed a nice tailor when along came Charlie, who quietly threw in a line next to where Bill was fishing. He too caught a fish, then the two mates went back to camp and cooked breakfast. After their meal, Charlie told Bill he was sorry he blew the river up, and he would not bomb any more fish.

They stayed at the mouth of the Warren River for a couple of weeks, and one day Charlie showed Bill a spot where there was quicksand. 'Don't go near there mate,' he said. 'I saved a lady there a while back. Up to her neck in quicksand she was. Dot Hanlon that was her name.'

The two friends enjoyed their break, living mainly on fish, then one day Bill told Charlie that he would like to go to Northcliffe for a while. Charlie laughed and said 'got a girl there have you mate?'

Bill was surprised that Charlie knew about Beatrice, because he had not mentioned her, and Charlie had never been to any of the Northcliffe dances, or at least not when Bill had gone.

When they got to Northcliffe, Bill asked at the store if there was any mail or messages for him, and he was surprised when Mr Leitch handed him a letter. The friendly storekeeper asked Bill how his family were, then after he told him that his father was much better, Bill hurried outside and sat under a shady tree where Charlie was having a nap.

The letter was from Beatrice, and Bill read out loud to himself, thinking Charlie was asleep. It was not unusual for Charlie to be able to nod off at the drop of a hat, so Bill continued reading;

"My dearest Bill,

I learnt from Vince about your father's sickness. I do hope that he is alright. I have missed you a lot Bill. My father is also very sick. He had a heart attack only a few days after you left here, so we have also put our farm up for sale and are moving to Perth. I do hope we will meet again Bill.

Love, Beatrice xxx."

Bill looked at the date of the post mark, but there was no stamp on the envelope, so he went back and asked Mr Leitch when he received this letter. The storekeeper told him that a young lady dropped the letter in to him only two weeks ago. Bill was upset at missing Beatrice by only several days, and was sorry to hear that her father was also sick.

Not sure what to do next, Bill asked Charlie what his plans were, and was surprised to learn that his friend was to box a bout in Manjimup soon. 'Don't know anyone that could act as my second do you mate?'

So the next few days were sorted out because Bill said, 'reckon I'd better come and keep an eye on you mate. You might blow the place up.'

Manjimup was about another twenty mile back past Pemberton, but the two friends were not in any hurry, so they rode their horses easily, stopping each day well before sunset.

After setting up a campfire, they would "spar" for an hour or two each day. Not having any proper boxing gloves with them, they wrapped some rag around their hands, then pulled a sock over each hand. Bill had never mentioned to Charlie that he was a trained boxer, so when they started "sparring" the first time, he hung back to let his friend show himself. Bill soon worked out that Charlie was a natural. He was fast with both hands, and his punches did not lack any power. Most boxers were either a left or right stance, but Charlie was neither.

For the first time in all his training, or in his many bouts, Bill was not sure how to box this man. Charlie would shape up as a natural stance fighter, then all of a sudden he would become a lightning fast southpaw, with a straight right that came out of nowhere. Bill took most of Charlie's punches on his socks that were acting as gloves, but when Charlie switched to his southpaw stance, Bill copped a few blows to his head. Whenever Charlie did hit Bill, he would apologize quickly. After a few afternoon sessions of just letting Charlie do all the attacking, Bill gradually started to box back a little.

Then one night after a meal of Marron that Charlie had snared in a river he said to Bill, 'why did you not tell me you can box good mate?' Bill laughed, and swallowing another Marron tail, he then told his friend all about his boxing history. 'You telling me that you, Bill Evans, that is sitting here eating Marron, next to Charlie Burns, has boxed against, and knocked out the world champion?'

Bill laughed and said, 'he was the former champ Charlie, and he was over forty years old.' He didn't want to show off about beating McCoy, and thinking back, if it wasn't for his father, he probably would never have beaten him.

The next day Charlie told Bill to stop hanging back, but to box properly. So they boxed a bit more seriously over the next several days, and they got closer to Manjimup each day. The last night they did not spar. Bill told Charlie it might be good for him to have a rest and be fresh for his bout.

The day Charlie was due to have this boxing match, the two close friends left their horses and their gear at a hostel, which had a stable. They planned to stay that night at this hostel, after the fight. Not long before start time, Charlie took Bill to his friend's house where they were given a meal, and Lionel, who was also a boxer, lent Charlie a pair of gloves. 'Thanks mate,' said Charlie. 'I'll buy my own if I win tonight.'

Bill and Charlie then went down to the town hall, and there out the front for all to see, was a big sign saying, " Boxing tournament tonight." Bill read the smaller writing underneath, which said that Charlie Burns, the local champion was to fight all comers over a three hour period, and that anyone that could beat him would win ten pounds. The sign went on to explain that to challenge Charlie, the fee was ten shillings.

Before Bill could tell Charlie that he was mad, his friend, who Bill did really think must be crazy to take on all comers, was inside the hall and was talking to a big bloke who Bill reckoned must be the promoter. 'This is my best friend Bill,' Charlie said to the other man.

The promoter after shaking Bill by the hand, and saying his name was Billy Jones, went back to sorting out with Charlie the financial arrangements for the night. Apparently Charlie had done this same type of contest before, and this promoter always tried to offer Charlie less money. Bill grinned as he heard Charlie say that he would not fight for less than the arranged four shillings a bout. Each bout was over three, four minute rounds, with only five minutes between each bout. Finally, Billy Jones sighed and said, 'you'll send me broke Charlie Burns, but it's a deal. You'll get your four shillings a fight.'

The hall was starting to fill up, mainly because there was not a lot of other entertainment to be had, and Charlie had a big following, which Bill was quickly noticing. Many of the crowd would wave and yell to Charlie, some saying that they had backed him, so he had better win.

Charlie led Bill out the back where they passed a room with about thirty men in it. Some already with their boxing gloves on. When Charlie took Bill into the next room, Bill asked him if he was going to fight all those men tonight. 'Probably might be a few more turn up after the Pub shuts,' Charlie grinned.

Bill only just had time to lace up Charlie's borrowed gloves, when Billy Jones stuck his big head through the door and said, 'let's go Charlie.' So the two of them made their way to the ring, one as a second, and the other ready to fight up to thirty men in one night.

The first bout was a mismatch, as Charlie's opponent had obviously had not any boxing experience. Charlie could have easily finished the fight with a first round knockout, but he did not want to hurt this young man, so after two very one sides rounds, the referee stopped the bout. The crowd, which had by now filled the hall, showed their appreciation at Charlie's leniency. Charlie told the referee that he did not need a spell, so the second opponent was ushered straight into the ring.

Much the same thing went on for the first hour or so. Bill figured that Billy Jones had probably sorted out the better boxers and kept them back, giving Charlie an easy time with the early opponents. After all, Billy was making six shillings a bout, as well as the gate money of sixpence admission fee. Bill reckoned there must be nearly four hundred people in the hall, so that worked out to be another twenty quid for Billy. This crowd was starting to get a bit bored with the ease that Charlie was winning, and some started to call for a proper fight.

Now Billy Jones was a business man, and he wanted more of these evenings when he could make easy money. So he thought he'd better bring out a better boxer, one that he was keeping back till later, just in case he did beat Charlie. This would have meant that Billy would have to pay out the promised ten pounds to any boxer that beat Charlie. No one had ever beaten Charlie yet, and unless they knocked him out, their chances were slim, because the referee just happened to be Billy's younger brother, Alan Jones, so a point's decision was not likely to go against Billy's man.

The next man that lumbered into the ring, was a giant compared to Charlie. Bill said to Charlie, 'do you know anything about this bloke mate?' Charlie just shook his head and told Bill that he thinks he is the bloke that they reckon is goning be the next heavy weight state title holder. 'Now you listen to me Charlie Burns. This man could be dangerous. You go out and box him. Don't get close, dance around and feel him out,' Bill was worried as he told this to his friend.

He was going to say more, but the promoter announced that the next opponent for the local champion would be none other than the heavyweight contender, Paddy Boxall. The bell went to start the fight, and Charlie darted straight towards this big fellow, who Bill had noticed had not taken his eyes off Charlie the whole time. To Bill this was a sign that he knew what he was doing, and was working his opponent out, as good boxers do. 'Stay away from him,' Bill yelled to Charlie, but the crowd noise was deafening now because Charlie in his keenness to get through as many opponents as possible, so he could make more money, was now laying on the floor.

The referee took his time in starting to count Charlie out. Bill watched as the count got to seven, and he was sure he seen Charlie look over towards his corner and give a wink. As the count got eight, Charlie got to his feet, and staggered around as if trying to get his senses back. This gave the big opponent more confidence, and as soon as the referee stood back and signalled for the two boxers to fight on, Charlie rushed at the big man in the same way as he had at the start of the round. This time though, when he got nearly to where the big opponent could reach him, as he had done a few moments ago, Charlie, with seemingly lightning speed, stopped going forward and did a little shuffle.

In the time it took Charlie to do his shuffle, the big man had thrown the same haymaker at where Charlie's head should have been, but was not. Bill then watched in complete amazement, as Charlie Burns seized the right moment. When the big man had dropped his defence to flatten him, Charlie delivered the sweetest knockout punch that Bill could ever wish to see.

The fight was over one minute after it started. The heavyweight contender had to be carried out of the ring. The promoter jumped into the centre of the ring and told the cheering crowd that his man, Charlie Burns had just knocked out one of the country's best prospects.

This got the crowd going, and many started throwing coins into the ring. 'Quick mate,' Charlie yelled to Bill. 'Pick them coins up before Billy does.'

So while Charlie did a victory dance and waved to the screaming crowd, Bill picked up nearly half a water bucket of coins. Charlie came closer to Bill and told him to stuff most of the money into his pockets as fast as he could. Billy Jones was too busy stirring up the crowd, who he wanted to come to his next night's entertainment that would be held. Too busy that is to see Bill filling his pockets.

When the crowd finally quietened down, Billy, who was thriving on the attention that he thought he was part of, told them that there would be an intermission of twenty minutes, and that there was drinks and food available in the supper room. Bill was taking Charlies gloves off when Billy Jones came over to see how much money the crowd had thrown into the ring.

Charlie had quickly told Bill that usually the coinage, that when collected, was shared between Charlie and his promoter, so now he told Bill to put some coins back into the bucket. 'Would have thought the lousy blighter's might have chucked a bit more than this,' the keen promoter said, as he divided the coins into two equal piles.

Bill could not believe how calmly Charlie was manipulating this promoter. 'Reckon I should get all that money Billy,' Charlie piped up.

Billy Jones, not knowing that all of Bill's pockets were full, told Charlie that he knew the rules, and that it was half each. 'What about giving my second some then, you lousy thing,' said Charlie?

The money hungry promoter said, 'you'll break me before you're finished.' But he now divided the money into three even heaps. Charlie and Bill took their shares and went to the room allocated to the boxer.

Charlie shut the door and pushed a table against it, then the two laughing mates counted out all the coins that the promoter had given them. 'Nearly three quid,' Charlie laughed. The laughter increased ten-fold as Bill emptied his pockets onto the table. They counted another seventeen pounds ten shillings, then added the two heaps together. When Charlie pushed half to Bill, he tried to refuse the money, but Charlie insisted that he take it.

So that night Bill pocketed over ten pounds. 'Heck,' said Bill, 'the farm wasn't making that much profit in three months.'

Bill was keen to ask Charlie what game he was playing when he fought that giant. Charlie said that he let himself cop the first punch so he could work out the big blokes weak spots. 'I did not want to have to go three rounds with that big fella,' he laughed.

Time was up, so Bill got his man ready again. It turned out that Charlie had another dozen opponents after the break, but none were any problem. Charlie only fought as hard as he needed to, and he made most of the bouts look interesting and closer than they could have been if he wanted. Billy Jones was happy that Charlie made the night a success, and he paid his boxer the agreed four shillings a fight. Charlie Burns had fought twenty one opponents that night. Bill told him that he had never heard of such a feat. 'I fought twenty four two months ago,' Charlie said.

The man that had lent the boxing gloves to Charlie, came over to congratulate him and to collect his gloves. 'Here you go Lionel, buy your kids and wife something, but don't drink it all away,' Charlie said as he handed his friend two one pound notes.

Both of them slept well that night at the hostel, and after breakfast they saddled their horses, packed their gear and prepared to head off. Before they left Manjimup, Charlie bought a full set of new boxing gloves, and Bill went to the music shop and bought himself a mouth organ. Bill had always wanted a mouth organ, ever since he had heard one of his cousins play one back in England.

So after buying some more supplies, Bill asked Charlie where they were going. 'Might try fishing at the mouth of the Donnelly,' said Charlie. Bill had heard there was excellent fishing there, but he thought that people could only get there by boat. But, as usual, Charlie had a plan. He knew of a track that could be ridden, and even though it was a bit further it took you right to the spot. Fish was the main menu at this spot, and to Bill's delight, the big tailor were biting.

Bill stared in wonder at the cliffs at this pretty spot. There were several caves near the top of the cliffs and as they were high and steep, nobody had damaged them. Charlie said he had climbed up to one of the caves a few years ago. Bill asked him if he found anything in the cave, and got a surprise when his friend pulled a pocket watch. 'There was a bundle of old clothes near this, and it looked like someone had been camped in there for a while,' Charlie said.

They had a great time there for a few weeks, then they both agreed it was just about time to move on. 'Anyway,' said Bill, 'one of these tiger snakes is bound to get one of us soon.' Hardly a day would go past without a near miss from one or more of these yellow bellied venomous snakes.

Bill had enjoyed this break, and he felt refreshed and ready to take on any challenge that life may throw at him. The pair of wanderers had kept fit by jogging along the beach and sparring each afternoon. It was much better using the new gloves that Charlie had bought with his winnings.

Still having over ten pounds in his kitbag, when they arrived at Pemberton, Bill posted a money order of five pounds to his parents in Perth. He put a letter in the envelope, mainly to let them know he was alright. Also he said that he was heading back to Northcliffe for a while, so if they could write to him there, he should receive any mail. Charlie Burns decided to stay in Pemberton, saying he would probably have another boxing night in Manjimup soon.

Bill did not hurry to Northcliffe, and when he did arrive, he went to the store to check if there was any mail, and found that his mother had written him a few weeks earlier. Bill was happy to get this letter, and was relieved to read that his family were doing well. His father was a bit better, and his mother sounded her normal self as she wrote several pages. Peggy was enjoying her job, and asked her mother to remind Bill that it was going to be her seventeenth birthday soon, and she was hoping her brother might be home for it. Bill smiled to himself and worked out that he still had over six weeks before Peggy's birthday.

Not quite sure where to go next, Bill mounted Blackie and headed out to the Sparrow's farm. There he found a sign saying it was for sale. The homestead was empty, and there were no stock anywhere, so he presumed that someone must have purchased the dairy herd and horses. Bill was right, as he found out from the only other settler that had not left this area out on the hungry sand where Bill's farm was a couple of years ago. The other farmer, whose block was only a short distance from the Sparrow's block, had seen Bill ride in, and had come over to see him.

This quiet farmer, whom Bill knew as Mr Gooch, told Bill that the Sparrow family had left him in charge of their farm. He said he had transferred all the animals to his farm, and was milking the herd in with his. Mr Gooch told Bill that he would pay the Sparrows for their milk each month, or when someone bought their farm. 'Don't suppose you want a job do you Bill?'

Bill thought for a moment, then told Mr Gooch that he could stay for a while. So they agreed it would be easier to bring the Sparrow herd back to their farm, and Bill could work it by himself.

So Bill was a farmer again, be it that it was only going to be for a while. He moved into the home on this farm, and set to work tidying everything up. Then he helped Mr Gooch drive the cattle back. They got them back in time for Bill to milk that afternoon, and he did not see Mr Gooch again for a couple of days.

The milk and cream carrier called again at the Sparrow farm, and Bill got to enjoy life as a farmer again. It did not take him long to work out the habits of each cow. This was important, because if you could keep a cow happy, well fed, and content, then she would repay you with more milk. So the pay check that the Sparrow family were to receive, went up accordingly. Soon though it was time to go to Perth for Peggy's birthday. Mr Gooch offered to run both farms for a few days so Bill could go.

The Evans family were back together again for a few days. It was for all four of them, a wonderful time. But time went quick, and it was not long before Bill was back milking the Sparrow's herd. Bill was in the middle of milking a few days after getting back, when he saw a group of people approaching the dairy. They waited until they could see that Bill could leave the cows for a while, then they approached and explained that they were the new owners of this farm. Bill invited them to go up to the house and said that he would join them shortly.

When he had finished milking, Bill discussed his future with the new owners. They said they would be happy to continue paying him the same wages that Mr Gooch had been paying him, if he could stay another month or so. Bill agreed, and during the next month he showed these people how best to run this farm. Bill wondered how they thought they could possibly make any real money here, but he did not say much to them.

As soon as the new owners were trained, and were happy, Bill packed up and rode Blackie to the Northcliffe store. There was a letter waiting for him. It was from his family and Bill read this letter outside. All was well at home, so he wrote a long letter saying that he would write them next from wherever he went, as he was thinking of heading to the wheat-belt. Bill put a pair of one pound notes inside the envelope, then addressed it to "The Evans Family" Oxford Street Leederville West Perth. Bill had only just posted the letter, when along came the "mail truck". It was not really a truck, as Bill noticed, but a big Buick car. Mr Alf Jones, who was the first mail contractor, took the mail each other day to Pemberton. He would then bring back any incoming mail for the settlers and townsfolk.

After buying some supplies, Bill decided to call at a few farms along Middleton Road. He stopped at most of the settlers places along this now graded road. One of the first was at the Flanagan farm, which he noticed now had a small sign out the front with their name painted on it. Bill stayed for a "cuppa" with this fine family that he had gotten to know over the years. Mrs Flanagan then packed him a bag of food. 'For on the way,' she told him.

James Flanagan wrote a reference for Bill, and he and all the family wished him well as he rode down their track to the front gate. Turning to wave to them, Bill got a surprise to see young Kevin Flanagan running along behind. Thinking he must have forgotten something, Bill reined Blackie in and waited for this fit lad to run alongside. Kevin told Bill that he was in training for the interschool sports. Bill asked Kevin what races he was planning to go in? 'Well I like the longer ones so I am hoping to win the mile race,' he grinned to Bill. The young runner then took off back to where his family were still waving.

Mr Brown also gave Bill a good reference, and wished him well, telling him that if he was around the Boyup Brook area, then he could call on a farmer named Ray Stephens. 'He might have a job there as it's soon to be seeding time.'

Bill camped that night where the Middleton Road met the Main Road to Walpole. Blackie woke Bill with a sudden neighing very early the next morning. Thinking something was wrong, he picked up his rifle that he always kept handy in case of Dingoes or snakes. 'That's a nice welcome mate,' came a voice that Bill knew well.

Bill was not surprised that his good friend Charlie Burns had somehow again turned up at a time when he couldn't, or shouldn't have possibly known where Bill was, or where he was going. 'Don't just stand there then Charlie. Light the fire and I'll cook us breakfast,' Bill said.

Long ago he had given up trying to work out how this man of many talents, "knew" things that were going to happen. Then as if by magic, seemed to turn up when he was least expected. They soon had a roaring fire going, and breakfast was cooked over red hot coals. Bill was going to ask Charlie if he would like to accompany him to the wheat-belt district, but before he could get the words out, Charlie said that he had just come to say, 'see you later.' Bill gave a smile when his friend then said, 'I'm not going to the place where you are going Bill. Too many spirits there for me mate.'

Bill had not told Charlie that he was going to Boyup Brook, or anywhere, but again he was not surprised that Charlie knew. The two friends rode together for a few hours, then Charlie stopped and looked Bill squarely in the eye. 'We won't see each other for a long time my friend. I must warn you Bill. Be careful. You are going to have some hard times, and you must be strong.'

Then Bill turned to get off Blackie to shake hands with his good friend, but he got a shock to see that Charlie had disappeared. 'Goodbye mate,' Bill yelled loudly, hoping that Charlie might hear him. The two had enjoyed many good times together, and both had learnt a lot from each other over the several years they had been friends. So it was with a strange and eerie feeling, that Bill turned Blackie's head to the east, and set off to face his next challenge.

Chapter Six
Too Many Spirits

It was another week before Bill reached the small town of Boyup Brook. He had camped along a big river called the Blackwood. The water in this winding river provided Bill and his horse, not only with good clean drinking water, but there were marron nearly as long as Bill's forearm. Bill boiled these fresh water crayfish in his billy most evenings for his tea. He also caught fish at his leisure, and they too, were plentiful and tasty. Blackie also was content as there was plenty of lush grass to eat. Life was good, so when he finally got to this small town, he felt rested and ready for work.

Seeing a sign saying, "Boyup Brook Café," Bill hitched Blackie out front and went in. His meal of steak and veggies was a good change. Afterwards, the proprietor directed Bill to the farm that Mr Brown had suggested he might find work. It was about seven miles to this farm, which Bill had no trouble finding.

An elderly, well- dressed man met Bill at the front gate of a neat looking homestead. 'What can I do for you young fella?'

Bill looked calmly at this farmer who seemed to be in a hurry, and said, 'Mr Brown of Northcliffe said he knows you Sir, and he gave me this reference to show you. I am seeking work Sir.'

The man did not take long to read Bill's reference, after which he shook Bill's hand, telling him that his name was Ray Stephens. He then suggested that Bill put his fine looking horse in the yard at the end of the lane, then come up to the house. Bill, a short while later, knocked on the front door of Ray Stephen's home, and was invited in by the polite owner.

Bill was shown into a large clean kitchen, where he was introduced to the lady of the house. 'This Bill, is my wife of twenty three years, Mrs Stephens, and this my dear is Bill Evans.' Ray Stephens went on to tell his wife that Bill knew their friend, Mr Brown of Northcliffe. With a smile, Mrs Stephens nodded to Bill and indicated for him to take a seat at the kitchen table.

Then Ray sat down and spoke to this youngster, who was from the same town as his friend that he had first met at a cattle sale at Manjimup. Bill answered the many questions that this farmer asked him, and as Mrs Stephens served tea and scones, he told Bill that he had a job here. 'Provided you give me your word to stay the whole seeding season, no matter what,' he said.

Bill was happy and accepted the job. After the morning tea, the farmer told Bill to call him Ray from now on. Then he took Bill to the living quarters, which were near the big shearing sheds. 'The wages are three pounds a week, for which you must work six days a week. We don't work on Sundays,' he explained. He then told Bill to choose his room and that he would see him in the morning at the shearing shed. 'I have to go to a funeral today, but Mrs Stephens will expect you for tea at seven o'clock sharp.' With that Ray left Bill to settle into his room.

There were three of these rooms, but the bed was made in one, and there were clothes and things on the bed. So that left two for Bill to choose from. After putting his gear into the room that he had chosen, he went out and tended to Blackie. Bill found that there were plenty of small yards, each with a water trough and a feed bin, so he chose the closest yard to the living quarters. He then fed some hay and oats to his horse.

When Bill got back to his room, he thought he might make a coffee. There was a separate shared kitchen at one end of these quarters, which had a Coolgardie safe, a stove and a sink. At one end he found a cupboard which contained plates and cutlery. He was just lighting the fire when heard a noise behind him. Thinking it may be the other worker, he finished lighting the fire, then turned around to speak to this chap. There was nobody there, so he looked in the rooms, but still did not find anyone. Back he went and made his coffee, which he took to his room, but just as he sat on the edge of the bed, he heard a noise in the kitchen. After a look, and finding that there was still nobody to be found, Bill went outside, just as a rider was yarding his horse in the yard next to his.

Bill waited until this chap had finished, and when he got closer to the living quarters he said, 'G'day mate. My names Bill, and I'm starting here tomorrow.'

Well Bill got the shock of his life when this chap pulled back his hat and said, 'pleased to meet you Bill, my name's Jenny.'

Bill was speechless. This person in front of him was not a man, but a pretty young lady of about the same age as himself. This lady told Bill that she works here, and that she has for the last two seeding and harvesting seasons. Bill told Jenny that he had just made a coffee and asked her if she would like a cup? Jenny said she would, but she would rather have tea as she did not drink much coffee. 'Just like my mother,' said Bill.

The two got on like a house on fire, and they talked for ages. Jenny told Bill never to call Ray Mr Stephens. While they drank, Bill queried her about the meal arrangements, saying that Ray had told him to be at the house at seven o'clock for tea. Jenny explained that Mrs Stephens always cooked the evening meal. 'Ray said that he had to go to a funeral today and it sounded like he might be a little late,' said Bill.

Jenny surprised him when she said, 'he will be late alright.' Then she told him never to approach Ray in the mornings, but to either wait at the shearing shed, or start work and he will find you. Bill was a bit puzzled, but didn't query Jenny any more.

Bill's new workmate then offered to show him around the farm. They rode together, Bill on Blackie, and Jenny on the farm horse. He noticed that Jenny was a good rider, but she was a bit wary of Blackie, and kept her mount a safe distance from him. They spent the rest of the day looking over the place, with Jenny explaining most things that she thought Bill should know.

Then when it was time to get ready for the meal at the main house, Jenny had a shower while Bill shifted his things to the other empty room. Jenny had told him to do so, saying that if he didn't shift now, then he soon would. Again Bill was puzzled, but again he didn't ask any questions.

On the way to the Stephens house, Bill asked Jenny if she had been in the kitchen earlier, when he was lighting the fire, as he thought there was someone behind him, but when he looked he couldn't see a soul. She shook her head and told him that he would get used to these things.

Bill opened the gate for Jenny and stood back allowing her to go first. 'Just like my dad,' Jenny smiled at him. As they got close to the front door Jenny whispered to Bill, 'watch out for Mrs Stephens after tea.'

The meal was like the ones his mother cooked, and Bill complimented Mrs Stephens on a wonderful meal. 'That's alright Bill,' she said. 'Now you can stay and help me do the dishes.' She then told Jenny that she could go, saying that she had helped last night. Bill looked at Jenny, but she quickly left to go back to the quarters.

Mrs Stephens surprised Bill by saying that she needed a hand to shift some furniture in her bedroom after they had done the dishes. She finished washing the dishes, and before Bill had dried them all, then she told him that she would be back in a minute.

When she did return she was wearing a change of clothes. She now had on a wide pleated skirt and a thin blouse. Bill was nervous as Mrs Stephens came very close to him and said that her husband would not be home till much later. A shock went through Bill as she told him to call her Rose tonight. She then took him by the hand and led him to her room. Bill asked which furniture would she like him to shift. Rose then put her arms around Bill and said, 'forget about the furniture for tonight Bill.' Nothing like this had ever happened to Bill before, and he wasn't sure how to handle this situation. Here he was, in a tricky position that he wasn't sure how to get out of. He didn't want to offend the boss's wife, but he certainly wasn't going to have an affair with her.

There was no way he was going to respond to the boss's wife's advances, so he quickly said, 'I'm sorry Rose, but I've had a terrible accident recently and I'm now what they call a horse when they say he's a "Gelding".

Rose became a changed woman. She moved away from Bill, telling him not to worry about the furniture, as her husband could shift it tomorrow. Bill started to leave, but was momentarily stopped by the now curt lady who asked him not to mention anything to anyone. 'And please call me Mrs Stephens Bill,' she said, as a nervous Bill left in a hurry.

When Bill got back to the quarters, Jenny was sitting in the kitchen drinking tea. She was in a bad mood and she snapped at Bill, 'didn't take her long to get you did it?'

Bill, wondering why Jenny was uptight about this, asked her if Mrs Stephens had made advances on other men. 'She is much younger than Ray, and he is often away drinking, so she does. I thought you were different Bill, especially when you reminded me of my father.'

Jenny then burst into tears, and ran to her room. Bill then realized that Jenny thought that he had responded to Mrs Stephens.

He followed Jenny to her room, and after knocking, opened the door and said, 'do you think I would have anything to do with the boss's wife?' Wild now, he yelled, 'for your information I did not touch her.' He stormed out to the kitchen and lit the fire to make a coffee.

It was not long before he heard a noise behind him, and thinking it was the whatever it was that he had heard earlier in the day, he yelled, 'and you can get lost too.' This made his new workmate cry even more. Bill turned, and there was Jenny crying her eyes out. Not sure how to react, Bill asked her if she would like a cuppa? So the two of them sat down and talked for hours.

Bill learnt that Jenny's father had died recently, and they were very close. 'I nearly didn't come here this season, but we need the money,' she said.

One of the jobs that the workers had to do each night, was to turn off the diesel driven generator, and Jenny, noticing that it was time to do so, asked Bill to accompany her. On the way back, Bill felt Jenny shake, then she started running to her room. 'Quick Bill,' she said, 'will you stay with me for a while. It's the stones.'

Following her to her room, which was lit up by a kerosene lantern, Bill said to her, 'what in the blazes is going on?'

He could hear stones rattling on the roof of the end room, the one that Jenny had told him not to bunk in. She held his hand as she explained that every now and then, stones would fall out of the sky, and land in the end room.

Bill asked her if she meant ON the end room. 'No Bill, they land IN the room. They somehow go through the roof and walls without making any holes.' The sound of these stones, went on for a few minutes. 'I still get scared, even though I know what it is,' she told Bill.

When she was game enough, Jenny led Bill to the end room. Bill opened the door and inside were dozens of similar sized gravel stones. Some were on top of the table, some on the bed, and lots more were scattered all over the floor. Bill looked up at the ceiling, and holding the lantern up high, he was expecting to see holes where these stones must have come through. 'Unbelievable,' he said. 'How did they get in here?'

Jenny was about to answer him, then they saw the lights of a horse drawn carriage coming up the farm driveway. She asked Bill to turn the lantern off, then explained that she didn't want Ray to see them. Sleep did not come easy that night for Bill, but when it did, he slept deeply. When he got up to light the fire next morning, he found it was already burning. Thinking Jenny must have lit it, he made two cuppas and called to her that her tea was poured.

It was a few minutes before she came out to the kitchen, then rubbing her eyes she said 'Oh I see you've lit the fire Bill. Thank you, I usually have trouble getting it going in the mornings. Looks like it's your job every morning.'

Bill was going to ask her if she didn't light the fire, then who did, but he reckoned he had just about enough surprises already. But he was about to get another.

Jenny took a sip of her tea, then said, 'thanks for being a gentleman last night Bill. I shouldn't have come to your room but I was still scared.' Bill couldn't remember her coming to his room, so he asked her what time she left, because she wasn't there when he woke up.

Jenny smiled and told him it was not too long before daylight that she went back to her own bed. 'Heck,' thought Bill, 'does that mean this lady spent some, or even most of the night in my bed?'

Jenny seemed in a happy mood as she made breakfast for them both, and when Bill had eaten the bacon and eggs she had cooked, he told her that it looks like it was her job each morning.

Ray Stephens was not at the shearing shed when Bill and Jenny reported for work, so they set about feeding the horses and mucking out the stables. Jenny told Bill that Ray took pride in his horses, so when Bill had finished the stable chores, he started brushing them, and had nearly finished when Ray called out good morning to him. 'Morning Sir, I mean Ray,' Bill answered.

Ray was obviously happy and said, 'good job Bill. That can be your first task every morning. I suppose Jenny has told you I like my horses. You've a pretty good looking stallion there Bill. Feel free to give him any of the oats that you want to.'

Jenny then came over, and Ray gave them both their jobs for the day. He explained that he would be starting seeding in a few days, so he would like them both to get the machinery in shape. 'Jenny knows the ropes Bill, so better work together as a team eh? That's what we are here, a team,' he said half to himself, as he headed back to the house.

The two of them did as they were told, and worked together. Jenny taught Bill a bit about machinery and explained Ray's way of farming, particularly the seeding techniques. After lunch Ray joined them, and taught Bill even more, especially about the way the seeder worked. The maintenance work kept them occupied for several days, but they finished getting things ready for seeding a day earlier than expected, so Ray told them to have a day off because they would soon be working long hours.

Bill and Jenny packed a picnic lunch, and rode about four mile along the Blackwood River, to a spot that Ray had told them was a gem of a fishing patch. So they fished for a while, then after a swim, they ate their lunch under the shade of a large shady river gum. The horse that Jenny rode was a retired racehorse that belonged to Ray Stephens. 'He's still fit and raring to go, so watch him,' he told Jenny.

They rode at a trot and canter only, on the way to their picnic, but on the way back Jenny challenged Bill to a race over the last half a mile or so. Bill grinned and said, 'loser lights the fire and runs the bath.'

Before Bill knew it, Jenny urged her mount into a full gallop, and the race was on. The track close to the Stephens farm was well used and firm. It was wide enough for two horses to easily run side by side. But Bill and Blackie were already a couple of lengths behind Jenny, who was urging on this former Perth race winner. Bill held the reins tight, until about two hundred yards to go, then he said, 'go Blackie.' Blackie drew level with them, then put his head in front, but Jenny's mount kicked again, and looked like pulling away. Then Bill shook the reins, and Blackie responded immediately.

Unbeknown to the two riders, Ray Stephens just happened to be outside, and being one who loved to see good horses run, he watched in disbelief as Bill's horse left Jenny and her mount several lengths behind. Bill got a shock when he saw that Ray was watching. 'Mighty good horse you have there Bill,' he said.

Both riders washed down their horses, then fed and watered them. Ray noted that Bill walked his horse to cool him down. There was a bigger stall that Bill had noticed earlier, and now his boss insisted that he make that Blackie's stall. This special stall had its own one acre paddock adjoining it, so Bill thanked Ray, and Blackie was now the kingpin of the farm horses.

When Bill and Jenny reported for work, after they had fed and groomed the horses, Ray Stephens was there to get them started on the seeding program. Ray's plan was to sow one hundred acres each of oats and barley, then three hundred acres of wheat. Bill was shown how to drive an eight horse team that pulled a fourteen foot disc plough which had a seeder attached. He was followed by Jenny, who drove a four horse team pulling a furrow leveller. This not only levelled the ground, but covered the seed. When Bill had finished ploughing and seeding a paddock, and had moved onto the next one, Jenny, who could level faster than Bill could plough, would change to a two horse team and tow a ground driven spreader. Ray would stand on the back of this spreader and tip fertiliser into it.

As the boss, Ray Stephens had explained, they must work as a team, and they did. This team worked from daylight to dark every day except Sundays. After a few weeks, Ray told Bill and Jenny that he was more than happy with their work, and if the rains come at the right time, he would be looking at paying them a bonus. 'After my wife gets her new dress that is,' he said.

Mrs Stephens, who was polite but cool towards Bill, handed him a letter at meal time one evening. Bill read it that night. It was from Beatrice. The letter had found its way to his parents place and his mother had posted it on. Beatrice wrote to tell him that she had met a nice man, and they were planning to get engaged. She said that she had waited for him to get in touch, but she just didn't know what to do. Beatrice ended her letter by saying that she was sorry that things hadn't worked out, but she wished he had been more aggressive and contacted her.

Bill did not sleep well that night, and the following day at lunch, Jenny asked him if everything was alright. After two days of Bill barely talking to anyone, she asked him if she had done anything to upset him. Bill told her that he would talk to her later. So that night after tea, when they were having a cuppa in their kitchen Bill told Jenny all about Beatrice. 'So Bill Evans, is that why you have not made a move towards me. What a fool I must be, and I thought you were just being a gentleman too.' With that said, Jenny stormed off to her room.

Now Bill was that upset that he went out to Blackie's stables and slept the night on a pile of hay. He was still there the next morning when Ray found him, still asleep. 'Talk about a man that looks after his horse,' he said to Bill. 'You had better have the morning off lad, but first go and tell Jenny that you're alright. She's been looking all over for you. I reckon she might be a bit sweet on you Bill.'

Bill rushed into the living quarters to find Jenny in tears. 'Bill,' she cried, 'thank goodness you're safe. I'm sorry if I yelled at you last night.'

Then Bill told her it was alright and that it was his fault anyway. They both ate a snack, then went to work, which made Ray smile to himself. 'Oh to be young enough to argue, then make up the very next day,' the aging farmer thought.

Work was a saviour for Bill, and as upset as he was, he realised that life was still good. Beatrice deserved her opportunity at life, and they had never discussed the future together. Bill also let some of his tension out by training a few times a week, especially on Sundays. He made a punching bag and hung it in the shed. He would also go for a long slow run each Sunday. Jenny was beginning to enjoy Bill's company even more, so she joined in when Bill did his training.

It was about six weeks after they had both started work on the Stephens farm, when Bill was woken by Jenny, just after midnight. She rushed into his room and said, 'it's the stones Bill. Can I stay here a while please?' Bill now could hear the stones. They were rattling on or in the end room again. When they stopped, and the couple could hear each other, Bill asked Jenny if she would like a blanket.

She shook her head and got into bed next to Bill. 'Don't mind do you Bill?' Bill told her that he was happy for her to stay. He reached over and turned off the lantern.

The next morning when Bill awoke, there was no Jenny, so he followed the smell of food, and to the kitchen he was led. Jenny had cooked breakfast, and as Bill sat down, she kissed him. 'Happy?' she asked.

Bill held her close and said in his casual way, 'just a little.'

They cleaned the end room of stones, then started seeding again. The first few paddocks that they had sown were covered with green, as the oats had received enough rain to get things started. This day Ray Stephens had told his workers that enough oats and barley had been sown, so they started on the wheat paddocks.

That night after turning the generator off, and having finished their evening cuppa, Bill asked Jenny what she knew about the stones. Jenny was a bit hesitant at first, then she said, 'promise you won't think I'm crazy?' Bill told her that he would never think of her as anything but a beautiful hard working young lady.

Jenny said to him that if he kept that sort of talk up then she not might have time to tell him anything. Bill laughed, then listened as Jenny told him all she knew about these mysterious stones. She started by saying that Ray had told her that there was possibly the spirit of an Aboriginal man responsible. 'Apparently Ray's father had employed a family of Aboriginals, and somehow their daughter died in the end room, and this spirit, according to Ray, is trying to set the girls spirit free,' she said.

Bill asked Jenny if she had ever gone near the room when the stones were falling. She told him that she once went for a look just as the stones stopped. Bill then asked her, 'did you see anything?'

Jenny again told Bill not to think she was crazy, then she told him that she had seen a fuzzy, moving outline of a little girl in that room. 'What did you do next?' Bill asked.

She then told him she ran back to her room and shut the door. She then said there was another worker, a middle aged married man named Jim staying in the room where Bill was now, and he had seen this spirit, or whatever it was too. 'He screamed nearly all night, and next morning he told Ray that he quit, then he took off.'

Jenny told Bill that she nearly left as well, but the Stephen's let her stay with them for a few nights after that. 'I haven't seen any spirits since, but I haven't looked either,' she said.

Bill didn't press her any longer, because he could tell that it was upsetting her.

The seeding was a complete success, and when the last paddock was finished, Ray Stephens thanked his two workers, and told them that if they wanted to stay for another few weeks, then he would pay them the same wages. Bill had been reading in ''The West Australian'' newspaper about the stock-market crash in America, and the world was in financial ruin. He knew that work, and therefore money would be a big problem for everyone. So after discussing it with Jenny, Bill thanked Ray, and they stayed and helped put up a new boundary fence around the farm.

When this was done, and it was now time to move on, Bill asked Ray if he could leave Blackie at the farm while he went to Perth to stay with his parents. 'Only if you agree to come back for the harvesting season,' his boss said.

Bill asked Ray if Jenny was returning, and was told that she said she would if he was. Bill accepted the offer, then worked out that he had a couple of months before harvesting began. On the spur of the moment, he went to Jenny and invited her to accompany him to Perth. 'You can stay at my parent's house,' he said.

Jenny told him that she would love to, but she promised her mother that she would go home. Putting her arms around Bill, she told him that they would be together again soon. 'Is that what you want Bill?'

Breaking her hold, Bill ran towards the stables, saying to the girl that he was starting to realize that he had strong feelings for, 'one last race before we go.'

They saddled their horses and rode for a couple of hours. Jenny stayed close as Bill said his good bye to firstly Blackie, then Mrs Stephens. Ray drove Bill and Jenny to Boyup Brook, where they parted, each going to their parent's homes. 'Will you miss me Bill,' Jenny asked.

Bill had been thinking for a while now, how much he was attracted to this fine young lady, so he let himself say what he felt like saying. 'Yes of course I will Jenny,' Bill replied as he held her close. Then he said, 'I'll be looking forward to the harvesting season.'

Jenny was happy at his words, but as usual she liked to put some humour in, so she said, 'I didn't know you liked farming that much Bill.' He was going to say something funny back, but Jenny didn't give him the chance, as she kissed him long and hard, then ran to her transport

Bill arrived at his parent's and sister's house just before dark, and surprised them as he had not told them he was coming. Mary Evans was the first to greet her son, then

Peggy joined in the hugging and happiness. 'Where's Dad?' Bill asked. With tears flowing down her cheeks, Bill's mother pointed to the lounge room.

He rushed in to see his father, the once proud and fit bustling man that Bill had respected and looked up to so much. The man who had the fortitude and gumption to bring his Family to this country, against all odds, to give them a chance at a better life. Then as Bill stood in the doorway, he heard his father say, 'look at you my son. You're bigger and fitter than Tommy Burns.' Bill knew that Tommy Burns was the famous Australian boxer who had made the mistake of fighting the vicious American Jack Johnson. This was the first time that Bill's father had ever spoken about boxing to his son. Bill went to his father and the two embraced, though Bill had to reach down to do so, as Joe Evans was now unable to stand. With just the hint of sadness this once proud man told his son that the diabetes had got the better of his legs.

Bill's mother and sister, sensing the mood, and the compassion of the moment, left father and son alone for a few minutes. Old Joe Evans spoke to Bill as he never had before. It was as though he sensed a changing in not only his life, but in his son's.

He spoke of his days back in England, when in his youth he had this dream of becoming a boxer. A smile crossed his face as he told Bill how he had met and fallen in love with Mary. 'The very best, that's who your mother is my boy. But you're no longer a boy are you Bill,' said this still proud man. 'Yes, I've been a lucky man, but I'm not finished yet Son. They tell me that there's a new drug that may cure this damn diabetes.'

The two talked for ages, Bill told his father all about his job at Boyup Brook, and how he enjoyed the seeding. Then he told him that Ray Stephens had asked him and the other worker to return at harvest time. Bill didn't mention that the other worker was a young lady named Jenny. Or that he felt that he was more than just a workmate towards her. 'What about the nice young girl from Northcliffe son? I was half expecting you and her to get together,' Joe said.

Bill would normally have just shrugged his shoulders, and not spoken about something so personal, but as his father was in such an emotional mood, he said, 'I got a letter from her Dad. She's engaged to somebody, so it's no good me thinking about her.'

It was tea time, so Mary Evans used this as an excuse to venture into the front room, where she thought that her husband and son could probably talk all night. 'About time they talked this way,' she thought.

Mary had prepared a wonderful meal yet again, after which the four happily reunited family adjourned to the front room to go over all of the happenings of the last few months. It was a time that this family enjoyed and didn't want to end. 'Sounds like you're a wheat cocky now son,' said Joe.

As soon as there was a bit of a break in the conversation, Peggy moved closer to her brother and held out her left hand. Bill was momentarily speechless as her saw the sparkling diamond engagement ring on her finger. 'Well I'll be,' he stammered. 'My little sister is to be married. Who's the lucky bloke Peggy?'

Peggy Evans told her brother that she was to become Mrs Harold Morris. So they talked some more, then some more. Bill looked at his family and thought that except for his father's illness, they were happy, and doing alright.

The next morning Bill got up at daylight and jogged around the streets of West Perth. When he got back Peggy was cooking toast and poached eggs for him. This reminded him of Jenny, so he told his sister about how he felt that Jenny was someone special. 'Do you like her much?' Peggy asked.

This made Bill stop and think. 'Yes, as a matter of fact my young and inquisitive little sister, I think I do,' he said.

Then Bill asked Peggy how things were going. Things like, did they manage on the money that they had. Peggy told him that they were really battling, and things were getting worse for everyone in the city. She explained that the depression that started a couple of months ago had spread. 'There are people out of work everywhere. To see once proud men having to line up at soup kitchens to get a feed is terrible. Every day we have to ration out any waste vegetables at the markets where I work. There is sometimes a line about a hundred yards long of hungry people just hoping to get some free left over produce. It's so shocking Bill. Who knows where or when this depression will end. My boss says there has to be a war to sort everything out.'

Bill gave his sister a five pound note to help his family, which brought a tear to her eyes. Bill had noticed that there wasn't any bacon left, so he said to his sister, 'could you buy some bacon for Dad's breakfast please?'

Peggy looked long and hard at her brother, and she almost broke down and cried. She knew how their father loved his bacon, but money was tight. Finally she just walked to her brother and hugged him. 'I will, if you'll walk me to work Bill,' she said.

After a quiet moment, Bill added his bit of humour to ease the tension. 'I'll walk you to work if you bring you Harold to meet me tonight. I want to see if he is good enough for my little sister.'

That night Peggy brought her fiancé to tea, to meet her brother. Bill and Harold got on well, and nobody else got much of a word in that night. They had a lot in common, both were in their early twenty's, they were of similar back grounds, and Harold's parents owned a house not far from the Evan's.

After Harold had gone home, Peggy asked Bill what he thought of her future husband, and he told her he seemed like a good bloke. 'But if he's not, and he does not look after you, then you tell him he'll have not only your father to answer to, but your brother also.'

Harold was an avid reader of newspapers, and would usually bring a copy of the latest daily paper when he came to visit. He would always leave this paper, which was usually "The West Australian" for Joe to read. Bill would sometimes have a bit of a read, and one day he read in the sports section how a horse called Phar Lap had just won the Victoria Derby. There was a photograph of what the newspaper described as a wonder horse, and Bill was surprised to see the similarities between his own horse and Phar Lap. A record crowd had turned up to watch this champion racehorse, who had recently won the Australian Derby in record time. Another story centered on a cricketer called Don Bradman. Bradman was rapidly becoming known as possibly one of the best batting prospects that Australia had produced for many years. A well reputed sportswriter compared Bradman with the great Bill Ponsford. Bradman first came under notice in nineteen twenty six, when batting for his home side Bowral, scoring three hundred runs when he was only seventeen. The following year he scored a century in his debut match in the strong interstate competition. Bill took this newspaper in to show his father, but Joe had already kept up with most of the stories, particularly the sports news. 'Don Bradman looks like the one man that might be able to face up to the new English speed bowler Harold Larwood,' Joe said.

Bill walked his sister to work most mornings, and would usually jog home afterwards. Then one morning, about a week after being back with his family, Bill noticed a poster stuck on the door of the Leederville town hall, which said, "CAN YOU BOX?" So he stopped jogging and read it properly. Apparently professional boxing was held in this hall each Friday night. Bill read that the promoter needed boxers, and was offering five pounds per fight, to anyone that could prove to him that they were capable. Bill went inside and after speaking with this promoter, he sparred a couple of rounds with a local boxer. 'Well Bill, I reckon you've passed the test. Can you be here at eight o'clock this Friday?'

So Bill, unbeknown to his family, did go that Friday, and for the next six or seven Friday's as well. He didn't have much trouble winning his bouts, and after defeating the main boxer on the programme, the promoter told Bill that he was now the main billing for next Friday. 'There will be an extra fiver in it for you, and another tenner if you win,' the smooth talking promoter told Bill.

The boxer that Bill had to face was a young up and coming middleweight named Steve Charlton, who had been undefeated in his twenty two fights. The poster out front read that Charlton was being hailed as the next good thing, and needed a warm up bout. Bill smiled as he read this poster on his way in that Friday night. Bill had purchased a new set of gloves, and had trained seriously since he had started these bouts at Leederville. He was feeling good, and was looking forward to his first real opposition, and also the extra money would be good for his parents. This gave him more will to win, which he did, though as he told Charlton after the fight, it was not an easy win, and he thought this young man would go a long way.

Bill had so far earned fifty five pounds from his boxing, so he offered to take his mother and sister shopping. He had another fifty pounds that he had saved from working at Ray Stephen's farm. It was a Saturday morning, and the city was busy as the three of them went from shop to shop. Bill's mother purchased a big aluminium kettle, which looked like it would boil about two gallons at a time.

Then Bill watched as she looked adoringly at a green teapot set, complete with a jug and six cups and saucers. Mary Evans picked up the teapot, then a cup, and Bill could tell that his mother really wanted this beautiful set. 'Too expensive,' she said as she went off to the clothes section with Peggy.

Bill took this opportunity, and quickly paid for the set that his mother had obviously fallen in love with. With the set packed in a box under his arm, he found his mother and sister, who had a parcel of new clothes each. They then went upstairs to a cafeteria and had a lunch of pies and veggies.

Peggy, noticing the parcel Bill was carrying, said to him, 'well now brother, don't tell me you've bought yourself a present, or is that for me?'

Bill just smiled back at his sister, then his humorous side got the better of him as he said back to her in a posh voice, 'could be that I've bought myself a new suit so I can take my sister dancing.'

He knew that Peggy didn't like dancing much, so he hoped that his being silly might take the attention away from what was really in the parcel that he wanted to surprise his mother with.

After arriving home some three hours after they had left Joe Evans by himself, Bill presented the box to his father. He explained what was in it, and how his mother had really wanted it. 'I thought you might want to surprise her with it Dad,' he told his grateful father. Bill smiled as his father pushed the parcel out of site behind his chair.

That night Peggy's fiancée came for tea, and he brought with him a copy of "The West Australian" newspaper. Luckily Harold showed it to Bill first, because it had a story about Bill's boxing bout, saying how he had defeated the bright prospect Steve Charlton. Bill asked Harold not to show the paper to his family, explaining how they did not know that he had been boxing. 'Dad does not agree with me boxing,' he said.

Harold just grinned and said, 'ok mate, I'll keep my Welsh mouth closed.'

Mary Evans put on a huge meal that night. Firstly she served lamb chops and tripe, with lots of fresh veggies that Peggy had bought from the West Perth Markets where she worked. This was followed by rhubarb pie and custard. 'You've done it again my dear,' Joe Evans said to his wife.

Peggy and her mother made them all a cup of tea, which Mary said they should drink in the front room. Bill and Harold helped Joe to his lounge chair, and just after he sat down, he reached behind his chair and retrieved the box that he had put there earlier. The three men chatted away, and when the ladies had served the drinks, Bill stood up, and all went quiet, as it was obvious that he had something important to say to them. 'I am heading back to Boyup Brook in a few days, and I could be away for a while. But there is one thing I promise. I will be back for the wedding.' He then handed an envelope to each of them.

As they opened them, each one, in turn thanked him in their own way. Firstly his mother embraced him, then told him he was a good son, and that she loved him very much. Bill's father put out his big hand and shook it so hard that Bill thought all his bones were going to break. Peggy and Harold opened their envelopes together, then gave Bill a group hug, and thanked him sincerely. Bill had put a ten pound note in each envelope, hoping that in would help get them through the tough times, which had now been officially called a financial depression.

There were tears of happiness all round, then to top it off Joe Evans presented his wife with the teapot set. Mary Evans could not believe her eyes. Never before had she had such luxury. 'Our son is the one to thank for this my dear,' Joe told his dumbstruck wife.

Mary took her new teapot set into the kitchen, and they all drank more than one cuppa that night. Then when it was time for the night to end, Harold shook Bill by the hand and asked him if he would be the best man at his and Peggy's wedding. 'I will be honoured to,' Bill answered, 'just let me know the date and I'll be there.'

Chapter Seven
Testing Times

Both Bill and Jenny arrived back at the Stephen's farm on the date given to them by Ray Stephens. Jenny had been there for about an hour when Bill arrived, and had lit the fire and the kettle was boiling. They talked for a while, Bill telling Jenny about his sister's engagement, and about his mother and father.

Jenny did not have much news, but told Bill that she had missed him. 'I hope you don't mind Bill, but I told my Mum about you and she said that you are welcome to visit or stay at our place anytime,' she said. Jenny then asked Bill if he intended going to his sister's wedding, and was a little quiet when he told her that he was to be best man, and he would not miss it for anything.

After they had finished their cuppa, they went to the stables to check out the horses. Bill said to Blackie, 'you've put on a bit of weight boy. We'll have to work that off you,' so they saddled up and rode for a couple of hours.

They had just finished hosing and grooming the horses, when Ray Stephens approached them. He said that harvesting looked like being delayed by about by week, 'but you are both welcome to stay till then,' he told them. Ray said that his wife was away visiting her sister for a few days, so they would have to make their own evening meals.

Bill then told his boss that he and Jenny would be fine to make their own meals every night, as he intended to ride Blackie each afternoon. 'I may be late back, and I don't want to put Mrs Stephens out,' he said.

So the big black horse was exercised each afternoon, even when harvesting started. Jenny rode with him most times, and the riding kept both horse and rider's fit. Blackie soon lost his fat and after a few weeks Ray told Bill that his horse was looking like a Melbourne Cup winner.

The harvesting went according to plan, and Ray was a happy farmer. 'Looks like a record crop,' he told his two workers one day. His workers were happy as well, not only with the harvesting, but with each other. They had grown closer together, and one night Bill told Jenny that he was expecting a letter soon telling him the date of

Peggy and Harold's wedding. Bill noticed that Jenny went quiet, like she did the last time he spoke about his sister's wedding. So he said, 'what's up Jenny?'

But she just shook her head and told him that nothing was up. Bill pulled her close and said that he would like it very much if she would come to the wedding with him, and also he would like her to meet his parents. This done the trick, and Jenny opened up. 'Well it's about time you asked me Bill Evans. It's over a month since you told me about the wedding.'

She was about to try to storm off, but Bill held her tight and said that he would not let her go until she agreed to go with him. 'Of course I'll go with you,' she said.

Bill was excited that he and Jenny were close, now that she was coming with him to Perth, he thought it was all too good to be true. Here he was, learning and enjoying the type of job that he felt he was made for, and earning good money doing it. But most of all he was happy. He was still getting over losing Beatrice, and still sometimes thought about her, and wondered if she was happy. Now he had Jenny, and they were very close, so things were good. Surely nothing could go wrong and spoil all this?

There had not been any episodes of stones falling since they had started harvesting. Then one night they were woken by the rattling, and as before Jenny held Bill close and started trembling. 'It's alright Jenny, they'll stop soon,' Bill said as he tried to console her.

The stones had been rattling for about ten minutes, when they suddenly stopped. Then they heard a noise that sounded like screaming, coming from the end room. Bill jumped up and started to go to investigate, but Jenny said 'don't go Bill.'

But he did go, and he did look into the end room. Bill's hair nearly stood on end as the saw the outline of a small child floating through the room. Bill could never remember being afraid in his life before, but he was now terrified, and he hurried back to their room. Jenny had lit the kero lantern and was huddled up like a ball on the bed.

As Bill got close, she reached out to him and clung to him tighter than ever. 'Stay with me,' she stammered. The silence was now deafening, and they did not get any more sleep that night.

The next morning Bill asked Ray if they could possibly have the day off work as they had hardly any sleep. 'Looks like rain in a day or so,' said Ray. 'Sorry Bill, but I reckon we better keep harvesting.'

So they did go to work, even though they were exhausted from lack of sleep. Something was telling Bill to refuse his boss and to take at least the morning off, but he did not. As he hitched his team of horses up to the harvester, he imagined he could hear his friend Charlie Burns saying, 'be careful Bill,' just as he had said to him several months ago. Bill shook his head, as if to clear it, and started work as Ray wanted.

As they did when they were sowing the crops, the three of them now worked as a team, to harvest what they had successfully sown some months ago. Bill and Jenny would each operate a horse drawn harvester. They worked in unison, one operating about fifty metres in front of the other. The crop that they were harvesting would shoot into a bin being towed behind the harvester. Then as each bin was full, Ray would drive his truck, which had a big bin on it, alongside and offload these smaller bins. Ray would then go back to his storage shed and empty his bin. This system seemed to work well, as the harvesting was not delayed by having to transport the small bins back to the shed each time they were full. The big bin could not be towed behind the harvesters as it was too heavy.

Bill was leading with his team of horses and harvester, so he did not see the tragedy happen. The bin on the back of Ray's truck was not fixed, mainly because he sometimes needed to take it off, so as he said, 'it was quicker this way.'

Seeing that Jenny had stopped harvesting, Ray presumed that her bin was full so he backed alongside her harvester ready to load her bin.

But Jenny had only stopped harvesting because she had noticed that there was a blockage in the worm drive, and wheat was starting to spill out. She had been taught by her boss that the best way to unblock this worm drive was to get out and hand clean away the grass that caused the problem. Ray had also shown her that if she could notice the blockage early enough, then it was quicker to back up the horses which would in turn reverse the direction of the worm drive and most times cleared the blockage. Jenny decided, that as she knew that Ray was in a hurry to beat the rain, she would try the quicker way.

She had not seen the truck that her boss had backed close to her harvester, but she heard a bang as her machine made contact with the bin on the back of the truck. Jenny jumped from the seat, and ran around the back to see what was wrong. Just as she got near she heard Ray scream for her to stop. But the call was too late to save Jenny. As she rounded the corner of the harvester, the bin fell from the back of the truck right on top of her.

Bill sensed something was wrong, and turned to see the bin fall. Not knowing that his Jenny was underneath it, he didn't really hurry, but went back to help put the bin back on the truck. He did hurry now though, as he heard Ray yell Jenny's name. Bill knew by the tone of his boss's voice that something was dreadfully wrong.

When Bill got there all he could see of the girl that he had grown so fond of, was one arm sticking out from under the heavy bin. Bill screamed her name and tried to lift the bin off her. 'Help me will you. Don't just stand there,' he called to Ray. But it was no use.

The bin was way too heavy. Bill told Ray to move his truck forward a bit, then he threw a rope over the bin and looped on the other side. 'Now slowly drive forward,' he yelled. It worked well, and the bin lifted enough for Bill to pull Jenny from under the bin.

As Ray Stephens ran from the truck, he heard Bill cry out in anguish, and he knew it was too late to save Jenny. Bill held her, and cried like he had never cried before. After a few minutes Ray tried to tell Bill that they should take Jenny to town. 'Go away,' yelled Bill to his boss. 'You shouldn't have backed in until you were sure she was ready. Go away and leave us alone.'

Bill was still holding Jenny's lifeless body when Ray returned with a trailer behind the truck. They wrapped Jenny in a clean tarpaulin and took her to the Boyup Brook Hospital. Bill stayed for a while, but there was nothing he could do, so he went outside and just walked. He didn't know what else to do. Somehow he finished up inside the hotel, and that's where Ray Stephens found him a few hours later. He tried to console Bill, but could not even get a word out of him. After paying the publican for Bill's drinks, he asked him to put his worker to bed when he passed out. Bill did eventually pass out from too much alcohol, and when he awoke he was in a hotel room. He lay there for a while, then the memory of what had happened to Jenny came flooding back to him.

Unable to stand the pain and remorse of the picture of his Jenny's lifeless body, Bill got up and staggered down to the hotel bar and drank himself into another stupor. He was now in a dream like state of unawareness, but the pain had gone.

For five days Bill Evans spoke to nobody, except to tell the barman to give him drink, or he would have to knock his block off. He only ate when he was too drunk to know what he was doing. Several times, Ray had tried to approach Bill, but each time he was pushed away and yelled at.

Unbeknown to Bill, Ray had sent a telegram to Jenny's mother, and she and Jenny's two brothers had come and organized for Jenny's body to be taken home. Jenny's brothers had tried to talk to Bill at the hotel, but all they got back was a drunken incoherent slur.

Ray had also opened a letter addressed to Bill, only to get an address, so he could send a telegram to let his parents know what a bad state their son was in and the reason why.

The first time Bill showed any sign of being alive, or aware of anything, was when Harold Morris was shaking him. He heard this voice that he somehow knew, but because of the alcohol still affecting his brain, he couldn't think who it was. Then the voice seemed to be shouting louder, right into his very soul. 'Wake up Bill. Come on mate, you must wake up.'

Then he heard his sister's voice. 'Peggy,' he cried out loud. Bill tried many times to get another drink, but his sister, with Harold's help, stopped him. 'Come on Bill, you have to sober up,' she said.

They made him shave and shower, then they took him to the local store and bought a suit for him. Peggy told her brother that she and Harold had met Jenny's mother and brothers and they were expecting him at her funeral tomorrow.

The funeral was held in Jenny's home district of Kojonup, and was attended by over two hundred people. Bill was asked by Jenny's mother to walk with her, in front of the funeral parade. Jenny's two brothers and four other family friends were the pallbearers.

After the funeral Bill, Peggy, and Harold were invited back to Jenny's mother's house. Mrs Williams told Bill that her daughter had told her all about him. 'She loved you Bill,' she told him through tears.

Bill told her he blamed himself for Jenny's death, but was stopped short by Jenny's mother, who told him that Ray Stephens had explained what had happened. 'He blames himself alone Bill, so do not feel any guilt. My daughter talked of you so much. Her last letter told me that she was going to Perth with you to your lovely sister's marriage.'

Mrs Williams up to this point in time had been able to control her emotions, but now the reality of losing her only daughter was starting to hit home, and the tears started to flow.

Then Bill suddenly realised that he had been feeling sorry for himself for the past several days. Here in front of him was Jenny's mother, who had given birth to, and raised Jenny to be what she had grown into. Did she rush off and try to hide a weakness that she could easily have had? Did she wallow in self- pity by drinking herself into a stupor so she would not have to face up to things?

Bill stood up and went to Jenny's mother, and putting his arms around he said, 'you are a wonderful, strong human being, and I can see your beautiful daughter each time I am lucky enough to look at you.'

Turning to include everybody, a somehow different Bill Evans said, 'can you all please find it in your hearts to forgive me for my selfish attitude these past days. I am so sorry that I put you through the unnecessary trouble and pain of having to worry about me at this terrible time.'

Bill continued to hug Mrs Williams, then he quietly said, 'I was going to ask Jenny if she would marry me.' Jenny's two brothers came over and joined in with their mother, and a sort of knowing silence came over everybody.

Peggy Evans and her fiancée Harold Morris, stayed with Bill at the Boyup Brook hotel for another two days. Bill's caring sister wanted him to return to Perth with them, but he said that he would not yet. 'I promise to be there for your wedding,' he told them as they boarded the train.

Still in somewhat of a daze, Bill paid the local courier to take him out to the Stephens farm. He was not looking forward to returning to the scène of Jenny's tragedy, but he had to get his horse and personal belongings from the farm.

Ray Stephens met Bill as he walked down the long driveway to the homestead. Both men were silent for a while, until Bill said, 'I firstly want to apologize for my behaviour towards you Ray. Also I sincerely thank you for organizing everything so well. I was a mess, and I was wrong.' Bill put out his hand and the two shook hands warmly.

Bill was surprised to see a tear or two in this tough old farmers eyes, as he invited Bill to have a cuppa. 'No thanks,' said Bill. 'I'll get my things and Blackie, then I'll be on my way.'

The man that had given both Jenny and Bill a job, was still standing in the driveway when Bill led his horse back to say goodbye. 'There will always be a job here for you Bill,' the farmer said as he handed Bill an envelope.

Bill didn't open this envelope, and as he was putting it in his pocket, Ray told him that he had paid Mrs Williams all of Jenny's wages. 'I know I don't have to tell you this, but I also paid for the funeral. Mrs Stephens and I are terribly sorry the way things have turned out Bill, and we wish we could change things, but we can't.'

The young man went quiet, then again shook hands with his former boss. He was about to mount Blackie, but something made him turn back to Ray and say, 'I know you don't like to talk about them, but if you could, I would like to know a bit more about the stones that fall through, and somehow into the end room.'

For a moment Bill was sure that Ray was going to refuse to talk about this paranormal happening, but the man in front of him then seemed somehow pleased to talk freely. It was almost like he was happy to get it off his chest. Ray firstly asked Bill to give his word not to tell anyone what he was about to tell him. After Bill agreed, Ray told him that, as his father did before him, he used to employ some Aboriginal families on his farm. 'Then one night a girl died in the end room. All the family members were screaming and wailing outside the room, and as I went to see if I could help, the Elder, or leader of the family stopped me and said that it was my Fathers fault. He then said that there was now a curse on this place. Then they all left.'

Bill could see that Ray was shaking as he continued, 'I was sorry to see them leave, as they were good workers and good people. The one thing I remember clearly was that as each family member left, they walked past the end room and threw a handful of stones at it.'

Ray was by now visibly upset, so Bill didn't stay any longer. Blackie did not need any prodding to head for the front gate, where Bill turned to wave goodbye. He looked for Ray but there was no sign of him.

He then looked up and said 'bye Jenny.' So a tired, and more grown up young man gave his horse a loose rein and said, 'take me somewhere Blackie.'

Chapter Eight
Gold Fever

For the next several weeks Bill followed rivers and creeks, where there was plenty of water and grass. Also the pools in these waters contained plenty of fish and marron, so both Bill and Blackie lived well. The solitude was good for Bill, and his horse loved having his master near all the time. At times Bill would ride Blackie hard to keep him fit. 'I reckon Ray was right,' he told Blackie one day after he had galloped him hard for about three miles, 'you probably could win a Melbourne Cup.'

The nights were the hardest for Bill, as he could not get Jenny out of his mind, and he would wake during the night expecting her to be there alongside him, but of course she never was.

Sometimes he would wake in a lather of sweat, and often he would be calling her name. Always his mind relieved the scene of the terrible accident and he tried to work out ways that he may have been able to save her. Mostly he could see her image whenever he was half awake, and almost always this image would fade away into the distance, and he would be trying to reach her, but never could.

After a couple of weeks he decided to start training a bit, thinking that this might tire him out and let him sleep better. He was right. The more, and the harder he trained, the better he slept. It was not long before Bill was running several miles, and shadow boxing for about an hour each afternoon. Most mornings he would let Blackie take him a few miles until they came to a suitable camping spot. Bill made a set of hobbles out of rope for Blackie, and this would let his horse be able to move around and eat the rich grass at his leisure. Blackie could only take small steps with these hobbles on, and could not roam far.

One of these afternoons, while Bill was hunting rabbits for tea, he heard Blackie neighing and squealing loudly. He figured he was about a mile from his campsite where he had hobbled Blackie, so he jogged back to see what was upsetting him. As he got close he heard a man's voice yelling, 'stay still you big mongrel.'

Realizing that someone was trying to steal his horse, Bill ran faster and sure enough there was a man trying to get hold of Blackie's short lead rope. Still holding his rifle,

Bill told the intruder that unless he wanted a bullet in him then he had better let go of his horse. The man turned to Bill and said, 'and unless you want a lame horse, you had better help me get this trap off his leg.'

Bill saw that Blackie did indeed have a trap secured to one of his back legs. He quickly got hold of Blackie and told him to lay down. Bill had been taught this trick of getting a horse to lay down upon his command, by Charlie Burns. Blackie did lay down at Bill's command, and as he held him, the stranger opened the trap and took it off Blackie's leg. They cleaned and bandaged the wound. 'Don't think it's too bad,' the stranger said, 'but it might be a good idea to bath it in salty water a couple of times a day mate.'

The other chap introduced himself as Alf Jackson, and Bill told him his name. 'Care for a cuppa while you tell me what happened?' Bill asked.

While they were drinking their tea, Alf told Bill that he was a professional dingo trapper. 'Been setting traps round here for a few years now,' he said to Bill in a slow drawl. This sort of easy speech was typical of the "bushies" who didn't see a lot of people to talk to. 'Reckon your fine looking horse must have walked on one of me traps. Sorry about that mate, but I don't often see too many folk around here you know.'

Bill asked him where here was, which started Alf laughing. 'You mean to tell me that you don't know where you are mate?' said Alf between fits of laughter.

When this dingo trapper had stopped laughing, he told Bill that he was camped on the banks of the Beaufort River, and the nearest place that a bloke could call a town was Wagin. 'That's about forty mile that way, as the crow flies,' he said.

They talked for a while, then Alf asked Bill if he would like to come and see his shack and maybe stay for a meal. 'The Mrs is a real good cook and she's sure to have enough to share,' he said as they headed off.

Bill had first packed all his gear and was now leading Blackie, who seemed to be only just limping. Alf's shack, as he called it, was not far, which pleased Bill, because he didn't want to make his horse walk too far.

Mrs Jackson, or Alice, as she insisted Bill call her, was a pleasant lady, but as Bill was to find out soon enough, could talk the legs off a table. 'Well hello Bill,' she said as her husband introduced her. 'We don't get many visitors out here you know, but we welcome you.'

She asked Bill of any news that had happened in the world or anywhere. Then if Bill tried to tell her something, she would be telling him all about the price of dingo scalps, or fox tails. She was though, as her husband had said, a fine cook. Bill told her so after the evening meal, and this started her off talking all about how weevils and ants got into the flour and sugar. Bill started to suggest that she might be able to use a dish of water under each container to stop the ants, but by this time Alice was talking about having to collect firewood, and how that was getting harder to find.

All this time Alf Jackson had hardly said a word, but now said in a loud voice, probably so he could be heard above his wife, who was still talking, 'reckon you better camp here for a while Bill. Won't do your horse a lot of good trotting around too much just yet.'

Bill thanked Alf and set up camp about a hundred yards up river from the Jacksons shack. He again checked Blackie's injury, and it looked alright, so he turned in for the night. During the night he got up to check on his horse a couple of times, but Blackie just neighed as if to say, 'I'm alright.'

Just after daybreak the next morning, as Bill was preparing his breakfast, Alf called out, then came near Bill's small fire he had lit to boil the billy and cook a damper. 'How's your horses leg?'

Bill had tended to Blackie before himself, and he now told Alf that the injury looked fine. 'Care to check the traps with me then?'

Bill nodded as he swallowed his last mouthful, and then they set off. He noticed that Alf carried only a club, and when the time come to check the first trap Bill learnt why. They had crossed over a shallow, but wide part of the river to get to where most of Alf's traps were set. But before they reached the first trap, Bill could hear a dog like noise, which was as he suspected, a dingo. As quick as a flash Alf rushed at the trapped dingo and clubbed it. 'Gotta get them fast Bill. They always back away for a few seconds, and that's the only chance a bloke gets, otherwise they'll chew you to bits.'

Standing back a bit, Bill watched as this trapper quickly pulled the now dead dingo out of the trap. Then with a piece of meat, which looked like rabbit, he re-set the trap. This process went on until they had checked all of Alf's traps. 'Not too bad eh Bill,' Alf said.

Bill had counted twenty traps, from which eight had been successful in trapping a dingo. Alf had re-set all the traps, and on their return trip he took the scalp off each dead animal. 'Five bob each scalp,' he told Bill.

Dingoes were classed as vermin, by the local governments, as they attacked and killed thousands of sheep, mainly lambs. To try to reduce their numbers, each road board, or shire, would pay licensed trappers five shillings for each scalp the trapper delivered to the road board office. Alf told Bill that he usually delivered his tally to the Wagin office, about once a month. He said that today was a good day, as sometimes he didn't get a single scalp. Alf said that Mrs Jackson would usually tell him when her supplies of tucker were getting low, and that's when they would harness up the horse and buggy. 'Mostly we take fifty or sixty scalps at a time,' he explained.

Bill stayed a week with the Jacksons, and when he left, Alice told him she was sorry he was going, because he was a good conversationalist. Bill grinned to himself at this statement, because he reckoned he wouldn't have gotten more than twenty words into their conversations all week. Blackie suffered no infection from his episode with Alf's dingo trap, and the small cut on his back leg healed quickly. 'I'll give you fifty quid for your fine animal,' said the man who Bill had thought was trying to steal Blackie.

It didn't take long to refuse this offer. 'No thanks Alf,' he said quietly. 'This horse is more than just a horse to me, and I wouldn't sell him for all the tea in china.'

He was a little sorry to leave the Jackson's camp, as he had enjoyed the company of this unusual, but close and genuine Aussie couple. He found that their humour had helped take his mind off Jenny's tragic death.

Alf Jackson had one morning, while they were checking the traps, told Bill that if he wanted to have the chance of having an adventure as well as the probability of making some money, then he should go gold prospecting. He explained that he had done well, and he had met his Alice whilst he was up that way. 'Now she's an adventure all by herself,' he laughed, as he told Bill this, in his form of a joke, as only Alf could do. Alf had given Bill the address of a friend of his, saying, 'this bloke is as honest as the day is long. Just tell him that Alf sent you and you'll be right as rain.'

So when he rode away, Bill didn't just give Blackie a loose rein, he directed his keen horse towards the goldfields, 'and who knows what,' he thought.

Bill had decided to take this old trappers advice and headed towards a small mining town named Southern Cross. Wagin was the first town on the way, and upon Alf's advice, Bill purchased a pack horse, so as to be able to carry extra supplies. 'Take as much water as you can possibly cart,' was Alf's last and best suggestion.

The tall timber country gradually gave way to shorter trees and scrub, which was somewhat easier for Blackie to move through. Bill decided after he left Wagin, that he would be better off now following the main tracks. After talking with the storekeeper that had sold him his supplies, Bill headed for Lake Grace, and from there he was told he should take the well-marked track to Southern Cross. This storekeeper told Bill to make certain that he carried at least fifty gallons of water when he left Lake Grace, as there was not much fresh water after that. 'And make sure you don't drink the water in the lakes as it's very salty.'

There were plenty of lakes, especially for the first fifty or so miles from the aptly named town of Lake Grace, and to Bill's amazement, some of these lakes were filled with pink water. Bill wished that his sister could see them, as she loved the colour pink. This made Bill think about his family, and in particular his sister's wedding. Peggy had told him that they would choose a day in March or April. He wasn't sure of the date now, but he knew that it was nearing Christmas, so he reckoned he had plenty of time to hunt for gold.

Thinking about the date reminded Bill that he had purchased a newspaper in Wagin, so that afternoon he read the sports section. He read how Phar Lap had come third in the Melbourne cup. Also the cricketer Don Bradman had continued to improve and impress. Playing for his chosen side, New South Wales, in the Sheffield Shield competition, he broke Bill Ponsford's world first class record score. Ponsford had set the world record score of four hundred and thirty seven runs, and at the close of play, when this story went to print, Bradman was four hundred and fifty two not out. After reading the date on the newspaper, Bill realized he had missed Christmas after all.

About a week out from Lake Grace, Bill had a strange feeling, or premonition, about his brother. He couldn't get him from his mind for some reason, no matter how he tried. Bill remembered how Don used to always want to be in charge whenever the two of them played any games. His brother was nineteen when the Evans family left the old country to come to Australia, which as Bill worked out, was nearly six years ago. Don had gotten engaged not long before their father broke the news about starting a new life in Australia. Bill could almost still hear his big brother standing up to his father, telling him and all the family that he was going to start his new life here, where he was born. Bill remembered how his mother had cried for days. There were no tears as their ship the "Ballarat" left port though. Don Evans had not come to see them off, saying that he could not stand goodbyes.

Then Bill's thoughts suddenly turned to his friend Charlie Burns, remembering that he also did not like goodbyes. These thoughts or daydreams were sometimes a good chance for Bill to clear his mind of Jenny's terrible accident. He still loved to think of her, and he missed her badly, but the way she was taken at such a young age was sometimes too hard to bear.

Thinking about other things was one way to ease his mind. Another way was to play his mouth organ that he had bought in Manjimup. It had not taken long for Bill to be able to play a tune or two, especially as Charlie Burns, who was a good player, had taught him a bit. Bill thought that there wasn't much that his Aboriginal friend did not excel at.

The mood was broken now, because just ahead of him was a fork in the road. There were no signs directing Bill which way to head. Both tracks looked similar, so he sat comfortably in the saddle trying to think which track to take. Bill reckoned that he was by now a pretty good bushman, but he could not make a decision. Then as he looked up the track that led slightly more to the right, he saw the shape of a man. Slowly he turned Blackie's head that way.

As he got closer, he saw that this figure was in fact a full blood Aboriginal, who was standing absolutely still. This proud man had one leg raised up so that the foot on this raised leg was resting on the knee of the leg that he was standing on. In his hand he held a spear, which he used as a support.

Bill stopped a few yards in front of him, and could see that he was a special member of the human race. The way he held himself erect, and the strength of character that seemed to somehow ooze from him, filled Bill with awe. Not sure how to handle the situation, Bill slowly unpacked some flour, sugar, and bacon. Carefully he placed these gifts on the ground, just in front of this still stationary God like man. Ever so slowly there was a moving of the right arm, and firstly he held this arm across his chest in a form of a salute, then he unfolded this arm and pointed up the track. Bill could tell that he was directing him which track to take, so he remounted Blackie and rode in the direction that the proud man was still pointing to. After riding about fifty yards, Bill chanced a look back, to maybe wave a thank you, or a goodbye, but there was nobody to wave to.

Bill didn't ponder for long on the ability of the Indigenous Australian's special way of being able to know what was happening all around them. More so he had recognized long ago, the fact that they could somehow see, or feel what was going to happen. In this case it was as though this man knew that Bill was coming.

With a clear mind, and confident that he was on the right track, Bill pulled his mouthorgan out of his saddlebag, and before long the desert was filled with the sounds of "Waltzing Matilda". Blackie had long ago gotten used to the eerie sound of Bill's mouthorgan, but not so the native animals. As they moved along this sandy track, Bill would occasionally see a pair of Bush Turkeys or "Bustards", rise from the scrub and spread their huge wings, only to circle and land a small distance away. Bill knew he could easily shoot and eat these birds, but he felt that he would survive without killing such a wonderful specimen of nature.

Now and then a Quail would flutter up and sometimes scare Blackie and his pack horse. Bill also liked watching the many Mallee fowl that were prevalent in this semi-arid country. The sandy soil soon started to change to a red colour, and naturally enough, this sand affected the colour of the coat of the native Kangaroo. Bill had only ever seen the south west Kangaroo, which is a grey colour, and at first could hardly believe his eyes when a mob of Red Kangaroos hopped across the track. Almost every time he played his mouthorgan, Bill would have an audience of up to ten or so inquisitive Emus. As soon as Bill would stop playing, the Emus would scatter, and Bill enjoyed stopping and starting playing, just so he could watch these long legged flightless birds run. The speed that they could muster over a short distance was phenomenal, and Bill reckoned that they would easily outrun a man. Then they would skid to a stop and look back. Mostly they stopped behind some scrub and all Bill could see was their head and long necks protruding above the bushes. Occasionally a goanna or a snake would either wriggle across the track, or lay dozing in the sun. Bill had seen photos of most of these native animals when he studied about Australia back in England, but to see them in real life was much more impressive.

The full blood Australian Aboriginal, had directed Bill in the right direction, and after enjoying the peace and solitude of the desert, which got more and more barren by the day, the small mining town named Southern Cross was reached. Bill's first task was to stable his horses, and not far from these stables he found, and booked into a boarding house.

After unpacking he went to the post office and sent a telegram to his parents, telling them where he was, and that he would stay for a while. As it was getting late in the day, he then had a meal at the boarding house. There were several other diners there, and as he went to sit at a single table, an elderly gentleman invited him to share his table. Bill was glad of the company, and they soon got to talking. As in most conversations, the weather was one of the early topics, but as this was a mining town, it was not long before the subject of gold was brought up. 'Tom's the name, young fella,' the friendly man said.

Bill willingly shook hands with this old local, then told him his name.

'Knew a chap by the name of Bill once. Dunno what happened to him though. Last time I saw him he was riding his push bike to Coolgardie,' Tom said.

There was no point in trying to stop him, and as their meal arrived, away he went again. 'Now that's where the gold is my boy, or it was, I should say. Paddy Hannan and his Irish mates, they found the first lot of gold you know. Now what were their names again?'

Bill did not have time to answer before he was told that it was Dan O'Shea, and Thomas Flanagan that were the other two lucky prospectors. 'Picked up a couple of kerosene tins full in a week they did Bill. Yep, Coolgardie that's the place.'

Bill listened intently for the next ten minutes or so, then Tom said he had to get home to his dog. The waitress served two plates of apple pie and custard, and not being one to waste any food, Bill did the right thing and ate both. He had not long finished eating when another chap came over to his table and sat down. 'Don't mind old Tom,' he said.

Bill was about to say he didn't mind Tom, when all of a sudden there was a commotion out the front of the boarding house. Most of the diners rushed out to investigate, so Bill followed them out. There were by now, about fifty people surrounding a man who by his grubby clothes and long whiskers was obviously a miner or a prospector. 'I've struck it rich,' he kept yelling.

Sure enough, he had struck it rich. He emptied a sugar bag onto the ground and out came a couple of handfuls of gold nuggets. 'Where did you find that lot?' came the question that was on everyone's lips. The gold-struck miner laughed and told them that he wasn't telling a soul where he found it. Bill was amazed at the interest shown by everyone in the gold that was laying in front of them. He found it hard to believe that people would get to the stage where the sight of gold affected them so much that they seemed to be in a trance like state.

Not yet having had a drink after his meal, Bill went back inside to have a coffee. Still sitting at his table was the stranger who had joined Bill just before the commotion started. Not sure whether or not he was ready for another ear bashing, Bill didn't start a conversation, but it wasn't long before this other chap continued telling Bill more about old Tom. 'He gets some of his facts a bit wrong, but he means well,' he started. 'Kalgoorlie it was that Paddy and the Irish lads found gold, not Coolgardie. I should know lad, I went there soon after and made a small fortune myself.'

Bill had finished his coffee and was ready to turn in, so he stood up and simply said goodnight. As he got to the door, he looked back to see that the chap had now wandered over to another table, and was starting to talk the ears off the couple sitting there. Bill grinned to himself, thinking that the sun must get to these miners or something. 'They sure can talk,' he said to himself as he headed up to his room.

There was a telegram from his family the next day, and Bill was pleased that things were alright, and the wedding was to be on the fifth of April. So knowing that he had some four months to try his luck at this gold hunting game, Bill didn't rush into it. Instead, he talked to several of the locals, asking them what tools he would need, and generally asking their advice. Then, fresh from a few days rest and good food, Bill Evans headed to an area that some of these locals had told him was a good starting place. Blackie and his pack horse were happy to be out of the stables and out in the open country. So too was Bill, and the first day he didn't even look for any of this shiny stuff that the people up here seemed to lose their minds over. He made a camp near a hill that had some breakaways on one side, as a few people suggested that this is the most likely sort of country to find gold. Then he searched for four days before he found even a speck of gold, and his first "find", was a piece of brown and white rock with several small pieces of what he thought was gold embedded in it.

After a week or so he moved on a bit, and found another likely looking spot. This time he found firstly an old campsite, with dozens of old Bully Beef cans and other pieces of metal and bullet cartridge shells scattered around the site. Bill did the obvious thing, and kicked a few of these tins. One that he kicked was an old tobacco tin. As it rolled away from him, Bill reckoned that he heard something rattling inside it, so he picked it up, and after several attempts, finally opened it. Inside was a brass ring, with an insignia of the Eureka flag emblazed on the front. Bill tried it on and it fitted, so he wore it. No gold found its way into Bill's bag though, so again he moved on.

This happened several times, then one morning as he was eating breakfast, he figured that he had better head back to Southern Cross, as his food and water supplies were getting low. He was going to pack up there and then, but decided to look around for about an hour first. Bill had already unhitched Blackie, but as he re-hitched him, Blackie, who thought he was going to be taken for a ride, reared up on his back legs, then pranced around as if to tell Bill that it was time to move on. Bill said, 'alright mate, I'll pack up now.'

After packing up and loading all his tools and empty supply containers, he walked over to Blackie and started to mount up. As his mounting foot hit the stirrup, Bill saw something reflecting the sun's rays. There was a bit of early morning dew, so the ground and rocks were damp. This made this piece of what now thought was rock shine even more. He was going to leave it, but as he moved his head to a different angle, the rock sparkled at him.

Not daring to allow himself to think that this rock could be gold, he jumped off his horse and picked it up. Hardly daring to breathe, Bill wet this rock, and when he suddenly realized that he had found a piece of what looked like solid gold, he was hit by what the old timers called "Gold Fever".

Bill held this nugget up to the sunlight and turned it over and over. He wondered where a loud yelling was coming from, and it took him a few moments to fully realize that it was him that was yelling at the top of his voice. Bill had truly been infected that day. He had caught the miner's disease.

Chapter Nine
Not So Easy

THE gold buyer at Southern Cross did not show any signs of emotion as he told Bill that his nugget was almost pure gold. 'Two and a half ounces,' he said. Bill didn't know that any nugget over about an ounce was usually worth more as a trophy nugget, or a jewellery piece. The buyer that resided in this small town knew this, and the nugget in front of him had something special about it. Probably it was the shape and the size. 'My current purchasing price is six pounds per ounce Sir,' he told Bill, who thanked him, but said that he didn't really want to sell his nugget.

This astute man wanted Bill's attractive piece, so he said that for today only, he was willing to give thirty pounds, 'and that Sir is my final offer.' Bill knew that he still had over a hundred pounds, so he thanked the buyer again, then left his office.

That night at the boarding house dining room, old Tom again asked Bill to join him at his table. As always, the talk turned to gold. 'Well boy, how did you go? Find your fortune?' the old man asked.

Bill pulled the first piece that he had found, and laid it on the table. Tom picked up this specimen, and after turning it over a few times, he said he thought that there was probably close to an ounce of gold in it. Bill was going to show Tom his new find, but something made him change his mind, so he left his good nugget in his pocket.

Seeing some gold must have started Tom remembering about the old days. 'Water was nearly as valuable as gold back around the turn of the century,' he told Bill. 'Hundreds of good men died of thirst trying to make their fortune, and many of them did not even get this far. They dropped like flies and we buried them where they fell lad.'

He went on to tell Bill that water was selling for up to two shillings a gallon, and many shrewd Afghans used camels to cart the precious liquid. He then told Bill that an engineering man by the name of C. Y. O'Conner was responsible for the laying of a much needed water pipeline from Mundaring to Kalgoorlie. 'Poor bloke never got to see the first drop of water reach us though.'

Bill who was now keenly listening, asked him the obvious question of 'why not?'

It was a question that he thought he might already know the answer to, but he wanted to give this friendly old man his chance. 'He couldn't handle the pressure of the Government interference any longer, so he committed suicide,' said Tom.

Then he continued, 'first drink I had Bill. I was waiting with me billy, and as all these official looking blokes started clapping, and trying to be the one to give a speech, in I darted and filled me billy up and I had the first drink ever to come out of this famous pipeline. True as I'm sitting here that is lad.' Old Tom kept up his story telling for ages, until finally he said, as he always did when he was leaving, 'gotta get home to me dog.'

Bill also left, and was going to have an early night, but instead he headed to the hotel, mainly to see if there was any potential gold buyers there. He saw that there were about a dozen drinkers lining the bar, and as he was a stranger, most of them looked at him as he walked to the bar and ordered a drink. The little barman repeated Bill's order loudly, 'one lemonade coming up,' he said.

Everyone went quiet now, and watched as Bill sipped his drink. Then from a few drinkers up the bar came a loud cocky voice, 'only sheila's drink lemonade.'

Bill took another sip, then unable to resist answering this insult, he calmly said, 'takes one to know one.'

The drinker with the loud voice was not one to be made look small in front of his mates, so he drank down his beer, then grinning widely, he pushed his way up to Bill. 'Did you just call me a Sheila sport?' There was no way of mistaking the challenge in this big bloke's voice. Bill didn't turn around, but he could see in the bar mirror all that he needed to know.

As he walked towards him, Bill could see that the big bloke leaned slightly forward with his left shoulder, so this meant that he would lead with his left hand and throw his haymaker with his right. Slowly Bill turned his head a little towards this man, who probably did this sort of thing most times a stranger came in for a drink. Bill knew that it wasn't the fact that he had ordered a lemonade, that gave this would be fighter the opening to insult him. He had been warned by old Tom that the miners who had been out bush were basically good men, but hard. They drank a lot when they came to town, and there was nearly always a fight. 'If they pick on you boy, don't walk away, you have to sort out the first loudmouth, then you'll be as right as rain,' Tom had said.

Bill did not want to fight, but it now looked like he might not have much choice. 'I don't remember using that name, but if the hat fits wear it,' he said as he turned to fully face this big bloke's challenge. Bill stared straight into his eyes, then saw them waver, and he knew that he wouldn't have to fight him.

Sure enough, the man's voice lost its threatening tone as he said, 'looks like I may have been wrong boys. Could be this here fine specimen is a man who just doesn't like beer, and in our pub he doesn't have to, does he boys?'

The big bloke stuck out his hand and said, 'names Colin mate. Didn't mean any harm, just having a little fun. Not much else to do round here.'

Bill accepted the hand shake, and told him his name, and that it was alright. 'I've just come in from the bush myself, so I know how you feel.'

The now less aggressive Colin, ordered two lemonades, and as he pushed one of them towards Bill, he said, 'new around here aren't you Bill?'

The ice was broken and everybody settled down to having a good time. Bill and Colin got on well and were having a good talk, mainly about gold of course. Eventually Colin asked Bill if he had found much, so Bill showed him the rock with the specks of gold through it, then the two and a half ounce nugget. 'That's a bit more like it mate,' said Colin. Bill was expecting him to ask where he found it, but he didn't.

Old Tom had warned Bill that there were plenty of "spongers", as he called them, who made a living out of finding out when newcomers had a strike, and could not help telling anyone that asked, where they found their gold. These "spongers" would immediately go and look for, and in many cases find, some of the precious metal that the newcomers had missed. Tom had told Bill that a few times these rotten gold grabbers had actually gone out and pegged the site, which meant that not even the people that found the patch could ever prospect there again. Satisfied that Colin was not out to rob or sponge on him, Bill asked him what he thought his nuggets might be worth.

Colin took a moment to think, 'not real sure Bill,' he then answered, 'I usually wait until I have found enough, then I take it to Kalgoorlie. They pay more there, especially for a nice nugget like that solid gold one of yours.'

This made Bill respect this man even more. Not only did he have the common sense to not fight when it was unnecessary, but he didn't try to buy Bill's nuggets cheaply, then sell them for more. The two talked for another hour or so, and when it was time to call it a day, Colin asked Bill if he would like to spend tomorrow prospecting with him. Bill accepted, and they met outside the hotel just after sunup the following morning.

Colin, like Bill had a pack-horse, and took enough supplies for a week or so. 'Never know, we might strike it rich and have to stay out picking up lumps for days,' he laughed.

They rode for what seemed like ages to Bill, and when Colin finally stopped, he pointed to a patch of ground that had white soil running through it. 'Almost like a white river,' thought Bill. They were on a rocky rise, and Colin showed Bill how the hill behind them had a lot of breakaways.

He explained how sometimes these breakaways released gold that over millions of years found its way to the lower gullies and creeks. 'That white stuff is sometimes a bit of a hint where some of this gold could be,' he told Bill.

Colin then showed Bill how to pick out a marker close to where they could see this different coloured soil. 'When you get down there, sometimes it's hard to find,' he said.

So they headed for a tree that was close to the chosen spot. 'Better have a feed and a brew first eh Bill', said Colin. They lit a small fire and boiled the billy, into which Colin threw a handful of tea leaves. Meanwhile Bill cut up some bread and covered the slices with plum jam, and the two happy gold hunters had smoko together for the first time. Little did either of them know that it was be the first of many?

The rest of the morning was mainly taken up with Bill being shown how, and where to look for the most likely spots that could have gold. After another food and cuppa stop, Bill decided to look around by himself for a while. He picked up a very small piece, then after a couple of hours, he headed back towards the area that Colin was working. 'Any luck?' Bill asked when he found him.

The big bloke smiled and pointed to a sugar bag that he had laid out flat. Bill went over to have a look and nearly fell over. There in a neat row, with the smallest on one end, and the biggest on the other, were six beautiful nuggets.

Bill gave a yell of sheer excitement, and could not help picking each piece up and holding it. 'See you've still got the gold fever eh Bill,' said Colin. The smallest of these nuggets was about a half an ounce, and the biggest was probably close to an ounce. 'Not a bad days work eh Bill,' said Colin, who was much calmer than Bill.

They worked this patch for another three days, but they hardly found any more gold, so both of them agreed that they give the patch where Bill found his nuggets a going over. 'Sure you don't mind showing your spot?' Colin asked.

Bill said that it was no different to him going to Colin's spot, so they headed back to town to get some more supplies, and while they were in buying these supplies, they noticed several men watching their every move. Bill knew that many prospectors did this in the hope that they might learn if anyone had had a strike. They called at the hotel and had a lemonade, then set off.

After about five miles Colin told Bill to follow him as he turned his horse in behind a clump of tall bushes. 'Keep out of site Bill, and get that rifle ready,' Colin said quietly.

They didn't have to wait long before, as large as life, three horsemen came round the bend. It was obvious to Bill that they were following him and Colin. With his rifle at the ready, as was Bills, Colin yelled, 'looking for someone?'

The three burley men were taken by surprise, but not for long. The one that had elected himself to be the leader of the pack, recovered first and said, 'just minding our own business, if it's all the same to you.'

Colin said, 'well as it happens, it's not all the same to us. We don't like spongers like you lot following us, so you better turn those mangy animals around and head back so you can sponge on some other hard working prospectors, then hope that they don't shoot you.'

Not quite so sure of himself now, the front man of the three said, 'are you threatening to shoot us unarmed honest miners?'

Bill had not spoken until now, so everyone got a surprise when he cocked his faithful Lithgow Rifle and calmly said, 'I see that not one of you has enough supplies to last more than a couple of days. I can also see that you all have a pistol tucked in your belt. Now this tells a bloke that you are up to no good, and my good friend here and I don't like the idea of being robbed with violence. So if you don't all get off your horses right now, then I'll have to clean the bore of my rifle by pulling the trigger.'

The tone of Bill's voice told these would be rogues and robbers, that he was serious, so one by one they dismounted. 'Now very carefully, with two fingers of your left hand slowly take those pistols that you said you didn't have, and place them on the ground.'

They did as Bill ordered, because Colin had also cocked and pointed his rifle. 'Now,' said Bill, 'remove your boots and place them on the ground.' This done, Bill told them to start walking back to where they came from.

As they started off, one of them asked if they could have a water bag, but was told that it was only a two hour walk back to town, and the exercise might do them good. Colin then said that he was a close friend of the local Constable, and that he would hand their pistols in to him and make a full report when they get back. Bill then grabbed the reins of the three horses, then to the dismay of these barefoot "spongers", as Colin had called them, he led them about a mile away, at full gallop and fired a shot in the air. The three hungry looking horses took off towards Southern Cross at a gallop.

When Bill got back to a laughing Colin, he said, 'don't reckon those blokes will ever catch them.'

Colin, when he finally stopped laughing, asked Bill why he didn't make them take off their socks as well. 'I not a hard man, besides when their socks fill with burrs they'll take them off anyway.'

After picking up the pistols Bill and Colin, both still laughing their heads off, headed to where Bill had found his pieces of gold a couple of weeks before. When they got to the spot Colin told Bill that it looked like a good patch. After setting up camp, they fossicked around, but didn't find any gold.

The next day was the same, and the next. Then on the fourth day Colin found two small nuggets, and Bill thought that their luck was about to change. But it was not to be. After a week they agreed to move on, but when several days later, they had had no luck, and their supplies were getting low, they headed back to town. 'Better keep an eye out for those spongers,' Bill said.

Colin told him that the Police Constable in Southern Cross would back up our story, 'especially when we hand these pistols in.' The Constable thanked Colin and Bill, telling them that it sounded like the three blokes from Kalgoorlie that were wanted for robbing several shops and hotels. He said there was a warrant out for them.

For the next few months Bill and Colin worked together, going over all the patches that Colin knew, and many different spots also. They found barely enough to keep them in food, but they survived and became good friends.

Bill was a bit saddened when Colin told him that he was going to move on to Coolgardie. 'Got a few mates there,' he said. He then asked Bill if he wanted come along also.

Working out that Peggy's wedding was only a month away, Bill declined the offer. So the two friends had a lemonade together, and shook hands goodbye. 'It's been good knowing you Bill,' Colin said. 'I've been wondering though mate. Would you have shot those would be robbers that day?'

A grinning Bill said, 'dunno Colin. Thanks for your friendship, and good luck mate. Now I've got a question for you. Why did you stop and hide behind those bushes that day? How in the heck did you know that those blokes were following us?'

Colin put down his empty glass next to Bill's, and as he got up to leave, he said, 'I really don't know Bill. My father taught me to always follow my gut feelings. Intuition he called it. Remember that mate, and don't get up please, I can't stand goodbyes.' With that he was gone.

Bill was not sure what to do next. Then he remembered that Alf Jackson, the good hearted Dingo Hunter, had told him of a friend that he knew here. Bill looked at his small notebook, which he kept in his back pocket and found the name of Alf's friend and how to find his place. 'Maybe I was meant to go there earlier,' he thought.

The next morning, after riding Blackie, and leading his packhorse, and with plenty of supplies and water, Bill found himself reading a sign on a gate. "IF YOU WANT TO LEARN HOW TO FIND GOLD COME ON IN"

Chapter Ten
Sunshine

Bill was met by a big, bearded man, with eyes that seemed to look at him with a certain confidence that Bill had rarely ever seen. 'Top of the morning to you,' smiled this happy man as he put out his hand. Bill introduced himself, and learnt the other man's name matched the one given to him by Alf Jackson. The name also seemed to match the nature and nationality of this still smiling chap, who had just told Bill that he was Paddy O'Reily, from Belfast Ireland. Bill told Paddy about his having met, and stayed a while with Alf and his good wife. He then said, 'Alf had mentioned that you may assist me in my gold prospecting.'

Paddy invited Bill to stable his horses, then to come in for a coffee at his house. This Irishman proved to be a good talker, and Bill was now sure that being out in the wilderness tended to make people talk more whenever the chance arose. The mug of coffee turned into two, as Paddy was keen to learn any news. He asked Bill how Alf was going, and Bill relayed the good wishes that Alf and Alice Jackson had sent, telling him how they were licenced Dingo trappers.

Bill got a history lesson about Southern Cross. He learnt that it was around eighteen eighty eight, that this town was settled. As nearly all the towns around this area, it was gold that brought people to live here. Paddy told Bill how the town was named after a famous constellation, which the prospectors used as a direction guide, when they found gold in the Yilgarn field. Paddy went on to describe how in the early days, it was easy to speck for gold, but now days most of the easy pickings have been taken. 'Most serious prospectors use a dry blower to make a living,' he said.

Bill was going to say that he wouldn't annoy Paddy by staying. 'I really only called because Alf suggested that I do,' Bill said.

Paddy quickly answered back, 'no lad, I'll not hear of it. You're here, and who knows, you might bring us luck.'

So as he was told to do, by this friendly Irishman, Bill set up camp in one of big Paddy's sheds, and yarded horses in one of the several paddocks behind the sheds.

Paddy O'Reily did not try to find any gold for a few days. Instead he gave Bill as many tips as he could, like where and when to look. 'With due respect Paddy, what difference could it make what time a bloke looks for gold?'

The happy Irishman laughed and said, 'might be best if I show you Bill. Better be ready early tomorrow, the weathers going to be perfect.'

Bill got up early expecting a fine day, but it was raining cats and dogs, so when Paddy came to pick him up, he said 'I thought you said today was going to be perfect mate?'

Paddy checked to make sure they both had enough supplies for a couple of weeks, then he said to Bill, 'couldn't be better, in fact it's just what the doctor ordered.'

So in pouring rain, the two prospectors set off. Paddy led Bill along the main road to Perth for about five mile, then turned down a narrow track. Bill reckoned they rode another ten mile, before Paddy called a halt and said, 'this is the place, I'm sure of it. Found a few bits here about a year ago and have been meaning to come back and check it out, but never got round to it.'

Paddy had brought along a big tarpaulin, and they made a rough shelter by tying it between four trees. They gathered a pile of wood and branches, and then lit a fire upon which Paddy placed a big billy. 'Crikey mate, that thing will make enough cuppas to drown an army,' Bill said.

Looking up to the sky, Paddy said, 'might be a couple of hours before this rain stops.'

He was right, it poured down until lunch time. Bill reckoned it was time to get something to eat but Paddy said, 'plenty of time for eating later mate. Now's the time to go specking while the gold is still wet and shiny.'

Paddy led the way to the where a creek that was dry a few hours ago, but was now running. 'The trick is to look where the water has washed away the dirt, sometimes there are nuggets that have been uncovered,' he explained to Bill.

They decided to speck one side of this creek each, and Paddy splashed his way over to the other side and soon left Bill behind. 'He must have good eyes,' thought Bill, who was moving much slower down his side of the creek. After about ten minutes he had trouble keeping his footing because the running water had made little tributaries that were sometimes several inches deep. Bill decided to follow some of these tributaries, and it wasn't long before he started picking up small pieces of gold. After collecting about twenty of them, he thought he could see lots of golden specks in the bottom of the water. He called out to Paddy, and the big Irishman came over and said, 'blimey Bill, I do think you've found something here mate.'

Paddy explained that sometimes where there were lots of small pieces, there were bigger pieces further back up the creek. Paddy put a marker where Bill had found the little specks, and they worked their way back upstream, again one each side of the creek. They did not have to go far before Bill started picking up more pieces, so Paddy crossed back over, and they both were putting small nuggets into their bags.

Again Paddy was moving faster than Bill and was soon out of sight. Bill looked around and worked out that they were now further up the creek than they first started. As he turned his head back to the ground to continue specking, something caught his eye, then he lost it. Bill turned his head away again then slowly turned it back in the same direction.

There it was. Something was definitely there and shining. Bill, excited now, rushed over and put his hand onto what he reckoned was a nice little nugget. He closed his hand around this little piece and tried to pick it up, but it wouldn't budge. The shallow water was dirty now, so unable to see this little nugget, Bill held on to it with one hand, and dug around it with the other. 'Must be a rock,' he thought, as he dug deeper.

Finally it came out in Bill's eager hands. It was now covered in mud, so he put it under the water and as he started to wash it, he caught his breath. Then he yelled, and he did not stop yelling, even when Paddy came running.

Paddy stopped near Bill and said, 'sweet mother of Mary, what have you got there Billy me boy.'

Both of them danced around, passing Bill's find back and forwards to each other. The big Irishman held the nugget in both hands, as if he was guessing the weight of it. 'Must be a hundred ounces,' he yelled.

Grabbing it back off Paddy, Bill lifted the glittering piece above his head, and said, 'it feels more like a flaming ton to me mate.'

When their excitement, which at times bordered on hysteria, finally died down, the two happy prospectors bagged all their finds, and went back to camp and had a feed and a cup of tea. 'I never thought I'd get gold fever again,' Paddy told Bill.

As the still excited man placed all their gold in a row along two sugar bags, Bill was putting a heaped spoonful of sunshine milk from a tin, into their mugs. 'That's what we'll call it, the "Sunshine Nugget", he said to Paddy. 'It was the sunshine that made it sparkle so if it's alright with you Paddy, then that's what we'll name this here piece.'

Paddy said, 'it's none of my business Bill. Yours it is me boy, you found it. You know what they say, finders keepers.'

Bill told Paddy that it was going to be shared equally between them both. 'So that is that. If it wasn't for you my friend then I wouldn't have even been here, so I'll hear no more of your nonsense then, Paddy O'Reily from Belfast.'

This started them laughing and passing the big nugget round again. 'So, Bill Evans, you who have brought the luck of the Irish, to me an Irishman. What do you say we go and sell this stuff then?'

They took the train to Kalgoorlie the next day, with all their gold in a Gladstone bag that Paddy had. Several people had seen Paddy and Bill heading for the station at Southern Cross, and some of them, knowing he was a prospector, asked him what he had in the bag. One bloke yelled out, 'going to sell your gold eh Paddy?'

They all got the answer that Paddy had worked out with Bill, 'the young fella here has got appendicitis and we're off to the doctor.' Paddy had asked his neighbour to mind the horses, as well as his place while they were away.

Bill was surprised how big Kalgoorlie was, and as the train passed the big open cut mine, Paddy said, 'the richest mile of dirt in the world right there Bill. They call it "The Golden Mile". Made many millionaires, that mile of dirt has made.'

They walked straight to the gold merchants in Hannan Street, and their Gladstone bag brought many a stare, as people guessed that the only thing anyone would be carrying into this merchant's office, would be gold. They took a seat and waited their turn, as there were already a half a dozen others before them. Finally they were called into one of the several rooms, where a bespectacled Scotsman invited them to lay the contents of their bag on a table.

This table had a set of gold scales, and the little man weighed and numbered each of the nuggets, then wrote down the details in a big brown ledger. Thinking that all the two prospectors' gold was on the table, the diligent Scotsman gave Bill and Paddy a list of each nugget's weight, with the price offered.

Bill was happy to see that the twenty seven small pieces that the Scotsman weighed, came to a tidy sixty eight pounds. 'That's thirty four quid each,' thought Bill.

He then looked at Paddy, who nodded, so Bill took their "Sunshine" nugget out of the bag, and laid it on the table. The merchant drew a deep breath, then said, 'excuse me gentlemen, I'll just go and get the owner of this business.'

It wasn't long before another man, also wearing glasses, returned with the first merchant. He introduced himself as John Sanders, and after shaking hands with Bill and Paddy, he picked up their big nugget and placed it on the scales. 'One hundred and nineteen ounces,' he said as he wrote the result into the ledger.

Then the eager gold trader picked up his special glasses, and for several minutes he studied this spectacular piece of gold. 'As pure a specimen as I've ever had the pleasure of inspecting,' he told the waiting two partners.

The serious looking merchant, who made a living out of buying and selling gold, took his time, playing out the moment, then said, 'gentlemen, at today's price your nugget is worth the princely sum of eight hundred and thirty three pounds.'

Bill was nearly shaking with excitement, and was mentally working out his share, but he nearly fell over when Paddy started packing up their nuggets. 'If that's the best you can offer Mr Sanders, then we'll have to go elsewhere,' Paddy said.

Then to Bill's amazement, Mr Sanders said, 'now wait on gentlemen, I only quoted you the value of your magnificent piece on today's price. Please allow me to finish my offer.'

This merchant, as Paddy obviously knew, could sell this nugget as a rare specimen, and get up to double the normal price. 'We're listening Mr Sanders, but please don't insult us with a ridiculous offer again,' Paddy said with a confidence that Bill could not believe.

Bill himself, was almost going mad with panic, and here was his partner, as cool as a cucumber. 'I won't be able to make even ten pounds myself, but my offer to you is one thousand pounds, and gentlemen that is my final offer.'

Paddy didn't flinch as he said, 'make it eleven hundred and it's a deal.' For a moment Bill was sure that Paddy had blown their chances of making any big money, then he nearly fell over backwards as Mr Sanders sighed and said, 'Paddy O'Reily, you are a hard and ruthless villain.' With that the now smiling merchant shook hands with both of them, and the deal was done.

Before leaving with the eleven hundred and sixty eight pounds, which Paddy insisted had to be all in cash, Bill looked at this magnificent nugget one last time. He knew he would always remember the excitement of finding this piece that nature had somehow managed to bring forth from its amazing supply of precious metals. The little merchant watched as Bill touched the specimen one more time and quietly murmured, 'goodbye sunshine.'

Chapter Eleven
Peggy's Wedding

THE new wallet was bulging in Bill's jacket pocket as he sat in the only first class carriage of the train that was taking him to Perth and his sister's big day. Bill had left Blackie and his pack horse, and most of his gear with Paddy, saying he would be back in a couple of weeks.

They had divided the gold money equally, and with the money that he already had, Bill counted seven hundred and forty seven pounds that he now had. Bill knew that he was lucky to have so much, particularly as most of the world was still suffering from the effects of the worst financial depression ever.

As he sat in his comfortable seat, which cost double the amount for a ticket than it would have for a normal class ticket, Bill thought back to how before he and Paddy left the area where they found their gold. Paddy had pegged the area, and while they were in Kalgoorlie he went to the Department of Mines, and claimed the patch, which meant that no other persons, or mining companies could take any minerals off his legal claim. Paddy had offered a half share in this claim, but Bill refused his offer saying, 'it's your patch my friend. I thank you for taking me there, but you keep it for yourself.'

Bill decided to lay down and have a sleep, especially as he was alone in this carriage. He had decided that because he was carrying so much money, that it would be safer away from any pickpockets that could be in the other carriages. These carriages were connected, and it was possible to move from one to another, as the conductor had to do.

He was almost asleep when sensed that there was someone else in his carriage. He knew the conductor had been and punched his ticket, so he jumped up, ready to face who he thought could be a robber. 'You wouldn't hit an old man would you son?' came a voice that he knew.

Bill quickly realized who the voice belonged to. 'Tom, what are you doing here?' Bill said.

Old Tom, as Bill remembered, used to sit with him at the Southern Cross Boarding House, whenever Bill ate there. Tom said that he always booked a cheap fare, then after a while the conductor would let him come up into this first class carriage. 'Much more comfortable here eh Bill?' He said.

As was the case when they used to eat together, Tom started talking. Bill liked this old man, and was interested in his life, so he asked him when he first came to the Goldfields? 'It was in eighteen ninety two,' he started.

Bill suspected he was about to hear Tom's life story, so he settled back in his seat and listened. Tom did not let him down as he said, 'I was working in York when the news of a big strike came through. A chap by the name of Bailey had picked up over five hundred ounces of gold, about a hundred mile east of Southern Cross. I chucked my job in, as did most blokes in York and other towns, and I started walking. Water was the biggest problem, not only on the journey, but on the diggings it was terrible. Nobody had a wash for weeks, unless it rained. Most blokes, including myself only had a one gallon water bag which sometimes had to last for four or five days. Many good men died, but I was one of the lucky ones Bill. If it wasn't for the soaks along the way, nobody would have made it. The Afghans had camels and they carted water, which saved hundreds of lives, but they charged an arm and a leg. They made good money though. Two bob a gallon they sometimes charged, but we had to pay it or die of thirst.'

Bill could sense the old man was reliving his memories. 'When I finally got to what they called "Bailey's Reward Claim", it took me about three weeks before I got lucky. Mainly because I couldn't get the hang of using those blasted blowing things. It wasn't until a fine Irishman by the name of Quin showed how me the right way, that I did any good at all. Then it sort of came easy. Everywhere I tried, I found at least some gold. Then in one day I dry blowed for only a few hours, and I had me forty ounces.' Old Tom's eyes started to mist over as he reminisced about the old days, and after a while it got a bit much for him, and he nodded off to sleep.

Very gently Bill shook Tom awake as they neared Perth, and as he woke up, the eager to talk old man said to Bill, 'now where was I?' And away he went again.

He told Bill how he, like hundreds of other onlookers lined the footpath, then squeezed into the Commonwealth bank when the famous "Golden Eagle" nugget was brought in. 'There was two Policemen there trying to stop us from getting into this bank, but they had no hope. People filled up the foyer, and then some climbed onto the counter, just to get a glimpse of this enormous nugget,' he said. 'A bloke named Larkin was the lucky blighter,' Tom continued. 'Not long ago it was. I couldn't believe me flaming eyes Bill. It took two blokes to carry the thing in. It weighed over eleven hundred ounces. Larkin told us how James Larkin junior was digging away with his pick, hoping to find a bit of gold, when his pick stuck into something and he couldn't pull it out. He got a bit of help and dammed near died of shock when they cleaned the dirt of one of the biggest pieces of gold ever found.' Bill could see the gleam in Tom's eyes as he relived these moments. 'Yes, "The Golden Eagle", that's what they called it,' he said.

As the train started to pull into the Wellington street station, Tom stopped his talking about his old days and asked Bill why he was going to Perth. 'Hope you are not thinking of living in the city young man. You are a country bloke through and through, and if you were to live in this hustle and bustle I reckon you'd just waste away.'

After Bill told him that he was only coming back for his sister's wedding, Tom was a happier man, and would have started his stories again, but the train pulled up with a bit of a jolt. The old and the young shook hands on the platform of the Wellington Street Station, and it was with a feeling of sadness that Bill watched as old Tom shuffled away. He had a strange premonition that he might not see this decent Aussie battler again. Bill was stiff and cramping a bit so he walked the two or so miles to West Perth.

As he did the last time he came home, Bill hadn't informed his family that he was arriving two weeks early for his sister's wedding, so they were surprised, but delighted to see him. Bill's father was still chair bound, but he hadn't lost his spirit yet. 'Good to see you son. You're looking well boy. I reckon you could give Jack Dempsey a run for his money lad,' he said.

Mary Evans shed a tear or two as she hugged her son and said, 'I'm so glad you have come home early Bill.'

The three of them talked, and drank cups of tea until it was time for Peggy to finish work. Bill, who as yet hadn't told his parents about his big gold find, said that he might head off and walk his sister home. 'Oh Harold does that each day,' Mary told Bill.

Joe then said, 'oh yes, then he stay's for tea, and he eats like a team of draught horses.'

This got Bill laughing with his father. Then his mother joined in, and the three were still in a happy mood when Peggy and Harold arrived. Bill quickly stood up and looked at his tall dark haired sister, then said, 'Peggy Evans, my sister, you have grown even more beautiful. And you Harold Morris, look like the king of the world.'

Mary and Peggy cooked a wonderful meal that night, after which they retired to the front room. Bill took the first opportunity in a lull in the conversation, which varied from Joe's health, to Peggy's job, to tell them all about his adventures and success in the goldfields.

Harold laughed and said he wished he could have been there when Bill and Colin chased those would be robbers away. 'Wish I could have seen the look on their faces when you made them take their boots off and walk back,' he said. Bill also told them about old Tom, then how he had been dingo trapping with Alf and Alice Jackson.

Finally he asked his parents how much did they need to by this house. Bill's father said that Peggy had taken over their money affairs. Peggy took Bill into the spare room where she kept all the records and accounts. She and Bill went over everything, and to buy the house for his parents, and to clear all outstanding accounts, the needed amount came to three hundred and forty seven pounds. Bill pulled out his wallet and gave Peggy four hundred pounds. He explained that there was an extra fifty pound there for their father's medicine. 'Oh Bill did you rob a bank?' Peggy squealed out loud.

Hearing his fiancé squeal, Harold came to see that she was alright. 'Look Harold,' Peggy said as she held out the money. After a while they went back to the front room, where Peggy told their parents what Bill had just done. Never before had either Bill or Peggy seen their parents break down and cry. They knew how tough it had been for them to battle on when things were hard on their farm, and it must have been heartbreaking for them when they had to sell up and come to the city. But now here were their two proud parents, arm in arm, crying like newborn babies. But it was a happy cry. A cry of relief and contentment, in the knowledge that they now had their own home. A home that nobody could ever take off them. At this time in life, their golden years, neither Joe nor Mary dreamt that they could be so lucky.

After a short time, Joe thanked Bill for his gracious act, and told him he was a good son. It was a few moments more before Mary could talk, but she also thanked her son and hugged him tightly. Then Peggy joined in the emotional hugging. Finally Bill said he would tell them all about his biggest gold find. He could almost feel the gold fever getting hold of him as he told them about the "Sunshine Nugget", and how he found it. We got eleven hundred quid for that single nugget,' he told them.

It was a late night at the Evans household, as they were all too excited to sleep, and Bill had plenty of stories to tell, and many questions to ask them. Then as Peggy walked to the door to say goodnight to Harold, Bill gave his parents fifty pounds so they could pay for Peggy's wedding. The next couple of weeks seemed to fly, and then the big day of the wedding was upon them.

All went to plan on the big day, Peggy was a few minutes late, Bill pretended to not be able to find the ring when the preacher asked the Best Man to pass it, and unbeknown to Harold, everyone in the church could see the word "Help" on the bottom of Harold's shoes whenever he had to kneel down. This was Joe's idea, but he got Bill to actually do the writing.

One of the highlights of the wedding was, as the Bride and Groom were signing the necessary forms, the organist played "Ave Maria". As soon as the first note sounded, Bill took his Mother by the arm and led her to the front of the church, but to one side near to organist, who stopped playing. There was now a silence as the guests wondered what was about to happen next.

Then Mary Evans sang the first verse of the song that the organist had played previously. Mary's high pitched voice was then joined by the baritone voice of her son, and the two blended together perfectly. Just as everyone thought that this was as good as it could get, from the front row came the deep voice of Joe Evans. Mary and Bill softened their tones to let this proud man sing the loudest. Then the organist started playing again, but ever so softly, but slowly increased the volume. By the time Mother and Son had finished the last verse of what was Peggy's favourite song, the organ was filling the church, and probably half of Leederville, with the sweet and moving sounds of "Ave Maria".

Peggy did not know that her mother and brother, then her father, were going to sing her song. So there were tears of happiness in her eyes as the preacher announced, 'Ladies and Gentlemen, I present to you, Mr and Mrs Harold and Peggy Morris.

Out of respect for Joe Evans, who still could not stand, nobody else stood either. Then everyone clapped and cheered as the Bride and Groom started to walk back up the aisle. The clapping momentarily stopped as Peggy stopped near her loving father, then knelt down next to him and said ever so quietly, 'I love you Daddy.' The clapping started again, even louder than before, and the cheering began as well, because Peggy had also gone and hugged her mother, and whispered to her also. Bill then helped his mother push the new wheelchair that Bill had bought for his father, and the three of them were followed outside by the still clapping guests.

As was the custom, many people stood outside the church to watch. There was something about a wedding that drew people to watch such a happy event, and this day being a Saturday, there were almost as many onlookers as there were invited guests.

The Evans family had sent invitations to several Northcliffe families, and as the bridal party mingled outside, before making their way to the reception, Bill was pleased to notice Vince Flanagan and his parents. When he got the chance, he made his way over and had just started to talk to them and a few other Northcliffe residents, when he was called away for the bridal party photos. He did get his chance to catch up with them all later at the reception.

In front of seventy eight people, the now ageing, but still proud Joe Evans welcomed all the guests and invited them to enjoy the wedding of his daughter and son in law. He got a loud cheer from the table where the Northcliffe people were seated, when he gave them a special mention, thanking them for not only traveling so far, but for carrying on the special bond that was started when they all came out together from the old country to start a new life.

He thanked his still beautiful wife for being what she is, the nearest possible thing to perfect that anyone could be. He spoke briefly of their family's life in England, and how their eldest son Don, had decided to continue the life that he had started, in the old country. Joe Evans then thanked his son Bill, saying how he had helped the family more than any son could ever be expected to do. Then sitting as tall and as proud as he could in his shiny wheelchair, he spoke about Peggy. He said how beautiful she looked tonight, and how happy she has been since she had met Harold, who they have already been pleased to have as one of their family. 'Now I ask you to charge your glasses, and toast the future life of Harold and Peggy.'

As best man, Bill gave a short speech, talking mostly about his Sister and his parents. Then he also welcomed Harold into their family, saying that it was just as well that these two newlyweds were moving to their own home, because Harold had nearly eaten all the food at their place. 'Never seen anybody eat so much as my new brother,' said Bill, amid much loud clapping and cheering.

As the celebrations finished, and it was time for the Bride and Groom to leave, everyone formed an archway by interlocking their hands. Peggy and Harold did their walk through this arch, and as people wished them well, some put an envelope in Harold's top pocket of his suit. At the end of the line, close to the door, waited Joe, Mary and Bill. It was an emotional send off, with plenty of hugs and good wishes. Bill told Peggy that she was the best sister in the world, and he said to Harold, 'I know I don't really need to tell you this mate, but if you ever hurt my Sister in any way, you'll have to answer not only to our father, but to me also.'

Harold shook Bill's hand and replied, 'I would expect no less from you, my new brother, but I give you my word that I will look after Peggy like you and your family expect me to.' Bill then handed an envelope to the newlyweds, and with one last hug from her parents, Peggy Morris left with her husband.

Chapter Twelve
Gold In Your Veins

The train trip back to Southern Cross was a long one for Bill, as he this time travelled normal class, which meant there was not as much room, and with no old Tom to talk to, time seemed to drag.

As the train got near Southern Cross, he felt an uneasy sort of feeling come over him, and he couldn't stop thinking about gold. 'Must be that I've still got the fever,' he thought. Then he remembered how Tom had told him that once you find gold, particularly if you find a big nugget, then a bloke sort of gets gold in his veins. 'You'll never get it out either,' the old prospector had warned him.

Paddy O'Reily was not at home when Bill arrived, so after he unpacked he took Blackie for a long gallop to give him some exercise. When he got back, Paddy was there, and he came out and asked Bill how the wedding went? They talked and had a cuppa, then Paddy said, 'I know you said before that you don't want to, but I was wondering if you may have reconsidered about becoming partners with me in my claim?'

Bill thought for a while, then told Paddy that he hoped to become a farmer one day, 'that is if I can get this gold out of my veins.'

Paddy then told Bill that in the time that he was away, a mining company had shown interest in his claim. 'Well it's up to you mate, it's your claim. I'm going to head to Kalgoorlie and try there for a while,' Bill said.

So the next morning Bill loaded his gear on to his pack horse, and saddled Blackie. Then he bid Paddy and Southern Cross farewell. He did stop at the store and stock up on flour, tea, sugar and coffee of course. 'Better give me some bacon and tinned meat, and four hundred rounds of twenty two rifle bullets as well,' he told the storekeeper.

The talkative man said, 'aren't you the bloke that found that big nugget out near O'Reily's place?' The storekeeper was very keen to talk about this, but Bill didn't tell him much.

Not being in any hurry to go anywhere, and glad to be out on his own again, Bill took his time getting to Kalgoorlie. He could tell that his horses were happy also, to be free from the small paddock at Paddy's place, so he did a bit of specking along the way. He didn't find much though, but then he remembered what Old Tom had told him about being more successful when he changed to dry blowing. So when he reached Kalgoorlie, he bought two dry blowing dishes, along with some extra supplies. He also remembered what Tom had told him about there not being much water the further east you went, so he bought another four two gallon water bags.

His pack horse was fully loaded when Bill and his two trusty and keen horses headed east. Blackie also had a saddle bag full of supplies and two water bags on his back. Bill and his horses had just over thirty gallons of this precious liquid with them, and fuelled with a bit of knowledge about where to look for water, he reckoned that they should survive for several weeks. He decided to buy a copy of the paper to take with him.

Paddy had suggested to Bill that Kanowna might be a good place to prospect, as there had been many reported "Finds" come in from there lately, and a few were said to be larger than the average nuggets, so he reckoned he might as well give it a go.

As he got to this small mining town, Bill remembered that Tom had told him that some of the miners were very protective of their claims, especially if they had found a bit of gold. Tom's advice proved to be good, because as Bill continued on past the tiny town, he noticed the unfriendly way he was looked at by them.

Continuing past the last of the diggings before the bush started, Bill stopped, and was going to ask one of last miners the normal friendly question, like do you mind if I peg a spot near here mate? But the two Italians who were watching Bill closely, picked up their shotguns, and one of them said in a surly voice, 'there is nothing for you here, so better you move on mister.'

Bill, who had a miners licence, knew that he could start mining anywhere that wasn't pegged, but he just nodded and moved away. Then he noticed a small camp close to the trees edge, and an older grey haired man who waved to him, so he went over and introduced himself. 'Pleased to meet you Bill, my names Dakota. Don't mind those unfriendly Italians mate, they think they own the place. Trouble is, they stick together like baby poo to a blanket. Also they get a bit too cocky, especially when there is a group of them.'

Bill accepted Dakota's offer of a coffee, over which he asked the older man if there was much gold around. 'Hardly making enough to buy coffee,' said Dakota. 'Could be there's a chance of finding a bit further out Bill. I took a look about a week ago and there is some pretty good looking country with lots of quartz on it.'

It was still a few hours to dark, so Bill took Dakota's advice and kept moving east for a several miles. He then set up camp near a rocky outcrop that had some white and brown quartz broken away from it. This country looked very likely to Bill, and he wondered why there was nobody else already working it? That evening he read in the newspaper that he had bought, how Don Bradman had travelled to England with the Australian test team, and in the second test had scored a test record three hundred and thirty four runs. Bill then read how an English flyer, Amy Johnson became the first woman to fly solo from England to Australia.

The next morning he took a look around, only to find several old camp sites, and lots of empty meat tins, which indicated that the area had been worked over already. Still, as he was already set up he thought he might as well try specking for a while. Remembering Tom's advice, he carried his rifle and bullet belt.

After working away from the rocky outcrop, and working downhill, Bill came to an old creek bed. He followed this creek, and after a short distance, the colouring of the soil changed to more of a white colour. Bill thought back to when Colin was teaching him to read the signs in gold country, and he remembered how Colin had liked to prospect in and around this white soil.

It was probably about two miles back to his campsite, so Bill figured that to work this area properly, he would need several days. So to save traveling backwards and forwards all the time he headed back with the intention of moving his camp to this new patch.

As he got close to his campsite, he sensed that all was not well, so he kept more behind cover and carefully crept closer. Then he saw them. There were eight scantily clad Aboriginals sitting in a group, and one, who was obviously the leader, standing in front of them. The leader, a tall very dark native, had already seen Bill, and without so much as a second glance at him, the tall one held out one hand and said, 'food.' The rest of the tribe stayed sitting, but watching.

Bill forced a smile, then laid down his rifle and indicated for this leader to also lay down his weapon. The Aboriginal did as Bill beckoned, so Bill slowly walked over to his supplies, and seeing that they had not been stolen or tampered with, he put some bacon, flour, tea and sugar in a bag. The group started to get up, but the tall leader said something in their native language and they all sat down again. A smile came over the tall black leader, as he accepted the bag from Bill, then he nodded to Bill and picking up his spear, he waved for his men to follow him and they left.

Breathing a sigh of relief, Bill made a mental note to bring extra supplies if he was to come back here. Little did Bill Evans know, but he was destined to return to this site at least one more time.

Not fearing these natives, Bill shifted camp down to where he had found the white soil, and in no time he was specking for gold. After a little while he found some very fine specks of gold, which gave him some encouragement.

Bill then decided to start dry blowing, so he started digging where he had just found the fine specks. When he had a fair pile of dirt heaped up, he got his two dishes and started tipping some of the dirt from dish to dish, allowing the wind to blow away the lighter dirt. Gold, being heavier than dirt, did not blow away, so if there was going to be any gold, it would be in the bottom of the dish after the last pour. This was done several times, and each time he felt he was getting better at this tricky way of finding gold. Bill was very keen, and started looking when there was still plenty of dirt, so he did not see the three small nuggets in the bottom of the dish the next time.

He was about to throw the contents of the dish onto where he was stockpiling the soil that he had checked, but something told him to tip the dish again. This time there was very little dirt left in the dish, and as he swirled the dish around, the heavier nuggets left the dirt and were easier to see. Remembering what Tom and Paddy had told him to do the minute he got what they called a "Strike", Bill pegged the area to the maximum distance that the directions on his licence told him he could.

Old Tom had, in one of his many stories, told Bill of times when a prospector had made a "Strike", but had forgotten to peg the area. This meant that any other licenced prospector could come and peg it, and it was then his and the original finder missed out. 'Unless of course, the first bloke didn't shoot the claim jumper,' Tom had said.

After bashing in his pegs, Bill had a good look at his three little pieces, and was surprised when he held them in his hand and "Guesstimated" that the total weight would be close to an ounce of pure gold. It was lunch time, so Bill stopped and had a meal of leftover damper and honey washed down with water, as he didn't want to take the time to light a fire to boil the kettle to make a cuppa.

It wasn't long before Bill was back digging another pile of dirt to look through. He had seen that all the other miners had dug only comparatively small holes, but he reckoned instead of maybe having to dig more than one hole, he would dig a bit wider, and a bit longer than the others. About two hours went by before Bill glimpsed any more of this much sought after precious metal.

He was about to pick out a piece that he thought might go a half an ounce when he heard a voice that he reckoned he had heard before. 'Had some luck have you mate?' asked Dakota, the chap that Bill had met the afternoon before.

Bill had been warned not to advertise any finds that he might have. 'Half the country will be at your doorstep before you know it boy,' Tom had told him.

Bill casually put down the dish, making sure that Dakota could not see inside it, and said, 'no luck yet mate. I was just going to knock off for a coffee if you're interested?'

Between them they lit a fire and soon had a mug of hot coffee each. 'Good brew Bill,' Dakota said. Then just as Bill thought this old miner hadn't noticed anything, he said, 'none of my business, but if you haven't found anything Bill, then how come you've put pegs in the ground?'

Bill thought quickly, then said that he was under the impression that a bloke couldn't start digging unless he had a licence, and that he had to have pegs showing where he was going to dig. Dakota started laughing loudly, then said, 'this must be your first time out here eh mate? You only put in your pegs if you find something, then no claim jumper can pinch your spot.'

Then Bill laughed with him and said, 'so I went to all that trouble for nothing?'

Dakota helped himself to another coffee, then as he finished it he said, 'see you've plenty of this stuff lad. I was wondering if you might trade me some, if you can spare it that is.' Bill poured about a quarter of his supply into an empty tin and passed it to the old man.

In return Dakota handed something to Bill, and to his surprise, it was a gold nugget of about two ounces. Bill shook his head and said, 'I can't take this, it's way too much.'

Dakota said, 'plenty more where that come from. Besides I can't drink metal can I lad.' Dakota then asked Bill if he had any trouble with the blacks yet, and when Bill said he had seen them, but they were no problem, the old man showed surprise. 'Be careful lad, they speared a miner here last year. That's why nobody will come prospecting here.' With that said, Dakota left and Bill didn't see him or anyone for two more weeks.

Not a lot of gold found its way into Bill's gold bag in this time. He was thinking of trying a new patch soon, then he started to find very small pieces in a narrow line, so he kept digging. Suddenly he got a feeling he was being watched. Bill had learnt from Charlie Burns, to take notice of these feelings or intuitions. So very casually he walked to his water bag, which he kept in the shade of a small tree. Also against this tree was his trusty rifle. Bill always kept a bullet in the breech and all he would have to do is pull back the safety lever and the rifle would be ready to fire. As he drank from his waterbag, he tilted his head further back than normal, so he could take a good look around. The scrub was only short, but there was a small clump of trees about a hundred yards away, so Bill looked closer at that. Sure enough, there was the outline of at least two horses behind the trees. Bill put down the waterbag and in one quick movement, picked up his rifle and bullet belt then stepped behind the tree. He half expected to hear or feel a bullet, but as this did not happen, he took a look. The horses now had riders on them and they were galloping away from Bill's claim. 'I better keep an eye out from now on,' he thought.

Then as he headed back towards his diggings, he saw a large group of Aboriginals coming towards him from the direction that the horsemen had been a moment ago. Bill was still holding his rifle, but as the natives got closer, he could see that their leader was the same tall one that he had given food to the other day.

Bill now realized that the horsemen probably were more scared of these Aboriginals than they were of him. All of the advancing group stopped, except their leader, who as he got within a few yards, also stopped, then put his spear on the ground. Bill then put his rifle on the ground. Both men looked each other in the eye, and it was Bill that said the word that he was expecting the other to say. 'Food?' The expected reply came back to Bill as the black man also said 'food.'

After giving the Aboriginals about the same as he gave them the previous time that they called, Bill slowly pulled out his pocket knife, and after showing it to them folded up, he could see that they didn't know what it was. Then when Bill folded out the blade, there were gasps of surprise and admiration, from all the group. Bill then indicated to their leader that it was a gift, and it was for him. Slowly this black man, who had probably only ever known a white man to be bossy and abusive towards his kind, took the knife, and after feeling the edge with a finger, he gave a yell. Then he gave Bill a big smile, and put a hand on Bill's shoulder, as if to say thank you.

Bill then sat down in the red dirt, and indicated for the other man to do the same, which he did. Then Bill took out a box of matches and showed them to the inquisitive fellow. After gathering up grass from where he could reach without getting up, Bill slowly opened the box and took out a match, then amid much murmuring from the group, he lit the match then set fire to the dry grass. There was now a lot of talking amongst the interested black men.

Suddenly the leader, who was still sitting opposite Bill, reached out to indicate that he wanted the matches. Now the whole group put down their spears and came closer to watch their fearless leader make fire magic. The first time he tried, the match didn't strike, so he yelled at the box and was about to throw it away.

This proud man had thought that the magic did not work for him, and he was losing face in front of his tribesmen. Bill carefully took the matches back, then he pulled his mouthorgan from his pocket and blew a few notes. The murmuring started again, and got louder as he kept blowing into his other piece of magic. Then he showed the leader how to hold the match against the box, then push it firmly along the rough edge.

Even though he was wild with this magic box, he needed to save face in front of his men, so he tried again. Bill played louder on his mouthorgan, and suddenly the match was burning and the proud leader lit a patch of grass. All his tribesmen jumped up in the air, then danced around yelling their praises for their great leader.

The tribesmen noticed that Bill had stopped playing, and at the same time, the match had burnt out. Obviously they thought that both these magic things worked in harmony, as did their leader who was clinging tightly to the box of matches. Bill knew by the way this man was looking adoringly at his mouthorgan, that he was about to lose it one way or the other, so he passed it to this leader who seized it with both hands, then he jumped up and yelled at one of his men to pick up the supplies, and they were gone. Bill stood and watched them start to jog away at a slow methodical pace that they could keep up for hour after hour.

The next morning, just as the sun was rising, Bill heard the sound of beautiful singing. It was slowly getting closer and louder. He had just been mixing a big dish of dry flour to make a damper, and had lots of this white flour all over his hands.

Now as he turned to see what, or who was singing, the sun which was just rising, almost blinded him, so he subconsciously raised his hands to shade his eyes. A lot of this flour then fell onto Bill's face and hair, and without realizing it he had made his hair and face white.

The group, that Bill could now see were Aboriginals, both men and women, who could not yet see Bill clearly enough to know that the white was actually flour, thought that he must be some sort of a spirit or something. Already they thought Bill was a magician, because of the matches and mouthorgan. This is the reason their leader had decided to honour Bill with a sing song.

Even though the sun was partially up, the early light was eerie, and the group was now singing with a certain nervousness or fear in their voice. The tall man held up both his hands, which was a signal for them to stop singing, but as soon as the group stopped, a lone woman's voice started. It was to Bill, a beautiful, but mournful voice that rose and fell in time with a clapping noise that was coming from the back of this group. Slowly the singing reached a crescendo, and then the group opened a narrow pathway between them.

From out of the group a young warrior, carrying a spear, came out dancing and making a sort of whirring noise each time he stamped one of his feet. This warrior, who was painted in many different colours and stripes, danced his way close to Bill, all the time waving his spear around. Not afraid, but not sure of what was going to happen, Bill stood as tall as proud as he could, mainly so he would not appear afraid. But as he stood a bit taller, the sun's rays now caught the top of his head and made the white flour look ghostly. Upon seeing this magician, who had somehow turned into a ghost, a loud scary gasp came from the group.

This new noise came just as the young dancer was about to lay his spear on the ground in front of Bill, but the crowd noise made him sense that something was wrong, so he looked up at Bill and saw what looked like a white spirit, with the sun burning up its hair.

The young warrior was in two minds. He knew that if he turned and ran, he would have to face the wrath of his feared leader. He now was also afraid, perhaps more than he was of the tall leader, of this thing in front of him. His orders were to honour Bill by dancing up to him, then to lay down his spear as a sign of friendship, then to deposit a bundle of gifts on the ground. Then he was told he must dance his way back to the group. Well he had done all these things, except the last two, so he quickly dropped the gifts and half ran and half danced his way back to the group.

Bill scratched his head in wonder, which made even more flower fall from his hands onto his hair that the sun's rays were still making it look like his whole head was burning. This was too much for all the Aboriginals, so at their tall leader's signal they left.

Still covered in flour, Bill went back to cooking his damper. Then after breakfast he remembered the gift on the ground, so he opened the bundle. Inside were some Aboriginal drawings, which were done on the bark of the paperbark tree. Each drawing was rolled separately, and inside each drawing there was something wrapped in a green leaf. Bill put all these little bundles together and looked at the drawings. Some were of Kangaroos, some of Emus, but most were drawings of the land. Bill could see more clearly, the real beauty of this semi-arid land in these works of art. 'Mum will love these,' he said to himself as he packed them away. Bill made a cuppa and pondered his next move.

He reckoned he may as well stay at this diggings for a few more days, then he would have to go for more supplies. As he drank the last of his drink, he remembered the rest of the native's gifts. Then when he opened the first leaf he could not believe his eyes. Bill quickly opened each bundle, and sure enough, there was the same gift in each. Excited now, he counted the bundles again, and each time he got fourteen. 'Fourteen gold nuggets,' he said out aloud.

He reckoned that each piece, which were all close to exactly the same size, would probably weigh an ounce. It was a good thing that Bill was given this gold, because for the next two weeks he hardly found a single piece.

Each day Bill reckoned that he had better head back to town to buy some supplies, especially as he thought that the Aboriginals could be back any day. Not sure as to whether or not he should return to this area after buying his supplies, he decided to have a look further afield to see if there was any promising ground. So he left his pack horse and most of his gear at his campsite, and riding Blackie, and taking only a waterbag and some damper, as well as his rifle, Bill left to check out some new ground. He spent four or five hours on this task, and finally did find a likely spot, then he headed back.

When he got close to his camp, he heard a commotion coming from where he had hidden his few supplies and tools. Pulling his rifle from its holster, he galloped Blackie straight to his camp.

Bill got a surprise to see the tall Aboriginal and a half a dozen warriors in a circle. Inside this circle were two of the Italian prospectors that Bill had seen a few weeks ago at Kanowna. These prisoners were not going anywhere in a hurry, because each of the warriors had a spear and were prodding their prisoners.

At the feet of these prisoners were Bill's remaining stores and his equipment, which meant that they had attempted to rob Bill's camp. It was obvious that if it was not for the Aboriginals, they would have been successful. On the ground were two shotguns that clearly belonged to these would be thieves. Bill picked up the closest one and saw that it was loaded, so he walked over to the tied up men. 'I'm not sure whether to shoot you mongrels, or let my friends spear you,' Bill said.

He then walked over and indicated to the tall leader that he would like to borrow his spear. When the warrior worked out that Bill was probably going to use his spear on these thieves, he smiled and handed his weapon over. 'I have given you no reason to come and try to rob me, so if you can't give me a good reason why I should not spear you, then I will,' said Bill as he prodded them with the sharp spear.

One of the captives then said, 'please no Mr. Please don't kill us.'

Both men were now crying like babies, which made the natives laugh. Bill gave the tall one his spear, then made a set of rope hobbles. He put them on the two screaming thieves, and told them that he was taking them to Kalgoorlie and the police. Then before leaving, Bill packed all his things onto his packhorse. But before mounting Blackie, he gave most of his flour, sugar and bacon to the Aboriginals. They accepted it and were turning to go when Bill stopped them.

He walked over to a tree and scratched a small target into the surface bark, which he knew would soon grow back. Then he drew his Bowie knife out of its sheath. Bill had practised throwing this knife, which was named after the Wild West hero Jim Bowie, who died fighting at the Alamo in Texas. He stood exactly nine paces from this target, then in one swift movement the knife was on its way to wedging its razor sharp point into the centre of the target. The tall one clapped his hands together and said something in his own language. This made the other warriors all point at Bill and they all repeated the same word over and over.

Bill, not knowing that they had just given him a new name, walked to the tree and withdrew his prized knife. He held it by the blade then slowly gave the knife, handle first to the tall one, indicating that he could keep it. A look of pride spread across this warrior, then he nodded to Bill and said the word that the other Aboriginals had spoken previously. Bill nodded back and as he backed away, the tribesmen jogged back towards their place of living.

The last time Bill looked the tall one was waving the Bowie Knife in the air and yelling. This started his fellow warriors yelling as well, and every few steps one of them would do a sort of dance, then start running again. Bill smiled to himself. He didn't think he would ever give away his knife, but as his friends had saved him from at the very least, being robbed, he felt that it was a fair reward for their leader. 'Anyway,' he thought, 'I can easily buy another knife.'

Dakota was the first to see Bill leading his two prisoners, and when he found out why they were tied and hobbled, he quickly packed his gear. 'I'm coming with you Bill. You never know what these blokes mates might do when they see the way these two are tied up.'

By the time the group had reached the other side of the small mining town of Kanowna, there were about thirty miners following them. Most of them were armed, and Bill wasn't sure whether they were going to try to free the thieves. As it turned out, he needn't have worried on that account. But he was now having serious trouble stopping the now wild and worked up mob, from actually wanting to string these two up. 'That's what we do to thieves and claim jumpers out here. Hang them,' several of the wild mob yelled.

Bill told the mob that it was him that they tried to rob, so it was up to him as to what to do. 'I'm taking them to the law in Kalgoorlie, and nobody had better try to stop me,' he said.

A few of the mob still yelled, and some threw stones at the prisoners, but after a mile or so, Bill and Dakota were left alone to take in these robbers. Finally they reached Kalgoorlie, still in charge of the exhausted prisoners. They took them straight to the Police Station, where the Sargent in charge took the necessary details, then locked the two of them in a cell. 'There will be a hearing at the courthouse tomorrow at ten o'clock, which you must attend gentlemen,' the officer told them.

The two miners booked into the Federal hotel at Dakota's suggestion. 'It's one of the better Pubs,' he said to Bill.

They had a room each, mainly because Bill knew that Dakota was a drinker and he didn't want to be tempted. A bell rang to announce that it was time for the evening meal, so Bill knocked on Dakota's door to tell him that he was going for a meal. He gave up after a minute or two, presuming that he must have already gone.

Bill was hungry and was busy reading the menu, when he heard a loud voice from a table across the dining room. He could tell that it was the voice of a man that had been drinking, perhaps a bit too much. Bill didn't want to get involved. He was more interested in getting some food, but when he heard a woman scream, he looked over.

The man responsible for the yelling was now wearing his meal. The young lady, who was obviously the waitress, now said, 'and if you ever touch me again, I'll pour a kettle of boiling water over you.'

Bill could see that the man was not going to let the matter lie, as he was now standing and heading towards the young lady in a threatening manner. It was obvious that he was about to strike her, and Bill knew he wouldn't be able to get there in time to stop him, so he started to yell to warn him off. He needn't have worried though, because as quick as a flash the young lady picked up a chair and threw it at him.

Then the hotel owner arrived and as Bill got there, he was telling the waitress in no uncertain terms, that she was fired. 'Hang on a minute,' said Bill. 'It was not the young lady's fault. This drunk was mauling her, and he got what he deserved.'

A few other diners voiced their agreement to Bill's words, but the owner was adamant that he was going to fire his waitress. He started to say that the customer is always right, but he never finished, because by now the offending drunk was on his feet delivering a haymaker to the face of the Owner- Publican. Down went the poor chap, with blood spurting from his nose.

This drunkard was not finished yet though. He turned towards the young lady, and if Bill had not stepped between them, he would have swung at her too. 'Well looks like I'm going to have to belt you as well,' snarled the troublemaker.

Knowing that he could easily handle this troublemaker, Bill said, 'okay mate I'll fight you. But not in here eh? Let's go outside where there's more room.'

The big man was still wiping his meal off his face as he staggered outside ready to belt this cheeky young bloke. Bill knew the cold air would help sober up this would be thug, so he walked a fair distance into the empty street before turning to face him. Several people had followed them, but were out of ear shot, so Bill told the trouble maker that he was a professional boxer. 'I'm giving you a chance to save face in front of these people. Either you turn and go home, or I'll give you the hiding that you deserve and then take you to the police.'

The big bloke, who was already sobering up, took a good look at this confident young man, who really did look like a boxer, then said, 'don't like fighting anyway.' He then turned and walked away.

Still hungry, and a bit annoyed at the delay in having his meal, Bill went back inside and sat down and picked up the menu. 'How did you get rid of him so easily?'

Bill turned to answer the waitress, who still appeared to have her job, and told her that the bloke changed his mind. 'Now could I please have a meal miss,' he said.

Then as he was waiting for his order to arrive, the Publican, who must have cleaned up after his injury, came over to him. 'Don't want a job do you young fella?'

He went on to explain that incidents like what had just taken place, were a daily occurrence here in Kalgoorlie. 'You handled that situation very well, so I'm offering you a job as a bouncer. Pay's good young fella. If you can start tomorrow then I'll give you a fiver a week and keep.' Bill's meal arrived, so he started eating without answering this brash Publican. 'Well can you start tomorrow?'

Swallowing his first mouthful Bill said, 'look, I'm trying to eat my first decent meal in three bloody weeks and all I get is interruptions. Come and ask me after I have eaten please.'

The young waitress brought Bill his apple pie and custard, then as she was about to leave, she turned and said, 'thank you kind Sir for your chivalry, even though I probably would have broken another chair over his head.'

Bill laughed and told her that he thought that she may well have done so, but he wanted some peace so he could eat his meal. 'My name is Bill, not Sir, Miss,' he said.

The girl, who Bill looked at properly for the first time, smiled and said, 'and my name is Annie, not Miss. And I'm very pleased to meet you Bill.'

They both laughed then, and again when Annie served Bill his coffee. As soon as he had finished his drink, the Publican was back asking him if he could start work tomorrow. 'No thanks' said Bill, 'I'm not interested in fighting, or working in this environment.'

The case against the two thieves that Bill and Dakota had brought in, was an easy decision for the Magistrate. There were two good reliable witnesses, so he found them guilty and sentenced them both to two years.

The next few days were easy for Bill. He had been back to the same gold merchant that had purchased the gold that he and Paddy had found. This time Bill had to accept the going price of six pounds per ounce. He had just over thirty ounces, so he pocketed nearly two hundred pounds.

Dakota was nowhere to be found, so Bill ate at the hotel three times a day and rested in between. Then one morning Dakota knocked on Bill's door, and asked him for a loan. Bill could see that Dakota was drunk, so he said, 'I'll not lend you any money for drink, but I will give you enough to buy some supplies so you can get back to your claim.' Bill gave Dakota a one pound note, and he didn't see him again.

Bill had become quite friendly with Annie, and one day the talk turned to where she was from. They only had a few moments to talk, because Annie was kept busy serving meals. Bill did learn that she was raised on a station that her father managed, and that she loved horses. So he suggested that they take his horses for a ride one afternoon. Annie had told Bill that she has the hours between two and five o'clock off work, then she would love to. 'Today is fine, if it suits you Bill,' she said.

Blackie and Bill's packhorse were stabled not far from the Federal hotel, so that afternoon the young couple saddled them up and rode for a couple of hours. Annie was a good horsewoman, and had no trouble handling this horse. 'Thank you so much Bill,' said Annie. 'This has been my best day since coming to this town.'

They talked as they hosed down and groomed the horses, and Bill learnt that Annie had come to Kalgoorlie only a month ago. The station that her father was on, was finding it difficult to make financial ends meet. 'Dad told me that if something does not happen for the good soon, then the owner may have to walk away from the station. So I came here to work,' she said.

Bill could tell that she was not happy, so he asked her if she liked working at the hotel. Annie thought for a moment, then said that she hates it, especially as her boss wants her to start serving behind the bar. 'But what choice do I have?' Bill now thought for a while, then asked Annie if she had any ties to keep her here. 'Do you mean do I have a boyfriend? If so, the answer is no.'

It was time for Annie to get ready for work, but Bill had an idea, one that could not wait, so he grabbed Annie gently by the shoulders and said, 'do you trust me Annie?'

She did not try to break away from Bill, but told him that even though she had only known him for a few days, she felt that she did like and trust him. 'Why do you ask me this Bill?' she said.

Bill said, 'go to work tonight, then ask for your pay, and tomorrow come with me to a world of adventure and chance. I have made as much in the last several months, by looking for, and finding gold, than I would have to work ten years for, to try and save. Annie, I have two horses, all the equipment we need, and a few hundred pounds. I will pay you the same wages, in advance, as you are making here,' Bill eagerly said.

Annie was speechless, but then finally she said, 'where will we go?' Bill then told her all about the Aboriginals, and how they had befriended him. 'They sound like "Wongi" Aboriginals to me Bill,' Annie said.

Then she told him that maybe they should take a bit more time to think about making such a big move. 'That's fine by me Annie,' said Bill.

The decision was probably made for them that night, because when Bill went for his meal at the hotel dining room, Annie was not there. Remembering that she had said that her boss was going to insist that she serve alcohol behind the bar, Bill looked in the public bar, and sure enough, Annie was being shown how to pour beer by her boss. Bill nodded to another bar attendant, a rough looking bloke, and ordered a lemonade.

Annie had not seen Bill come in, so he sat quietly and watched. He could see that this nice young girl, who he now realized he had taken a liking to, was not happy.

Suddenly Annie's voice was raised, as she yelled at her boss, telling him to keep his hands to himself. The publican said, 'If you want a job here my girl, then you'll have to get used to it,' and he put his arm around Annie again.

Bill could see that she was struggling to free herself, so he said, 'take your hands off my girl, or I'll have to climb this bar and break both your arms.'

The Publican let go of Annie, and was about to front Bill. Then he remembered how easy this young man had gotten rid of the big trouble maker the other night, so he was a bit wary, saying that he meant no harm.

Calling Annie over, Bill asked her how much this slime-bag owed her in wages. She told him it was about seven pounds. 'Give the lady seven pounds, and I'll consider not knocking your head off,' said Bill to the Publican.

The money was given to Annie, who stood close to Bill as they left the Bar. Then Annie asked Bill to accompany her to her room while she packed her bags. Bill, with Annie near him, went to his room and did the same. 'Where to now?' Annie asked.

Bill said, 'first I'll pay what I owe for my board and lodgings, then if it's alright with you, I'll book two rooms at another hotel. Then we'll talk about things after that.'

As they left the hotel, Annie told Bill that the Publican that he had just make look small, has a new bouncer. 'I think he will send him after you Bill.'

They hadn't gone much further, when a real big ugly brute stepped in front of them and said, 'boss reckons you owe him.'

Bill ushered Annie aside, and said back to this bouncer, 'why doesn't your chicken hearted boss do his own dirty work, instead of sending an ugly thing like you to try to prove that he is a hero?'

Bill was deliberately trying to get him riled up, because a riled up man is not a thinking man, so he teased him a bit more, by saying, 'what does it feel like to have to do as your creepy boss tells you to do? I suppose you lick his boots too?'

This was too much for this bully, who was not used to being belittled. By now there were about a dozen or more bystanders and he didn't want to look afraid, or small for his new boss, so he did what Bill wanted him to.

The big bouncer charged straight at Bill with his right hand pulled back ready to throw a haymaker at Bill's head. He did exactly that, but Bill's head wasn't there. Side stepping this clumsy bully, Bill hit him in the solar plexus, which doubled him up, then he hit him like a sledge hammer, right on his jaw. He was ready to give him another blow to the jaw, but the bully was out cold. Bill casually walked over and helped Annie with their luggage and they went up Hannan Street and booked into the first hotel they came to.

Bill tried to book separate rooms, but Annie said that she would be too worried that the Publican or his bouncer might try to get her. Luckily there was a family setup available, which had separate bedrooms. Bill was still hungry, having missed out on his tea, so they ate at the new hotels dining room. Afterwards they went to their room and talked for ages. Annie then thanked Bill for rescuing her yet again. 'Seems you're my knight in shining armour,' she said.

This got Bill thinking about the famous Australian outlaw Ned Kelly, who had become a legend when he and his gang faced overwhelming numbers of police and troopers at Glenrowan. Ned and his gang were dressed in heavy bullet proof armour, so Bill asked her if she knew about Ned Kelly.

Annie said she had heard of him, and that there is still a "saying" that she had often heard people repeat. 'As game as Ned Kelly,' she said. 'That's what you were tonight, when you took on that big bouncer Bill.' Then she leaned closer and gave him a kiss on the cheek.

Chapter Thirteen
Annie Gets A Gun

THE next morning, after breakfast, Bill asked Annie if she had given thought to his offer of going prospecting with him. 'Yes,' she answered, 'I have given your kind offer a lot of thought, but I can't make my mind up Bill.'

Not being in any real hurry himself, Bill told her that it would only be a business deal, if she decided to accept. 'We can become partners if you like. I could pay you the wage we discussed, always a month in advance, and we share any gold we find, sixty forty.'

Annie asked him if she could have a bit more time to make up her mind. 'Of course you can. In the meantime, how about we go riding,' said Bill.

That night, after a meal, Annie said, 'Bill you have asked me to go bush with you, yet you don't even know my surname. For that matter, I don't know yours either.'

Bill laughed and said, 'a name is just a lot of letters to identify someone. My way of knowing or liking, does not need, or is not changed by a lot of letters. A name in feeling, is more important than a name in writing. Annie is what you are to me, and I like and respect you, and you have my word that I would never hurt you, or let anyone else hurt you.'

She looked at him, then as she wiped a tear from her eye, she said, 'Bill whatever your name is, my dad would have loved to hear you say that, and if he had of, I'm sure he would have shook your hand and said, take care of her. So Bill, we are forty sixty partners. When do we leave?'

Bill put out his hand to seal the deal, and was surprised by the strength of Annie's handshake. Then he took out his money bag and asked her how much does a month's wages come to. 'That slime-bag, as you rightfully called him, was paying me three pounds ten shillings a week, so I suppose that works out to fourteen pounds per month, partner,' she said.

Bill paid Annie the fourteen pounds, then said that they needed to go shopping in the morning, so she had better make out a list. Shopping they did go. First Bill asked Annie if she could shoot a rifle, to which she said, 'Dad taught me pretty good.'

So the first thing they purchased was another Lithgow single shot rifle, the same model as Bills. With this came a bullet belt and five hundred rounds of ammunition. Then Bill took Annie to the livery stables and told her to choose a horse that she liked. Annie walked over to Bill's pack horse, the one that Annie had been riding, and said, 'I choose this one partner.'

Bill laughed and said 'well it looks like I'll have to buy another packhorse.' After learning that there were only two suitable horses for sale, and if he was to buy them both, the liveryman would let them go for eight pounds for the pair, Bill bought both. So they had a horse, and a packhorse each. Now all they had to do was to purchase enough supplies for the two of them, and their horses, as well as about a dozen Aboriginals, to last three or four weeks, then they could head off. They did all of this with no problems, and by mid-morning the two partners were on their way back to where Bill had been prospecting before the two robbers caused him to go to Kalgoorlie.

The two new partners talked a lot on the long trip. One of the things Bill found out, was that Annie's surname was Oakley. It was about five minutes before he realized that she had the same name as the famous American trick shooter. Bill had seen comic books and Buffalo Bill Albums with pictures of this Wild West Heroine. 'Did your parents really name you after her?' he asked.

Annie replied, 'Mum died giving birth to me, but Dad loves the cowboys and cowgirls, though he never told me that's why he named me Annie.'

Bill said ' I'm sorry to hear about your mother. It must have been hard growing up without a mum.'

They talked and then talked some more, and Bill learnt that Annie had led a quiet life on a huge cattle station in the Kimberly's. She told Bill that she didn't have any brothers or sisters. 'Dad looked after me so well Bill. I suppose after Mum died, I was all he had. He never married again, in fact I don't think he ever looked at another woman.'

Bill was quiet for a while, then he said 'love does that to a bloke.' Before Annie could comment, Bill said, 'look, there's Kanowna.'

The two mining partners still had some fifteen mile to travel to Bill's diggings, and as they came to the patch that Dakota had been working, they noticed a new chap working it. Bill stopped and chatted for a minute, introducing Annie. Then he asked this Chap, who said his name was Robert, and that he was from Ireland, if he'd had any luck? 'As a matter of fact, I have been blessed with a few pieces, Bill,' he said as he pulled three nice little nuggets from his money belt.

Bill told him that they were going a fair way further, then he explained how he was nearly robbed a while back. 'Better be careful, there are some desperate men out here Robert,' he said.

They reached Bill's diggings with still an hour or so to go before sunset, so after unpacking their gear, and setting up the small tent that Bill had bought for Annie, they gathered firewood. Then by the time they had cooked a meal, it was time for sleep. 'Night partner,' said Annie, as she went to her tent.

Bill slept nearby, on his bedroll, and just before going to sleep, he called to Annie, 'night girlfriend.'

Annie stuck her head through the tent opening and said, 'that's the second time you've called me girlfriend Bill. I'll have you know that I've never had a boyfriend.'

Bill laughed and said, 'no offence meant partner.' Annie did not move back into her tent. Instead she said, 'how about a coffee?'

So away they went talking again, and upon Annie's insistence, Bill told her his surname and how his family came out to settle at Northcliffe. Annie was a keen listener and a good talker, so they had more than one coffee, during which Bill had told her probably most of his life's story. 'Sorry to hear about Jenny Bill. Did you love her?'

Bill found it too difficult to answer this personal sort of question. It still pained him to think about Jenny's tragic death, but he felt easier when Annie told him to try to remember the good times that he and Jenny had together. 'Thanks Annie, I'll do that,' he said. Just as Annie was about to go back into her tent, Bill told her that if she heard the Aboriginals singing, or sees them, not to worry. 'They won't hurt us,' he told her as she tied down the tent opening.

The happy young lady beat Bill up the next morning, and was cooking breakfast just as the sun was peeking its head up. 'Morning Annie' he said. 'How did you sleep girl—I mean partner?' A big plate of bacon and eggs was Bill's answer.

Then she then sat down and, still not speaking, ate her plate of food. 'Everything alright partner?' Bill asked as he poured two coffees.

Annie sipped her coffee, then without looking at him, she said, 'I've never had anyone call me girlfriend, and I liked it when you said it Bill.'

He tried to explain that he was only having fun, but Annie took it the wrong way and started crying which in turn upset Bill. 'I'm sorry Annie, it's just that I'm not sure how you feel, so I use humour as a way of covering up my true feelings,' he said.

Annie then said, 'I want you to tell me your true feelings Bill Evans. You have looked after me like a father, made me a partner, paid me good wages, in advance and all, but?'

She was going to say more but she couldn't, because her mouth was covered by Bill's hand. 'Listen,' he said. Then he pointed to the trees, where Annie could now make out the figures of a group of Aboriginals. Annie instinctively went to pick up her rifle, but Bill motioned for her not to. 'Just stand still,' he told her.

Bill then packed a bundle of supplies, including four loaves of bread that he had bought especially for this occasion. He carried this bundle a few steps towards the group and placed it on the ground. He then walked back and sat on the ground. 'Sit down girlfriend,' he smiled to Annie.

Sitting next to him, she looked at him then said, 'Bill Evans, I told you not to call me that unless you meant it.'

He told her to sit still, then said, 'I did mean it.' He then felt his hand being squeezed. Annie did not take her hand away, even when the leader of the Aboriginals came forward and sat opposite them.

Bill nodded to him, then pointed to the lady that was still holding his hand and said, 'Annie.' Bill then pointed to the black man and said to Annie, 'Tall one.' Annie nodded to this Aboriginal, then started talking to him in a language that Bill couldn't understand. Both Bill and the tall one were taken by surprise.

Then the proud native, without talking back to Annie, stood up and indicated for Bill and Annie to follow him. Bill looked a bit pensive, mainly because he didn't really want to leave all his supplies unprotected. Sensing this, the Tall One said something to his warriors, and four of them stayed to look after his camp. Bill and Annie, carrying their rifles, were taken to the Aboriginal's campsite. On the way Annie told Bill that the tribe was Wongi, the same as the area around the station where she was raised. She told him that she learnt to speak their language as a child.

As they walked into the centre of the camp, which consisted of about ten shanties, or lean to type shelters, Bill could not see any sign of life anywhere. The Tall One pointed for them to sit near a fire that had burnt down to just hot coals.

He then clapped his hands, and this brought six or seven Aboriginal women out from where they were hiding. These women all sat a little distance away. The Tall One then waved for one of the women to come and sit alongside him. He spoke to her for quite a while, sometimes pointing to Bill, and sometimes pointing to Annie. After he stopped speaking, the woman spoke. She told Annie that she was the wife of their leader, as she pointed to the Tall One.

Then in her own language still, she explained that their custom didn't allow the men to speak to other women, and that is why she is talking for him. Annie spoke back, saying that she understood and respected their ways and laws. Then she told her that her name was Annie, and that her man's name was Bill. The Aboriginal woman smiled and repeated this to her husband. Annie had to correct them a few times, but they finally could say Annie and Bill. Then Annie told the lady that Bill had chosen the name, The Tall One, for her husband. When she repeated this, The Tall One smiled and nodded to Bill.

Talk was conveyed backwards and forwards for a while, then another woman came to the fire and threw in a Bungarra and some Kangaroo meat. When this was cooked, Bill and Annie joined all the tribe in a feast. The Tall One then broke some of the bread that Bill had given him. He nodded his approval and shared it around and everyone murmured their delight at this new type of damper.

When the meal was finished, The Tall One clapped his hands again and most of the Aboriginals jumped up and started dancing. Then from seemingly out of nowhere came about twenty children, who also joined in the dancing.

After several minutes of this, their leader said something, and everyone sat in a circle. One of the warriors then placed a pole in the centre. Then The Tall One, stood up and walked to this pole. He looked first towards Bill, then he drew out the Bowie Knife that Bill had given him. He took nine steps backwards, then in one movement, he threw the knife. His aim was perfect, and with the stance and swagger of a true chief, he withdrew the knife from the centre of the pole. Bill clapped loudly and then everyone clapped and cheered.

The Tall One then said something to his wife, who then conveyed the message to Annie. She then told Bill that The Tall One would like to see him make his gun throw something at the pole. Bill nodded and walked to the pole, and taking out his new Bowie Knife, that he had purchased in Kalgoorlie, he marked a small target. He then stepped out thirty paces then aimed for, and hit the target. This pleased the group, but they all went quiet when the leader pointed for Bill to shoot from further away. Bill stepped out another ten yards and fired. Again he hit the target.

The Tall One then gestured to Annie to have a shot. Not wanting to make Bill look small, she went out and took a shot, but she missed on purpose. This made the Aboriginals think that their hero, or magician, was still the best.

Time went quickly, so Bill asked Annie to thank The Tall One for his hospitality. Then they headed back to their camp. The four warriors who had been guarding their camp, jogged away as soon as Bill and Annie got back. 'What do you want to do now?' Bill asked Annie.

All was quiet for a moment, then Annie said, 'let's find some gold. I've never done that.'

Bill was somehow hoping that they might have continued talking about the way that they felt about each other, but he took her to his diggings and explained his method of specking, then of dry blowing. It wasn't long before she got the hang of both methods, and Bill smiled when after only about an hour, Annie held up her first ever piece of gold. It was a nice little nugget of about one half an ounce. Annie was that excited with her discovery, she ran to Bill and threw her arms around him and kissed him.

Bill was surprised, and said, 'I hope you find more pieces of gold soon girlfriend.'

Annie blushed and said, 'so do I Bill.' Then they started looking for more of what drives people to travel hundreds of miles to find. But they didn't find any more gold that day.

It was about a fortnight before the young couple found any more gold, and Bill was happy as Annie, although not as excited as she was before, still gave him a kiss. 'That's more like it,' Bill said.

Memories of old Tom came back to Bill now as he held this small nugget. 'If you ever find a really rough piece of gold, then it means it hasn't travelled far. So look at the countryside and dig towards the most likely looking, or probably the closest, breakaway or hill. Particularly if the breakaway has white and brown quartz around it.'

Bill did as Tom had once told him, and sure enough, there was a small breakaway only about fifty yards to the north. Annie asked him what he was thinking about, so he explained about old Tom, and his gold theories. 'Let's start digging then boyfriend,' she said.

He noted that Annie had subconsciously called him boyfriend, so he was now smiling as he started with his pick and shovel. The two partners had developed a good working system. Bill would dig the soil and rock, putting it in a heap, on one side of the trench. Then Annie would sift the dirt, leaving all but the fine sand and dust in the bottom of the sifter. Then she would tip this coarser dirt and rock into one of the dry blowing dishes. Holding this dish about shoulder height above the ground, she would then tip the contents into another dish below. This worked better if there was a wind to blow away the fine soil as it fell into the bottom dish.

For two days they worked without any luck, but then on the third day, just as Bill said, 'that's enough for today,' Annie gave a loud scream. Thinking something was wrong, Bill climbed out of his now deep trench in a hurry.

With both hands firmly holding a piece of the metal that drives all prospectors, Annie said, 'good golly miss Molly. Look at this Bill.' Annie was holding a beautiful nugget, which Bill estimated must weigh at least five ounces.

They danced and yelled for ages, waving the nugget around. Then Bill said, 'this beauty could be worth more than a kiss Annie.'

The digging continued for the partners, and over the next week or so they collected several nice nuggets. The biggest was still the five ounce piece, with three others around the two ounce size. So far Bill calculated that he and Annie had nearly twenty ounces to show for three weeks work. 'It's not work Bill,' she said, 'it's the best fun I've had for a long time.'

Annie then moved closer to Bill and thanked him for everything. 'I'm not sure what I would have done if it weren't for you Bill Evans.'

Before Bill could think what to say or do, Mother Nature supplied the answer. 'Rain,' they both yelled at the same time. The skies opened up as torrential rain threatened to wet some of the supplies. Both of them got soaked as they put anything that may spoil in Annie's tent. Wet but happy, they then put out any containers that they had to catch this precious water.

Then satisfied they could do no more, the both of them stripped off and grabbing a block of velvet soap each, they had their first real shower in weeks. Annie had been making do with a small dish of water each day for her wash, so to her, this was heaven.

They spent nearly half an hour in the rain, then Annie went into her tent to dry herself. It was starting to get dark by now, and still the rains came down. Bill managed to dry himself under a small canvas lean to that he had made to cover the horses feed. He was trying to set up his bedroll under this canvas, when he heard Annie call him.

So thinking she may be in trouble, he rushed into her tent. 'Close the tent flap Bill,' came her voice. Bill could hardly see, but he could make out Annie's figure. She was half under her blanket, and as Bill got closer, she moved over and motioned for him to hop in beside her.

The next morning, the sky was blue, and all the containers were full of fresh water. Bill woke to find himself still in Annie's bed, but there was no sign of her. He got dressed and went outside, and there was Annie, cooking breakfast. Without either of them saying a word, they ate heartily, then drank coffee. It would have been obvious to anyone watching, that these two youngsters were embarrassed. Annie was especially shy, but she broke the silence by saying, 'Bill, about last night. I hope you don't think I was to forward. I mean I have never been with anyone like that, and I don't want you—.' She didn't get a chance to finish her sentence, because Bill had walked over to her and silenced her with a long loving kiss.

Finally he stopped, long enough to say 'Annie Oakley, I could only ever think of you with the greatest respect, and I think you are one of the most beautiful and–.' This time it was Annie that put an end to anymore conversation for the next hour or so.

They decided not to do any mining that day, instead they went hunting. Bill had figured that if they could supplement their supplies with some fresh Kangaroo meat, then they could get by for another two weeks or so. Because of the rain, they had plenty of water, so with rifles in hand, they set off in a direction away from the Aboriginal's camp. Bill didn't want to fire any bullets in their direction, for fear of hitting or annoying them.

They had walked about a mile, when Annie suddenly shouldered her rifle, and before Bill had even seen what she was aiming at, Annie had shot a young Kangaroo. Bill ran over to make sure it was not suffering, but was impressed to see that the bullet had been a brain shot. 'Good shot,' he said.

Bill then looked back to where Annie had fired from. 'Do you realize that you hit your target from about a hundred yards,' he said to her. 'Now tell me the truth, did you aim for a brain shot, or was it a fluke?'

Annie just giggled and shrugged her shoulders, so Bill thought that it may well have been a lucky shot. Bill then watched as Annie kneeled next to the dead Kangaroo, then said something. After they had skinned it, they buried the unwanted pieces. On the way back, Bill, who was still not sure about Annie's good shooting, stopped and said that he wanted a spell. After placing the meat on a clean piece of rock, Bill asked Annie again if she had aimed for a brain shot. 'I always hit what I aim for,' she replied.

Bill reminded her that she had missed the target at the Aboriginal's camp. She then told Bill that she had aimed to miss. 'Why would you do that girlfriend?'

Annie said 'because you silly man, a woman's place in the Aboriginal's way of thinking, is in the background, not beating her man. The Tall One was testing me out.'

Bill thought for a moment, then said, 'so you could have beaten me that day?'

Now Annie laughed and said, 'I didn't say that Bill.'

Up jumped the young man and marked a target fifty yards away. Then he picked up his trusty rifle and shot the target dead centre. 'Your shot,' he said.

Annie said, 'there's no need to do this Bill. It doesn't matter who is the better shot, let's just go back to camp and cook some of this Kangaroo.'

Bill, thinking he was going to win, then said, 'loser cooks tea for a week.'

So with a smile, Annie Oakley picked up her rifle and hit the target. This shocked Bill, so he jumped up and shot the target from another ten yards further away. Annie was in hysterics of laughter now as she walked another ten or so yards further away. When she stopped laughing she turned her back on the target and turning her head enough to be able to line up the sights, she fired. Then without looking to see if she had hit the target, she said, 'start cooking boyfriend.'

Bill, not believing his eyes' walked over, and sure enough Annie's bullet had hit dead centre. Not wanting to be beaten, he fired his next shot from another ten yards further back. His bullet just hit the edge of the target. 'Nice shot,' said Annie, 'don't know if I can beat that.'

This made Bill full of confidence now, 'you have to try, or otherwise you'll be chief cook for the next week.'

Annie walked another ten yards, then she again turned her back on the distant target. This time she fired from a bent over position with the rifle between her legs. Again she didn't bother to check the target, but Bill did. 'You missed,' he yelled.

Annie walked up to the target on the tree, then told Bill to have another look. He could not believe his eyes, when Annie pointed out that her last bullet had hit in almost the same hole as her previous shot. Bill knew he was beaten. 'Annie, I have never seen anything like it. Well done,' he said as he gave her a kiss.

Not sure whether to tease him or not, Annie said, 'that was nice, but it won't save you from having to cook for the next week Bill.'

The next week went fast, but without much gold. They did get a visit from the Aboriginals though. This time The Tall One brought his wife with him and a guard of six warriors. Annie and the black Lady talked freely for a while in Wongi language. Then The Tall One said something to his wife, who knowing that Annie had understood, nodded for her to pass the message on to her man. Annie told Bill that the group had been watching, as she and Bill had their shooting contest that day a week ago. 'He now wants me to show them some of my "clever" shots.'

Bill played the part he was expected to and stood up and pointed for his woman to shoot. Shoot this young lady surely did that day. Annie shot at stationary targets from all angles, and from between her legs, and never once did she miss. Then she got Bill to throw pieces of wood as high in the air as he could. Not missing any of these flying targets, Annie shocked even Bill, when she asked him to hold a stick out to his side. Annie then walked about fifty yards from him, and facing him she yelled first in English, then in Wongi, 'don't move my man.'

Whilst she was walking away from the group, unbeknown to anyone, she had fitted a mirror to the butt of her rifle which enabled her to be able to see a target behind her.

At the spot where she had indicated she was going to shoot from, she turned her back on Bill who was doing his best to hold the stick still. Annie looked into this small mirror, and when she could see the target she fired. The Tall One not knowing that this woman had a trick mirror, jumped up in bewilderment and wonder as the stick that her man was holding was shot in half. He pointed to Annie, then said something to his wife, which made the other warriors start singing and dancing. Then The Tall One walked to Bill and placed a parcel on the ground. In return, Bill gave him most of the supplies they had left.

As fast as they had appeared, some thirty or forty minutes previously, the group were gone. Annie was interested in the gift that they had left, so Bill, knowing that it probably was gold, told her that she had better open it. 'I think it's a present for my woman,' Bill laughed.

Annie said, 'I'll give you "your woman", you cheeky Magic Man.' Then she unwrapped the parcel. 'My goodness, there's gold in here Bill,' she screamed.

There was the same amount of nuggets that the Aboriginals had given Bill before. 'You keep them for yourself, they are not a part of our business arrangement,' he told the excited Annie.

The rest of that day, the happy partners talked, and started packing. Bill had decided that they must go and get more supplies. Annie told Bill that The Tall One had given them both names. 'That's what he was saying after my shooting exhibition that you ordered me to put on.'

Bill thought back to the time when he had flour all over him, remembering how the Aboriginal leader had pointed to him and said a name to his warriors, so he asked 'what did he name us then?'

Annie answered, 'well it seems that you are named "Magic Man," and I'm to be called, "Gun Woman". That's what the Aboriginal's have decided.'

Whist they were drinking a mug of coffee, Annie told Bill that she would use the gold, and her wages that he had paid her, to enrol at the University. Bill was interested, and asked her what she was going to study. 'I have always wanted to be a Chemist,' she said.

Bill now started to think he may lose her and was not happy with this idea. 'I've heard you need high marks to study Chemistry,' Bill told her.

Annie said that she had received all "A" results at her high school graduation. 'Dad wanted to put me through Uni, but money was too scarce.' Bill could see that she really wanted to become a Chemist, so he suggested that when they get to Kalgoorlie, she should enrol at the University for next year. 'My Dad is going to like you Bill Evans,' she said.

They went back to Kalgoorlie, where Annie, with Bill's help, filled in the necessary forms to enable her to be enrolled at the University starting January next year. Then after buying their supplies, they headed back to their "Paradise", as Annie called it. This time they were followed by two or three groups of other prospectors, who after seeing Bill always returning, must have reckoned that he was on to a patch. Bill said to Annie that they might be better off trying a new area for a while, or there will be miners everywhere.

Both Bill and Annie had written letters to their families, and had posted them in Kalgoorlie. They also collected mail, and all was well with both. Annie was an only child, so her only family was her father, and he obviously missed her, because he had written about twice a week, so Annie had several letters to read. She, on the first night that they camped, read parts of these letters to Bill, and he did the same with his mail. 'I hope you don't mind Bill, but I told Dad that we are partners. I also told him that you are trustworthy and a gentleman,' she said.

Bill said 'well I've told my parents nearly all about you too.' Then he grinned as he added, 'I also told them that you were a cheeky lady, but I couldn't tell them all the cheeky bits.'

To which Annie replied, 'oh, did you now. Tell me which bits didn't you tell them about boyfriend?'

Bill said, 'these bits,' as he chased her, then held her close.

Ever so softly, Annie said, 'I told my Dad that I like you,' Then she said, 'do you like me Bill?'

Bill and Annie shifted several times over the next week, and each time they were followed by one or more other prospectors. Not wanting to indicate where they had been digging before they were followed, they only dug in ground that looked unlikely. Then finally they were free to go back to where they wanted to be, because all of the followers gave up.

When Bill and Annie did set up camp, the Aboriginals were waiting for them, or at least, four of them were. The Tall One was not one of them, and when Bill tried to offer these two some food, they both shook their heads and indicated for him and Annie to follow them. Two though stayed to guard their supplies.

The Aboriginal camp was a hive of activity when the two warriors took Bill and Annie there. The Tall One and his wife met them, and the relayed message was that they were to be taken to a special place, where there is much shiny metal. So The Tall One, with an escort of six warriors took Magic Man, and Gun Woman to this special place. It was not far from the tribes camp, but very hard to find.

They were led through thick scrub, which was covering a narrow entrance to what opened up into a huge underground cavern. Not far into this cavern was a creek, with crystal clear water flowing in it. Bill now knew where this tribe was getting their water. There were several hand carved bowls on the edge of this underground creek, and each warrior stopped and drank some water before crossing over. The Tall One signalled for Bill and Annie to drink, then he told two of his warriors to stand guard at the cavern's entrance. Then in semi-darkness, The Tall One stopped, then as he pointed to one side of the rough and crumbling wall, both Bill and Annie drew an extra breath.

As they stared in disbelief, the proud leader of the tribe, picked up a handful of the glittering metal. The Tall One passed the nugget to Bill, who got a shock at the sheer weight of it. Not sure what to do next, Bill showed the piece to Annie. Then for the first time, and only because his wife was not there to pass on messages, The Tall One spoke to Annie. Annie knew what to do in this situation, as she and her Dad employed Wongi Aboriginals on his station.

Annie went and stood behind Bill, out of sight, and changed her voice to make it sound like Bill's. Then she told Bill each time a statement was made. Then, repeating what The Tall One had just said, she told Bill, 'please help yourself, Magic Man.'

Gun Woman spoke Bill's answer, 'thank you Tall One, but as this is your special place, we cannot take any of your precious metal, but we are honoured by your kind offer, and your friendship. Thank you Tall One for showing us here today. We will never tell anyone about this place.'

The Wongi chief spoke again, through Annie. 'Magic man, you are not like any of the other greedy ones who come to our land. They take our precious metal, and give us nothing. Our people have lived here for as long as there is time, and we have looked after our land and our animals. We watched as your special woman, the one who speaks our tongue and knows our ways, killed one of our animals. Then she praised the animal, saying she was sorry to have to kill it. She will make you a good wife. Now you Magic Man. You treat us as equals, and you give us food, and also weapons. This is a good knife. Now you are given the opportunity to have all the precious metal you want, but you honour us instead. Others of your tribe would, and have, killed for less of this metal that is so valuable to the white man. I see you work for this metal, and yet you cannot take the easy way of becoming rich.'

Bill answered almost immediately, 'Rich, you say to me. I am already rich, as are you Tall One. We are born to appreciate and be content with what nature has given us. That is a richness than cannot be bought. You say I treat you as equal. This is because we are equal. We may have different colour skin, but we are all only here until nature takes us to another place. Neither of us can change that, so while we are all here for such a short time, we should all treat each other as equals. I apologize for the ill treatment that some have given you, but you were right when you called them greedy. The world is full of greedy men, and we must all try to change them, or it will be too late, because they will destroy the whole world. I do not like to take too much from your land, but I need some of this precious metal to be able to live in this changing world. From this special place, I and my woman want to take only a little of your water, and a lot of your wisdom and friendship.'

Bill then signalled to Annie that he had more to say. He wanted to have a little fun with her, without dishonouring this proud tribesman. So knowing that Annie wouldn't say what he was going to tell her next, he said, 'thank you Tall One for your kind words about my woman. You are a wise man, but even wise men can sometimes be wrong. This woman that you have named so honourably, is not really a good shot with her gun. She is also not a good cook. Also I have to belt her more than one time each day.' Trying not to laugh, Bill then nodded to indicate that he had finished speaking.

Annie also had trouble keeping herself from laughing, but she said everything exactly as Bill had meant her to. That is until she got to the last part, the part about herself, which she changed, as Bill knew she would. Annie said, 'thank you Tall One for your kind words about my woman. You are a wise man, because she is a good woman. She looks after me very well, and I love her very much. My woman can shoot better than me, and I need her, so I hope she will accept me as her husband so we can have many children.'

When they arrived back at the Aboriginals camp, there was no one in sight. The Tall One indicated for Bill and Annie to sit near him, then as he clapped his hands, his wife came and sat near them. Even though she sat alongside Annie, and the two had become friends, she did not talk. The silence remained until The Tall One again clapped. Then the whole tribe appeared from seemingly out of nowhere. Each one of them was painted, ready for something special. Bill and Annie were that day, treated to a full tribal coroberrie. Then as the Digeridoo player stopped, each member of the tribe walked past and gave Bill and Annie a gift. They then sat in a circle around their leader and his guests. The Tall One then stood and drew out his knife. He then invited Bill to stand near him. Not knowing what to expect, Bill watched as the tribe's leader first cut his, and then Bill's arm. The Tall One then placed both the bleeding arms together. Then for the first time he spoke, 'we are now brothers,' he said, and Annie translated. Singing now echoed through the Aboriginal's camp as all the tribe sang a song to honour Magic Man and Gun Woman.

The two young prospectors, with their gifts under their arms made their way back to their camp just as the sun was setting that day. Bill was not surprised to see that there were two of The Tall One's warriors guarding his and Annie's camp. The two of them saluted Bill, and nodded to Annie as they left.

That night Bill asked Annie what she had said about herself to The Tall One earlier. With a cheeky smile she said, 'you'll never know boyfriend.' Annie was still smiling to herself when she went to sleep.

The next morning, Annie woke Bill saying, 'let's look at our gifts that our friends gave us yesterday.'

Bill had forgotten to open them, and jumped back in amazement when he saw that each small bundle contained a nugget of similar size. 'I told him not to give us any of their gold,' Bill said. There were about forty of these nuggets, which Bill told Annie, would weigh over an ounce each. 'I'm taking them back,' said Bill, as he started packing them into a bag.

Annie stopped him, 'no Bill, you must not. My Dad refused a gift from an Aboriginal once, and the poor man was dishonoured by his tribe.'

So Bill gave in and accepted that all this gold must be theirs. The next time the tribe came, Bill gave them all their supplies. He then got Annie to tell The Tall One that he and his woman are going away for a long time, and this handshake is not goodbye, but farewell until we meet again. Annie passed on this message, and as the proud Aboriginal nodded to him, Bill and he shook hands in the way that Charlie Burns had shown him how to. So the two blood brothers parted, and if Bill Evans, or Magic

Man, as he so named by this incredible man, had known that it was to be the last time that they would see each other in a happy way, when everything was good, then he would have lingered longer in his farewell.

As it was, neither of them hurried, and Bill did get a strange feeling of nostalgia, as The Tall One stood tall and saluted him and Annie. Bill was so moved that he unstrapped his Bowie Knife and pouch. He then presented it to The Tall One and asked Annie to pass on his message, 'your knife looks lonely, and so here is another to go with it.' Now for the last time they looked each at each other with equal respect. Then this proud group of true Australians were gone. Bill stood for a long time, staring at nothing, until Annie broke the silence, 'what's up boyfriend?' she asked.

'Don't really know love,' Bill said quietly.

'Did you just call me love?' asked Annie.

Bill snapped out of his strange feeling, and realizing that he had just subconsciously called her that, he said, 'didn't you want me to?'

Annie smiled and said 'yes it's all good boyfriend,' as she quickly kissed him on the cheek.

But the mood of this young man was not yet broken. He was still worried that his Aboriginal friends were in some sort of danger. 'Something is telling me that it's time to move on Annie,' he finally said.

So they packed, and to their horse's joy, they headed off. 'Where are we going love?' asked Annie.

This time Bill smiled as he replied, 'I reckon we might try our luck where Old Tom made his start, Coolgardie, if it's alright with you Annie Oakley.'

Kalgoorlie was the first stop, as they wanted to check for any mail, and sell some gold. There was mail, and after reading that all was still well at his parents, and his sisters households, Bill noticed that Annie was excitingly re-reading the same letter over and over. 'I can't believe it Bill. Look, a letter from the University, and I've been accepted for chemistry.'

Bill joined in Annie's jubilation, then he said, 'wow, that means you can make plans for next year.'

Annie quickly said, 'no boyfriend, not next year, they said there is a vacancy next term. That means I have to be there in three weeks' time.'

Realizing what this meant, Bill went quiet. Not only had he lost Beatrice, then Jenny, but now he was going to have to say goodbye to Annie. Bill had not allowed himself to be attracted to Annie for ages. Now after opening his heart to her, he was going to lose her too.

But Annie seemed to have other ideas. 'Oh Bill,' she said. 'We can leave soon, but I want to go and see Dad first. You'll like him Bill, you and him are so much alike.'

It was too much for Bill, and he sat down on a bench and invited Annie to do the same. 'Annie Oakley, what are you saying? Do you plan to include me in your life? We must talk girlfriend,' he said.

Annie looked surprised, 'maybe I was presuming too much Bill. But we seemed to be, I mean, oh Bill you've never told me how you feel, but I love you.' Annie burst into tears, and started to walk away.

Bill grabbed her and sat her down again. 'I meant that we should not rush into things, but I can see now that we must. Annie Oakley, I will be happy to come with you to meet your father. Then girlfriend, we will talk, because I think I love you too.'

Annie stopped crying and said, 'oh Bill I hoped you would say that.'

The two partners, who Bill thought to himself, might become more than just prospecting partners, embraced in the main street of Kalgoorlie. There were still not a lot of cars in this mining town, but the few that were passing, tooted their car horns when they saw this young couple embracing. Bill then said, 'well as it looks like our gold hunting days may be over girlfriend, we better go and sell what we've found.'

Annie nodded her agreement, then said, 'I was hoping that our days of being boyfriend and girlfriend may be over too Bill.'

Thinking that she had just changed her mind, Bill asked her what she meant. Then Annie said that she would love to be able to introduce him to her Dad as her fiancée.

Chapter Fourteen
There's Life In The Kimberley

Annie's Dad met them at the airport of a large town that was regarded as the capital of the Kimberley cattle industry. Annie got her wish, 'Dad this is my fiancée, the man I wrote you about, and the man I love, Bill Evans.'

Bill shook hands with a strong well suntanned man of about fifty years. 'Pleased to meet you Bill, call me Henry,' he said as he picked up his daughter's luggage.

Bill grabbed his pack also, and he felt the immense tropical heat bounce back off the tarmac and hit him in the face. 'Always this hot here Mr Oakley?' he asked.

Annie's father said, 'call me Henry please Bill. This is a rather mild day today mate. Gets hotter than this most days.'

Annie nudged Bill and said, 'we'll get him used to the weather up here eh Dad.'

As they drove down the main street, Bill got a history lesson. 'This is Derby Bill. Most of our northwest cattle come here to this town's jetty, and are shipped to all parts of the world. But mostly our station's beef goes to Perth.' Bill stared at the funny looking trees that lined the street. 'Boab trees they are,' Henry said as he stopped his old Rio truck near the huge wharf.

Bill wondered how the cattle got down to the ships, because the ocean seemed about twenty feet below the top of the wooden jetty. 'We have some of the biggest tides in the world here in Derby,' said Annie. 'That ship you can see down there will rise up about seven yards later today.'

Bill then got out of the truck and thought he might go down the bank and soak his feet in the ocean. He was half way there when Henry said, 'wouldn't go there if I was you Bill. Don't want to lose you yet mate.'

Bemused, Bill looked to where Annie's Dad was pointing. He had to look hard, then he made out the shape of a crocodile laying just out of the water under the shade of a mangrove tree. 'That's a small one Bill, but its parents are probably working out which one of them is going to have you for lunch,' said Henry.

They stopped in town, and Annie wanted to shop for supplies for the station. It wasn't all that often that Henry came to Derby, so it was a good time to stock up on all the goods and chattels that he needed to run his cattle station. The station that Henry Oakley managed, was over two hundred mile inland from Derby, and as it was still only eleven o'clock, he said to Bill, 'feel like a drink before we head back mate. Annie can drive the truck to the co-op to get the stores. Pick us up in about an hour love.'

Annie said, 'I'll be there in half an hour Dad. I'll toot the horn, and if you're not out in two minutes I'll see you back at the station.'

The barman said, 'Gooday Henry, the usual for you eh, what about the young bloke with you? What will it be mate?'

Bill said back, 'name's Bill mate and I'll have a lemonade thanks,' he told the talkative barman.

Then, 'one beer and one lemonade coming up,' the barman said to nobody in particular.

Bill looked around and noticed there were only a few other drinkers, and they all waved to Henry, who waved back. 'Only a small town Bill, so a bloke gets to know mostly everyone eh?'

The prospective Father and Son in laws talked away for a while, and Bill noticed that Annie's dad drank his beers down fast. By time they heard the truck's horn, Henry had put away ten glasses of beer. 'One for the road Henry?' the barman asked.

'No thanks, better be off, it's a long walk back to the station,' he said as he and Bill left the quiet hotel to join Annie in the station truck. 'Better you drive Princess,' Henry said as he climbed into the back seat and stretched out to obviously have a nap.

Annie was a good driver, and as she drove down the dusty street, she tooted to several people, who waved back to her. 'Your Dad knows a lot of folk here too,' Bill said.

Then Annie explained that people are mostly different up north, especially here In the Kimberly. She stopped the truck not far out of town, and showed Bill a huge boab tree. It was about forty feet in circumference, and was hollow with a narrow opening. 'They used to lock prisoners in there,' she told Bill. 'The story is that the Police once locked twenty seven Aboriginals in there for a night.'

Bill was then she shown a cattle trough, which was fed water from a bore which didn't need a pump. Apparently the water just spewed from the ground to fill this huge water trough, which Annie said was claimed to be the longest one in the world.

They had travelled for about an hour, then Annie stopped again. 'We'll have to walk a bit here Bill,' she said as she led him down a narrow winding track. Then as they squeezed through an opening in a cliff, Annie pointed up and said, 'mind your head boyfriend.' Bill looked up and there was a python, which was a very large snake, curled up in a crevice on the rocks. 'That's Oscar. He won't hurt, he lives here in these Oscar Ranges,' she said.

Annie then led Bill to a wider opening in this cliff, and he drew in his breath with wonder as they entered a huge cave. Annie took off her boots, and Bill did the same then he followed her into a creek. It got quite dark as they waded waist high through the cold running water. 'Don't worry if you tread on something and it moves, it'll only be a freshwater croc. They don't usually bite,' she said.

When they had crossed the creek, it got lighter, and after climbing over rocks, Annie pointed out some Aboriginal drawings etched into the smooth rock face. 'Those were painted over thirty thousand years ago,' she told Bill who was staring in wonder at these amazing drawings. Bill wondered how these first Australians had the ability to draw so well. They somehow chose the rock to draw with that would stand the test of time. There were some red and brown, and even a tinge of yellow blended in with the predominately white paintings. It was hard for Bill to grasp the fact that some thirty thousand years ago, these peaceful Aboriginals, were so more advanced than the Europeans, who were not to come even close to the intelligence needed to be able to do works of art like this for still thousands of years. No, thought Bill, even today no other race could possibly paint pictures like this. Annie had been quiet for a few minutes. She remembered how she was amazed by these paintings the first time her father had brought her here. Now she broke the eerie silence by saying, 'you like this place don't you Bill.'

He nodded to her and said in an unusually soft voice, 'just a little.'

When they had returned to the other side of this underground creek, Annie stopped and pointed up again and said, 'that's where an Aboriginal named Pigeon, who had been wanted for murder, hid when the Police chased him into here in eighteen ninety five. They finally shot him.'

Bill asked what the place was called, and Annie told him it was Tunnel Creek. 'The next place just up the road is Windjana Gorge,' Annie told him. 'It's a sacred place to the Aborigines, and it was the Ongkomi people that named this place.' She went on to tell him that Windjana is their rain god, and his figure is in most of the native paintings throughout the Kimberley.

When they reached this sacred gorge, Annie showed Bill the ruins of the old Police station. 'This is where Pigeon killed a Policeman and freed twenty prisoners,' she said.

Then as they walked a bit further, they came to several pools of clear water in this massive gorge, which had beautiful river gum trees lining most of the banks. 'If you look close Bill you'll see the odd freshwater croc, and look at the birds,' she said.

Bill looked and saw several of these crocs, and many dozens of different birds. 'Peggy would love it here in your Kimberley,' he said. 'This beautiful place is so alive.'

Annie smiled proudly as she said, 'oh yes boyfriend, there's life in the Kimberley.'

Henry was still sleeping, and did so until Annie stopped the truck at a wire gate. 'Why didn't you two wake me earlier? I wanted to show Bill Tunnel Creek,' he said.

Annie then had to explain that she had done that for him, while he was busy snoring. The track that they took was just before a sign that said "Kimberley Downs", and Henry told them that there was to be a big rodeo and gymkhana there the coming weekend. 'That's only two days away Dad. I hope you've been practising your whip cracking,' Annie said as she swerved the truck to miss a big pothole in the middle of the homestead track.

Henry then asked, 'ever cracked a stockwhip Bill?'

Again they all hung on as Annie had to avoid another big pothole. 'Just a few times,' Bill finally answered.

Annie then said, 'Dads won that title for as long as I can remember, so maybe you better give him some opposition this year,'

The three of them seemed to get on like a house on fire, and before long the truck was parked in front of a beautiful big house. The house was on stilts and Henry explained that sometimes it rains a bit up here. The homestead was surrounded by a sea of green. 'There must be a hundred trees around the house and sheds,' Bill thought to himself. As he got out, he also saw that the whole area was under green grass, which seemed to accentuate the white homestead.

'Keeps the place a bit cooler, all this green,' Henry said to Bill.

Annie proudly showed her fiancée around the house, and to which was his room. 'You do mean our room don't you girlfriend,' Bill smiled.

'Sorry Bill, Dads a bit old fashioned, and he still thinks I'm his little girl,' said Annie.

That was settled, so Bill looked round his room and was impressed. It was the biggest bedroom he had ever seen, and there was a fan above his bed and a large window with fly screens. 'Keeps the beasties out,' Annie told him.

The rest of the house was equally impressive to Bill. There was a huge kitchen, a big study, and a large dining and living area. There were four other bedrooms, and Annie smiled when Bill asked her which one was hers.

It was now late in the day so Annie started cooking their meal while her father showed Bill around the sheds and the stockyards. There were several good looking horses stabled near the stockyards. Each stable had its own yard of about ten acres adjoining it. Looking at these fine animals, Bill got to thinking about his own horses.

He had stabled Blackie and his pack horse in Kalgoorlie. The livery man was happy to buy back the other two pack horses that Bill didn't need any more. Annie had suggested to him that he may as well sell all his horses, but Bill told her that he would never sell Blackie. Between them they had received over six hundred pounds for their gold that they sold at Kalgoorlie. As partners they should have taken half each, but

Bill took three hundred pounds, which left three hundred and forty seven pounds for Annie. Bill added his to what he already had, and he now had just over seven hundred one pound notes in his new wallet. He had also bought a new Bowie Knife to replace the one he had given to The Tall One.

Bill told Henry that he was impressed by the size of, and the clean way his station was set up. Annie's father then told Bill that things had been very tough, but he had sold and got good money for two thousand head of cattle last week. 'Looks like the bank manager might leave us alone for a bit longer mate,' he said.

Bill took this opportunity to speak man to man with the father of his promised bride. He nervously said, 'Mr Oakley, I'm sorry I did not show you the respect you deserve, and ask for Annie's hand in marriage. I do though give you my solemn oath that I will always do my best to look after her, in the way that you have brought her up. If you have any objections to me marrying your daughter Sir, then please tell me.'

Henry Oakley turned from leaning on the stockyard rails, and faced this well-mannered young man that had won the heart of his only daughter. 'Well Bill, do think for one minute that I could change my daughters mind. For a start young man, I'll tell you what Annie has probably already told you. She has been the one thing that has kept me going since my Mary died. Without her I don't know what I would have done. So Bill Evans, thank you for being so straight forward with me. One thing I probably don't need to say, but I will, is this Bill. If you don't do as you have promised, or if you harm my daughter, I will find you son.'

Bill held this proud man's eye contact and said, 'I would expect no less from you Henry.'

The silence that threatened to take over, as the two men recovered from an emotional and straight from the heart conversation, was broken by the very one that they were talking about. Annie Oakley called to the two most important men in her life. 'Come and get it,' she bellowed. Both men laughed, then headed to the homestead dining room.

Sleep did not come easy for Bill. The night time temperature only dropped a few degrees below the daytime one, which was over a hundred degrees. But when he did finally nod off, it was a deep dreamlike sleep. 'Take care Bill, take care, take.. .' Bill woke in a lather of sweat, yet he felt cold. Then he relived part of this dream that had woken him. A picture of his friend Charlie Burns kept flashing through his mind. Then as he almost drifted back to sleep, a vision of a snake also flashed across his mind. Bill was sure that it was only a dream, but he knew that if Charlie had anything to do with these messages, then it must mean something.

Bill opened his eyes, and seeing that it was almost light, he sat up. Just as he sat forward, he felt a movement and saw a blur behind him, where he had been laying one second ago. In one quick action, he jumped out of bed and picking up the blanket, he threw it over this thing that had just tried to hit him. Bill then used the bedside table to hit this wriggling thing under the blanket. After about fifty blows, Bill stopped belting the blanket.

He did not realize it, but he had been yelling at the top of his voice the whole time. This had woken the household, and in came Annie and her father to see what was wrong. They both exclaimed in horror as Bill pulled off the blanket to reveal a big brown snake. It was not a pretty sight. Bill had belted it to death, and just as well Henry told him later. 'The King Brown is the most vicious and deadly thing here in the Kimberly. Don't know if you would have survived if he had bitten you Bill.'

Henry then tried to work out how the snake could have gotten into Bill's bedroom. Annie walked to the window and seeing that the flywire was open as well as the louvers, she said, 'I should have told you not to open the flywire Bill, this is where it got in.'

There was no more sleep for the family, instead Annie took Bill to the kitchen while her father got rid of the deadly snake. Coffee, then bacon and eggs done the trick, after which Bill asked what he could do to help today. 'I thought you might want to settle in today son,' Henry answered.

Bill thought for only a moment before saying 'Reckon I'll settle in better if I can help out Henry.'

So after breakfast, the three of them saddled up and set off to shift cattle from one paddock to another. Annie chose a big chestnut gelding for Bill, who had no trouble getting him to work the cattle as directed by Henry. They drove about four hundred two year old steers into a holding yard which was next to the main stockyards. From this holding paddock it was Bill's job to herd them into a race. Then as Annie then urged them along the race, Henry treated them for worms and ticks, then they were directed into the main yard. Once they were all treated, Henry opened the gate into the chosen paddock and Bill and Annie drove them into it. 'Good job you two,' said Henry. 'You don't make a bad team.'

After a big lunch Bill said, 'what's next boss?'

To which both father and daughter laughed and laughed, so much so that Bill joined in. Then he asked them, 'what was so funny?'

Annie was the first to recover, so she told Bill that the word "Boss" is usually only used by any Aboriginals that her Dad sometimes employs. 'It sounded so funny when you said it Bill,' she said.

Not sure whether to or not, Bill decided to tell them about his dream, and how his friend sort of sent him a message about the snake. 'If I hadn't of sat up when I did I reckon it would have bitten me for sure.'

Henry nodded and asked Bill if his friend was an Aboriginal? When Bill told him that he was, and that he was born up here in the Kimberley, Henry said, 'don't worry, we believe you. Happens all the time up here, eh Princess.'

Then Henry said that he might get his stockwhip out and practise a bit. 'Care to have a go Bill?' he asked.

Annie said she had washing and things to do, so the two men went out into an empty paddock and practised cracking Henry's twenty foot long whip. It took Bill a while to get used to this long whip, as the one he owned was much shorter. 'Young bloke called Nathan Griggs from Queensland makes these special whips,' Henry said as he did a double forward then a double back that he called his quadruple.

After a while they took a break and Henry said, 'Annie tells me you can fight a bit Bill.'

Not too sure where this was heading, Bill said, 'just a bit.' Henry then told him that there was a boxing tournament at the coming gymkhana, and the winner usually takes home twenty quid. Bill just nodded, then said that his father didn't like him to box. They were about to start practising again, when out came Annie on a magnificent brown mare. 'Sit down and watch this Bill,' said Henry.

As the two men retreated to the fence of the big paddock and sat on the railings, Annie galloped her horse straight at them. Bill thought she may have overjudged her run, but at the very last second she pulled hard on the reins and her horse stopped on a dime and stood on its hind legs. The hooves of its forelegs were missing Bill and Henry's heads by only a foot or so, as this proud little mare pawed the air with them. Then at Annie's command, it was off and galloping in an ever increasing circle. At its master's command, this well trained animal slowed to a canter, then Annie stood up in the saddle and the circle became smaller with each revolution, until the sprightly horse stopped and stood on its hind legs, allowing Annie to land in the saddle, backwards. Then to the hand claps of Annie, this amazing horse marched in time with the clapping.

The tricks went on for several minutes and when the pair had seemingly finished, Annie again galloped her horse straight at the two watchers on the fence. Again Bill thought she may have overshot the mark, but as horse and rider got very close Annie jumped from the saddle at the last moment. She did a roll as she hit the ground and as she stopped close to Bill and Henry, she turned and told her horse to go away. The little mare galloped for about thirty yards, then stopped and turned its head and looked at its master.

Annie then yelled, 'alright come on back.' At this command the obedient animal trotted back, then as it got close, it somehow folded its forelegs and knelt in front of its master. Annie stood alongside her beautiful horse and bowed to the onlookers, who burst into applause. As Annie continued to bow, deliberately overacting, the clever horse got up onto all fours and just as Annie was bowing, it butted her with its head, nudging Annie in the backside. Still overacting, she fell forward, then jumped up and pointing her finger, she pretended to scold her horse. Then both horse and rider bowed again and the show was over. Bill allowed Annie's father to go and congratulate her first, then he did the same, telling her that it was the best trick-riding he had ever seen.

That evening after their meal, they all retired to the activity room where Annie served them cold drinks. Bill and Annie had a lemonade, and Bill noticed that Henry refused the offered beer saying, 'I only drink when I'm not on the job, Bill, and a blokes always on the job out here. Never know what can happen eh.'

Talk turned to the coming gymkhana, and Bill asked Annie if she was going to enter the trick riding contest. 'I always do Bill, and I always come second to Alice Watson,' Annie said.

Henry then said, 'Alice Whatshername has the ability to show enough of her body to sway the goggle eyed judges. That's the only reason she wins.'

Bill said that two can play at that game. 'What about giving us a fashion parade Annie?' So Bill and Henry sat back to watch as Annie came out dressed firstly in the outfit she wore most years. 'Looks good, but too plain,' said Bill.

This went on for a while, and when Bill said the same thing after the fourth parade, Annie thought that she would show him. Bill's eyes nearly popped out of his head when Annie next wore a yellow skirt that didn't quite reach down to her knees. For a top she had on a sleeveless white blouse, and this was mostly covered by a fawn coloured leather jacket, which was also sleeveless. 'Well Princess, if that doesn't wow them judges nothing will.'

Annie looked at her fiancée and asked him if he thought it was a bit too revealing. Bill sensed that he had better answer the right way. 'My beautiful lady, to me it would not matter how you dress, I see deeper than just clothes and flashy arms and legs when I look at you. I see a wonderful beautiful human being that should not need to resort to these tactics to win a contest. But it seems that we must, so give em hell love.'

Henry drove them to The Kimberley Downs Station the next day. They arrived early enough, so Bill helped Annie unload her little horse, while Henry went off to enter them in the events that they, or more so, he, had chosen. Annie was not yet dressed for her event, but kept her clothes in the cab of the truck.

Then it was time for the annual gymkhana to start, and the Emcee duly welcomed every one and wished all the contestants good luck in their events. Then he said, 'to get the show on the road, we have a bush poet, who has written a poem about our Kimberley. So please welcome Neil Contro.'

An elderly gentleman, dressed in swaggie clothes, made his way to the loudspeaker. The crowd went quiet as he recited his poem.

'To a stranger who may be passing through,
It may seem like there's not a lot up here.
But newcomers way up here are rather few,
And they don't get to see what we hold dear.
They don't see the rugged beauty that's so dear.

Or the colours created by the rising sun,
And oh, if they could see it when it sets again.
These things are not appreciated by everyone,
And they are hard to describe by mouth or pen,
But us that see it, always come back again and again.

Back to this rugged country that we all love,
Back to where we know we want to always be.
Where we appreciate what we have,
Where both man and animals can run free.
Oh yes, there's life in our Kimberley.

Up here a man's word is Gospel.
If he says something then it will be.
The folk up here are true, we can tell,
Yes we up here, those that can truly see,
Know that there's life in the Kimberley;'

The old man bowed to the strong applause he received. Annie clapped loudly and a little longer than most. She also held her hands quite high, and Bill could see the diamonds shining in her engagement ring that they had chosen before leaving Kalgoorlie. Annie then moved closer to Bill and said, 'quick boyfriend, kiss me.'

Not having seen as much of her as he was used too while prospecting, Bill didn't hesitate. 'Don't look, but Alice Watson is headed this way, so hold me close Bill,' Annie told him.

Sure enough, the girl that Annie wanted so badly to beat in her trick riding contest, came over and said to Annie, 'aren't you going to introduce me to this handsome man, Miss Oakley?'

Annie took a moment to move away from Bill, but still held his hand as she said, 'Bill darling, this is miss Watson. Miss Watson this is my fiancée, Bill Evans.'

Alice held out her hand to Bill, but he didn't let go of Annie's hand as he said, 'hello.' Alice was not used to being snubbed like this. Mostly she could manipulate a man by flashing her eyes and moving her body in a suggestive manner, but now that she really wanted to show Annie up, it wasn't working. This upset the prudent young snob, and Bill made things worse by ignoring her, and giving all of his attention to Annie. She turned to go, then as she walked away she took off her coat to reveal her riding costume. 'I see what you mean,' said Bill to Annie. Alice was wearing a skimpy low cut dress that didn't leave a lot to one's imagination.

Meanwhile Henry had nominated them for their events and was now having a drink at the bar. He got into a conversation with another station manager that he knew and it wasn't long before the subject of whip cracking came up. Then Annie's chances of winning the trick riding was discussed. Unbeknown to Henry, a friend of Alice Watson was drinking not far along the bar. So when Henry told his friend how they had a plan to sway the judges, many an ear was trained to this conversation. Henry let slip how Annie was going to also wear revealing clothing, to take away the unfair advantage that Alice gained each year.

Henry had finished his second beer, so he made his way back to Annie and Bill. Meanwhile Alice Watson's friend was hurrying to tell her what he had overheard.

The stockwhip championship wasn't on for a while yet, then the trick riding was to follow. So Bill thought as he had spare time, they could take a look around. Henry suggested that they have a look in the boxing tent. Bill was not keen, but he thought that he better go along, especially as Henry seemed so eager. There was already a bout in progress as they sat down. Bill could feel the urge of the boxing ring, and he found himself following the moves and stances of each boxer. 'Makes you want to have a go doesn't it mate.' Henry said to him.

Bill was so intent watching the bout, that he didn't hear Henry, so Annie spoke a bit louder, 'you're on next boyfriend,' she said.

This time Bill heard and he laughed back, 'don't think so girlfriend.'

Henry waited until the round ended, then he told Bill that he had in fact entered him, and he was down to fight the next bout. Bill was about to go crook and refuse, but Annie said, 'it was my idea Bill, I thought we could use the twenty pounds.'

Now he did get upset, and walked out of the tent, only to be followed by Annie, who said, 'I'm sorry Bill. You don't have to fight if you don't want to.'

Bill stopped and said, 'that's right Annie, I don't have to if I don't want to. But it is presumed that I can be expected to, if you say so. I do enjoy boxing, in fact I love true boxing, but this is not what I love. This tent fighting is just that. Fighting, or slugging it out. Knowing that if I use my skills and knock out some of these thugs, some of them half drunk, then I'll be made to feel like a murderer. That is what it would be Annie, murder, and for what. Twenty flaming quid. Now if I don't go and honour the entry, I will be called a coward by others. That I might be able to handle, but I won't be able to bear you thinking of me as one. Can't you see that you have forced me into a corner girlfriend?'

Tears flowed now as Annie realized that she was badly wrong. 'I'm so sorry Bill. But I will never think of you as anything but the bravest sweetest man I have ever known. Can you please forgive me?'

Bill had cooled down enough to hold her and say, 'yes of course I forgive you my Annie, but what will your father think of me if I don't go in there and put on a show. There may be a good boxer there but I doubt it, which means I'll have to pretend that I'm trying.'

Annie hugged her man tighter and the two of them went back to sit with her Dad. 'Everything alright you two lovebirds?' asked Henry.

Bill nodded to him, as if to motion that everything was fine. 'He doesn't even understand,' he thought.

The bout that Henry had stayed to watch was over and the announcer called out Bill's name as one of the next contestants. Annie held his hand tightly, then whispered, 'you can say you're injured.'

Bill bent and kissed her, then shook hands with Henry. 'Should I put a bet on you Bill, or should I keep my money in my pocket son?' To hear this man call him son, made Bill feel good, so he asked him how much did he have in his pocket? 'Down to me last fiver Bill,' said Henry.

Bill now felt guilty. Here was a good man, down on his luck, yet still willing to look after and call him son. 'Go and put all your money on me Dad. I won't ever let you down.'

Henry walked over to the corner where he knew the bookie was taking bets and said, 'what price the tall skinny bloke mate?' Thinking that Henry wanted to bet against Bill, the bookie offered six to four on. Pretending to be a bit drunk, Henry slurred his speech and said, 'well what price the bloke who hasn't even got togs or sandshoes?'

The bookie laughed and said, 'blimey he's four to one old timer.' Henry pulled out his last five pounds and stammered, 'I'll put five quid on that Bill bloke then. That's twenty quid if he wins. Is that right mate?'

The bookie wrote out Henry's ticket and took his money. Then he said, 'your bloke can't win old timer, that's Don Travis he's fighting. He hasn't lost a bout in my tent for ages.' Henry tucked his ticket into his pocket and went back to sit with his daughter.

Annie said, 'I saw you pretending to be drunk Dad. What price did you get?' When she learnt that Bill was at four to one, she went over and placed a bet. When Henry asked her how much she had bet on Bill, she told him that she'd seen him fight, so she put five pound on him to win.

Just as she had finished telling her father about her bet, the announcer introduced Bill Evans as the challenger. Then gave his opponent a huge wrap, saying he looked like being the most promising boxer to be seen for a long time. He said, 'it gives me great pleasure to introduce Don Travis.'

Bill should have been more prepared, because for the first round he had trouble getting going. It wasn't until he got belted on the face, that he started to box well. As like other tent boxing tournaments, this bout was scheduled for only three rounds, and by the end of the second round Bill knew that in a properly run contest, he would be in front on points. He also knew that this was not run by the Marquis of Queensberry rules, so a point's decision would nearly always go to the boxer that the organizers wanted to win. So to win Bill realized he would have knock his opponent out.

The bell sounded for the last round and Bill used his trick of double leading with his straight left, then feinting to use it again and sure enough, his opponent was wide open for Bill's right cross. The referee had no choice but to count Bill's opponent out and raise his hand, declaring him the winner. Bill looked across to see that Annie and her father were jumping about with excitement, but he for some reason did not feel excited at all. As he went over to shake hands with the other boxer, Bill noticed that they were having trouble getting him up off the floor. Someone said, 'better get a doctor.'

Bill felt a cold chill run through his whole body, and he thought the worst. Then he saw the young man start to stagger to his feet and shake his head. Bill waited until he was sure that the other man was alright, then he went and consoled him, telling him he fought well and he would become a good boxer. As he returned the gloves to the promoter, who was waiting in Bill's corner for them, he was asked if he could be ready for his next bout in one hour.

Bill still had a sickening feeling after the thought that he may have badly injured young Don Travis, so he took his time answering this eager promoter. When he did, he hardly knew what he was saying as he told him that he wasn't going to fight again. 'Please give my purse to Don, and I would appreciate it if you would let him continue in my place,' he told the promoter.

Bill then went to where Annie and Henry were sitting, but they weren't there, so he sat and waited. After a few minutes they returned and Annie was all excited, as was her father. 'Look Bill, we both won twenty pounds on you. Isn't it wonderful,' Annie said.

Henry was counting his winnings as he said to Bill, 'glad you told me to back you mate, this is great, twenty flaming quid. Wow.'

Bill looked at the two people that were going to be a huge part of his life when he married Annie. 'They haven't even said congratulations or asked me how I am, or how is the poor bloke that I had to knock silly just so they could win some money, 'Bill thought.

Feeling a bit upset, Bill used the excuse of needing the toilet so that he could be alone for a while. Afterwards he found a food van and bought a pie and a coffee, then sat alone on a bench. It wasn't too long before Annie found him, 'what's up boyfriend?' she asked.

Bill tried not to show his feelings, so he simply said, 'I'm just hungry.'

Annie said that she wanted to go and get changed ready for her trick riding contest. So Bill accompanied her as she first attended to her little horse, then followed her as she went to the cab of the truck to get the special outfit so she could change into it.

Annie yelled, 'Bill my outfit. It's gone.' They looked through the truck but there was no sign of Annie clothes.

'Maybe your Dad might have them,' said Bill. Annie told him that her father had already gone to the whip cracking area so he couldn't have them.

Neither of them saw the friend of "Evil Alice" as he watched Annie despairingly search for the skimpy clothes that she thought that she needed. Neither did they hear this scheming Miss Watson laugh as her friend reported back about the frantic action at the Oakley's truck.

Bill, no longer thinking about his boxing, said to Annie, 'well girlfriend, you'll just have to go out there and woo them judges dressed as you are. You Annie Oakley are already the best looking woman here, by a country mile at that, so go get em girlfriend.'

He then pinned a corsage to Annie's jacket. This picked Annie up, and as she led her horse to the acceptance area, she was feeling more confident. Annie didn't even look, and she pretended not to hear as "Evil Alice" said, 'oh look everybody, here comes plain Annie.'

Alice then looked towards the judges, and to her horror saw that they were all women. She knew she wouldn't get any votes for being dressed in hardly a stitch, but it was too late to change. 'Alice Watson will be the first rider,' called the announcer.

This scheming woman got the votes of most of the men in the crowd that day, but not the votes of the five female judges, who thought this contestant was a little hussy. There were three other riders and they all performed well. Then the announcer called out, 'miss Annie Oakley please.'

Henry had just arrived back and joined in the loud applause as his daughters name was called. Bill turned to him and asked him if he won the stockwhip title. 'I thought I did alright, but some young fella beat me. He was good to. I learnt after the contest that he was the same bloke that made most of the country's whips. Griggs that's his name. Natham Griggs. The organizer told me that Natham had recently finished second in the Australian titles. Maybe I shouldn't have had those two beers earlier. Don't ever turn to drink to drown your sorrows Son,' he said.

Bill remembered how he had turned to drink after Jenny died, so he knew how the man next to him must still feel. Annie had told him how her mother had died giving birth to her, and how her father never got over losing his Mary. Now he felt a bit more close to, and a bit more sorry for this man who had carried on with his life, and gave Annie a proper upbringing. Bill reached over and shook Henry's hand and said, 'congratulations Henry, there's no disgrace in coming second. I wish I could have watched you.'

Henry then thanked Bill, and asked him how come Annie was not wearing her new outfit?

Bill told his future father-in law, 'some mongrel pinched them.'

All talk ceased now, because Annie and her little mare had started their show, and what a show they put on. The crowd showed their appreciation, which turned to laughter when Annie amazing little animal did its trick by nudging Annie in the backside, and Annie fell over. Then when she told her horse to go away, and when it came back again, the now big crowd cheered wildly. Annie smiled at the judges, then she rode her horse to where Bill was sitting. The horse stood on its back legs and pawed the air, then as it came down on all fours, Annie took the corsage from her vest and threw it to Bill. As he caught it, he stood and blew her a kiss.

Never before had anyone received an ovation like Annie Oakley and her wonderful horse did that day. As if it knew, Annie's little mare bowed it's head then after pawing the air again, turned and, with Annie waving to the still cheering crowd, away it galloped.

The judges did not take long to announce that Annie and her mare Mary, were the winners of the trick riding competition of The Kimberley Station for nineteen thirty two. It was a great result and Annie thanked Both Bill and her father as soon as she got back to the truck, where they were waiting for her.

Henry asked them if they were ready for home. Annie looked to Bill, who said, 'I have one or two more things to do more things to do if it's alright.'

Then Annie asked if she and her father could come with him, but he said that he would meet them at the boxing tent in a while.

Bill did not have a lot of trouble finding the person he was looking for, because she was the least dressed person at the gymkhana. Alice Watson was near the drinking area, surrounded by wide eyed males, all of them jostling to buy her a drink. Slowly, Bill pushed his way through the group and said to Alice, 'gee you were unlucky to lose. I thought you were easily the best rider there Miss Watson.' These are exactly the words that Bill knew that she wanted to hear, so he carried on with his ploy by saying, 'and you were also dressed well, I know if I were the judge..'

He was cut short by the person he was really looking for, who said, 'aren't you that Annie Oakley's boyfriend?'

Playing out his game Bill said, 'not any more, she off with another man by now.'

The bloke that Bill reckoned was the one who took Annie's clothes, now fell into his trap. 'Yeah she wouldn't have got our vote, even if she had worn these,' he said as he held up Annie's stolen clothing.

Expecting Bill and everyone to laugh along with him, the loudmouth thief got the shock of his life when a plain clothed Police Constable grabbed him and said, 'you're under arrest for stealing.' Then the Policeman turned to Alice and told her that she also was under arrest. Bill nodded to the Policeman, who he had asked to listen in to the conversation that he had set up. 'Thank you Mister Evans. I'll need you to sign some forms later please.'

A content Bill Evans made his way to the boxing tent, and after a brief word with Annie and her father, he went over to the boxer who had earlier knocked out. He knew that this promising young man had won his way through to the final, which was due to start soon. Bill said to him, 'well done Don in making the final. I was wondering if you might like another second in your corner for the final.'

Don Travis answered Bill with a smile and a handshake as he said, 'sure Bill, I reckon I could use your help. Thanks for letting me fight in your place, and for the prize money. I don't know your reason for not fighting on Bill, because you would have easily won this final.'

So the two Oakley's sat and watched as Bill acted as Don's second. The chap who had been assisting Don previously, was happy to act as towel man, as he wasn't trained as a second and had only been helping out for the first time. Bill didn't say a lot to Don, in fact he let him do his own thing. Then at the end of the first of three rounds, Bill suggested that it might be time to step up the pace, 'but keep your left hand up a bit higher,' he told Don.

The rest of the bout went all this young man's way, and he won by a unanimous points decision. After the fight Don thanked Bill again and asked him if he had fought any top fighters, and was flabbergasted when he learnt that Bill had fought against a former world champion. 'How did you go against him,' Don asked.

Bill said, 'pretty good, I actually knocked him out, but he was forty two.'

He then asked Don how old he was, and was surprised to learn that this promising youngster was only eighteen. 'What are your plans,' Bill asked.

Don said that he wanted to go to Perth to improve and maybe become a professional, but he didn't have anywhere to stay or anything. The youngster said that he didn't have any parents, and he had been living with his Uncle. 'But soon I have to move out, because my Uncle is sick and has to go into a home.'

Bill thought for a moment then wrote down the address of his parents place. Then he told Don that he would be down in Perth in a couple of weeks. 'I can't promise anything but if you look me up I may be able to help you get started.'

Bill was just about to go back to Annie and her Dad, but young Don said, 'hope you don't mind Bill, but I feel I must tell you that I'm part Aboriginal.'

A surprised Bill told him that lots of his best friends are Aboriginal. 'It doesn't make any difference to me or my family, so I'll keep a lookout for you in a couple of weeks Don.'

Before heading back to the station, Bill, as requested by the Police Constable, went to the Police station. Annie and Henry came in also. Bill smiled when he saw the two clothes thieves locked in a cell. Annie and her father knew nothing about how Bill had organized the capture of Alice and her friend, and they were shocked when they also saw them. 'Now Annie Oakley, as owner of the stolen items it is up to you to press charges,' the Policeman said.

Annie asked this law officer if Bill could act as her adviser, and when permission was given, Bill started by saying, 'if the two thieves are brought out Officer, then we may be able to work something out.'

So with everyone concerned sitting at a table, Bill told the Officer that if the two thieves wanted the charges dropped, then retribution of five pounds each must be paid forthwith to the claimant. Everybody thought that was all, but Bill continued. 'Also both of the defendants must apologize to the claimant immediately, and a record of all that has happened is to be kept by the Police, so that if this event is ever repeated, then this charge shall then be brought before the courts.'

The Policeman then asked the two prisoners if they agreed to the demands of the claimant. Having spent the last two hours locked up, both of the nervous defendants were more than eager to grab the chance to be out of the Police station. Alice told her friend, who was used to jumping at her every command, to pay the nice Constable, 'so that we can be out of here.'

As usual the son of a rich station owner from near Fitzroy, did as he was told and paid the ten pounds to Annie. It was obvious to the experienced Constable, that these two had not really learnt their lesson, and noticing them getting up to leave, he snapped, 'sit down. You have not been released as yet.'

Bill smiled as the Constable continued, 'there is now the matter of cost to the law. The decision of the law today is that there is a fine to cover costs. This fine has been set at two pounds ten shillings each, which must be paid before the prisoners can be released.'

The male thief, who had been identified as Bruce Crampton told them that they had no more money. The policeman was enjoying himself now. 'As has already been stated by this hearing, if this said fine is not paid now, then the prisoners will be held until such time that the fine is paid.'

The Constable then proceeded to lock Alice and Bruce back in the cell. Then just as he was going to turn the key, Bill said, 'I don't wish to interfere Constable, but the accused have not yet apologized to Miss Oakley.' The Constable then told Alice and Bruce to apologize.

Bruce was so wild at having been locked up again, that he said, 'I'll be dammed if I'm going to say sorry to that bitch, or her drunken father.'

Then to make things worse, Alice piped up and said, 'if my father was here you lot wouldn't get away with this. Anyway I should have won that contest not that..'

Alice never finished her sentence, because the Constable opened the door and told Annie to accompany him to the desk. Then he said, 'I'm sure that your father and your fiancée have something to say to these two foul mouthed thieves.'

Henry pushed past Bill and walked up to the woman who had cheated her way through life and said in a voice that made her cringe and draw back, 'Alice Whatsername, you are nothing but a spoilt brat, and if you were a man I'd knock your block off.'

Then Henry Oakley really lost his temper. He turned to Bruce and said, 'now you are not a real man, but this is for both of you.' Bill watched as Annie's Dad hit Bruce with all his force.

The Constable then came back and let Bill and Henry out of the cell. After locking the cell door he looked back, and pretending to notice Bruce laying on the floor, he said, 'you had better watch that floor Mr Crampton, it's a bit slippery. You could fall and you might hurt yourself.'

Bill was about to thank the Constable, when he heard Alice call out, 'Daddy. Oh thank goodness you are here. Get me out of here please Daddy dear. These awful people have locked me up for nothing. I knew you would come and tell these liars a thing or two.'

Mr Watson was then told by the Constable to follow him outside. Bill and Annie plus her father were also asked to follow him out, leaving the Alice and her semi-conscious friend in the cell.

After explaining the whole situation, except the slipping over of Bruce, the Constable told Alice's father that once the fine was paid then the prisoners would be released. Mr Watson started to open his wallet but got a shock when this Policeman, who had just about come to the end of his patience, told him that as it was now after hours, he would have to come back tomorrow. Then he corrected himself and said, 'sorry Mr Watson, but the station is closed on Sundays, so you'll have to make that Monday morning.'

The drive back to the station homestead was a happy one for the three of them. Bill helped start the humour by saying, 'I bet Miss Smarty pants is cold in that cell dressed in those clothes.'

Henry added, 'you mean undressed in those clothes, don't you Bill?'

Annie then said, 'she'll be right, she's got her servant Bruce to keep her warm.' More jokes followed and the three of them hardly stopped laughing all the way.

Then one time when it seemed there might not be much more to say, Bill said, 'what about that knockout punch that put Big Bad Bruce on the floor.'

Annie said, 'tell me about it Dad, I didn't know you would do that.'

Henry could hardly stop laughing, but he finally said, 'I thought the Constable already explained what happened Princess. He slipped.'

Annie gave her father an envelope the next morning, and when he opened it he was too overcome to speak for a while. Finally he hugged his daughter, then he passed the letter to Bill, 'I'd like you to read this too,' he said. Bill read the following,

> *" My wonderful father. As I find it hard to be able to say what I feel, I have decided to try to convey to you my deepest feelings. You are the best father any girl could ever hope for. You are always there for Me, and have raised me to be what I am, which I hope is just like you. I have always felt so guilty that I was given life, but my mother, your wife was taken from you. I wish I had known my mother. She must have Been a wonderful person, and I can see by the photographs that she was very beautiful. We my Daddy, have had a good life together, and from the bottom of my heart I truly thank you. Soon we will be saying goodbye, But we shall always be together in spirit. I know that you and your Mary are together. Sometimes when you don't think I am listening, I hear you talk to her, and I cry.*
>
> *Now I believe that I have met my kindred spirit, and I seek your blessing, for in a few days Bill and I will be heading to a new life. My ambition to become a Chemist, looks like coming true, and it's thanks to you for not only giving me the opportunity, but for also teaching me to have ambition and belief. I hope I can do you, and Mummy's memory justice. Daddy, I probably haven't told you enough times that I love you, but I hope you can tell that I do. I will always try to come back to your beloved Kimberley to see you. I do hope that I can take some of the spirit of both you and the Kimberly with me.*
>
> *As you have remembered your wife, my Mother, please know that I will always remember you in the same way Dad.*
>
> *I will always be proud to say that I am your Princess.*
>
> *XXX'*

Bill slowly put down the letter and walked over to where father and daughter were still hugging. He then put his arms around them and felt the true emotion that had been brought out by Annie's letter to her father.

The next few days were some that Bill knew he would never forget. Henry showed him all around the huge cattle station. The two of them rode for hours each day, taking enough food and water, they used the opportunity to check and clean the windmills and water troughs. 'There's forty four of these troughs, and the same amount of paddocks,' Henry said.

Bill asked him how many acres does that come to, and near fell out of his saddle when he was told that there was near enough to a quarter of a million acres all up, including the two paddocks on the other side of the Fitzroy River. Then Henry showed Bill a brown stain on the side of one of the sheds. He said, 'that's how high the floods came up to a few years back. We lost all of our stock and feed. I reckon we would have all drowned if we hadn't of perched on the shed roof. We took enough tucker for a week luckily, because we were up there for nigh on a week.'

Annie didn't come with them, but packed their food each day, and always waved them off each morning at daybreak. During the day Annie would study, preparing herself for her Chemistry course that she was so looking forward to.

The last day came too quick for Bill. He was enjoying the farm life, and he told Henry that he could easily live up here. 'Well Bill, today we're going fishing for a Barramundi. If you want to, that is son.'

It didn't take long for Bill to say that he would love to have a go at catching this famous fish. So off they went with heavy gauge fishing lines and chicken meat for bait, to put on the biggest fish hooks that Bill had ever seen. Henry took his three-o -three rifle along and gave Bill a twelve gauge shotgun. 'For the crocs,' he said.

It took them a couple of hours to reach the mighty Fitzroy River as they cleaned out the two remaining water troughs on the way. The two lines were ready, and the hunt for the much sought after fish was on. Henry had given Bill the rundown about the crocodile situation. 'Never turn your back on the river, especially when you're close to the water's edge, which I advise you not to do,' he said.

They kept their guns within reaching distance at all times, but after several minutes had past, Bill got a little careless and started to fish a bit close to the edge of the river. Henry was experienced at this risky game though and he told Bill to stand back. Just in time he stepped back another few yards, for a huge croc poked his massive head out of the water, about where Bill had been standing. 'Time to move,' said Henry.

They also moved their horses that were tied well back out of the crocs reach. The new spot that Henry chose was on a higher bank, 'the hungry big lizards can't reach us here,' he said to Bill as they both threw their fishing lines.

No sooner had Bill's line hit the water when something grabbed it. 'It feels big enough to be that croc,' he said.

'Don't pull too hard or you'll pull the hook out of his mouth,' yelled Henry. Bill eased off a bit but kept the pressure on by keeping his line tight. 'That's it Bill. Don't let your line loose, but slowly pull him. Yes, that's it boy, wow he's a big one,' Henry said.

Bill gradually won the battle, then after ten minutes he had a big Kimberley Barramundi flapping at his feet. 'What a fish. Thanks for bringing me Henry. It's the biggest fish I've ever seen. Whacko, I wish Charlie Burns could see it.'

He couldn't remember being this excited since he found that big nugget with Paddy O'Reiley back in Southern Cross. It wasn't long before Henry also hooked a big one. They were satisfied with two fish, so they started heading back to the homestead. Henry took a slightly different track home, and Bill soon learnt why. As they both pulled the reins tight to stop their horses, Bill saw an old Aboriginal step out of a rough shelter. Henry spoke to this old man, then passed him one of the Barramundi. The proud old native smiled and said something back to Henry, then he waved goodbye to them. Annie was waiting for them when they got back, and was excited with the thought of fresh Barramundi for tea. She was happy when Henry told her that they had each caught one. 'How was Sandman then Dad?' Annie asked.

Bill later learnt from Annie that the old man had worked for them, but was now too old. 'He just told Dad one day that it was now time to go home and journey to his ancestors. Dad and I miss him, and always call to see him, especially when we have been fishing,' she said.

What a meal they had that last night at Henry's station. Bill always thought of it as Annie's father's station, even though he was managing for someone else. 'I can't eat another mouthful,' Bill said as Annie offered him his fourth helping of the tasty fish.

That night the three of them sat out on the big veranda, which was fully enclosed with a heavy duty fine mesh to keep out anything from mosquitos to snakes. They sipped ice cold fruit juice, and talked. Mainly the topic was, as is mostly the case out in the wilderness, about station problems. Bill could tell that Henry did not want this last night to end, so as soon as it looked like the talking might be over, he would bring up another subject, just to hang onto his daughter as long as he possibly could.

Bill could see the pain and anguish that Henry was going through, so to leave father and daughter alone, he stood up and said, 'goodnight, I'll see you in the morning.' It was much later that he heard Annie come to bed.

Chapter Fifteen
Wrong Chemistry?

The plane trip back to Kalgoorlie was a quiet one for Bill and Annie. They had decided to fly back to where Bill's horses were stabled, then with them in the stock carriage, Bill and Annie would travel to Perth by train.

First though, they went to the Kalgoorlie Post Office, and Annie squealed when she was handed a letter from her future University. 'I hope they haven't changed their minds,' she said as she tore open the official looking letter.

Annie was excited as she relayed the contents of the letter to Bill. 'Oh boyfriend look, they've offered me a room on campus, starting next week. Bill this will make it much better for me to be able to study. The library will be close, and the tutors may be able to offer extra studies.' Bill had an uneasy feeling, but didn't say anything as Annie was still talking in her excited way. 'You don't mind do you Bill? I mean I hope you won't stop me from accepting this offer.'

So without much input from Bill, it was decided that Annie would fly to Perth, so she could go straight to the on campus facilities at the University, and Bill was to follow by train. 'Bye Bill, come and see me as soon as you can won't you,' Annie said as she hurried to catch her plane.

The uneasy feeling was still hanging over Bill, but he knew he had to snap out of it and take Blackie and his packhorse, plus his and Annie's gear, to the train.

The first stop when he got to Perth was to stable his horses, and as luck would have it, Bill found one behind the West Perth Markets, which was not too far from his parent's house. Joe and Mary Evans were again happy to see their son. Bill had written them several times since he had been home last, so they knew he was engaged to be married. 'Where is your Annie?'

This is what Bill was asked after he had greeted his Mother and Father. So he told them the whole story, finishing with the news that his fiancée would not be staying here with them. Bill could sense the same uneasy feeling that he had, spreading to his parents. His Dad said, 'that's probably the best thing for the Chemistry's future, but is it the best thing for the future of both of you?'

Bill somehow knew that his father was trying to tell him that to live apart, changes the heart. This was an old saying that he had heard his mother quote on more than one occasion.

Peggy and Harold visited that evening, and after a big meal, Bill and Peggy said that they would do the dishes. This gave both brother and sister a chance to talk. Bill learnt that their father was doing well and would not have to have any surgery at this stage, as his new medication was working. Bill of course, had to retell all of his adventures, and all about Annie. Like her parents, Peggy didn't seem to like the idea of Annie living away. 'There's plenty of room here and Mum would like another woman's company,' she said.

The day after arriving back in Perth, Bill travelled out to Annie's University. He found her with a group of other students, who were, obviously discussing Chemistry or the like. Bill who was at this stage unnoticed, sat on a bench a short distance from the group. Then Annie saw him and waved, but stayed talking with the other students.

Finally a bell sounded and Annie came over to him. She kissed him on the cheek and said, 'sorry Bill but you've picked a bad time to visit. That tall fellow over there, the one with the suit on is a Professor and he majored in Chemistry. He has just now offered to tutor any keen students after our lectures finish each day. Isn't that great Bill, everything is working out better than I hoped.'

They chatted for a while then Bill said that his Mum was expecting her to come back to meet the family. 'You don't mean tonight do you Bill? I have a lecture in a few minutes, then I was hoping to take up Professor Blinton's offer of extra studies.'

Annie was getting ahead of herself now, as she said to Bill, 'why don't I come out to your parents for tea the day after tomorrow, because tomorrow there's four lectures, and I really can't miss any.'

Bill was getting more and more annoyed, then he stood up and said, 'how are you going to get to our place?'

Annie's mind was already on her Chemistry, so she didn't realize what she was saying when she told Bill that she can get a lift. 'Tell your parents I'm sorry about today and I'll see them next time,' she said. Then picking up her books, she gave Bill a quick kiss and she was gone.

Bill was confused and a little upset as he made his way back to his parent's house. He knew that he agreed to his fiancée's wishes to go to University, but the sudden decision by her to live on site, caught him off guard. Now he had to tell his parents that she won't be meeting them for a couple of days yet. Already Bill was starting to wonder if leaving the open air and country living was a good idea, or whether it was going to work out. Joe Evans couldn't help noticing that something was making his son become unusually quiet and moody. So after a while he said, 'What's up Bill?'

Not wanting to annoy or upset his father, Bill just said, 'oh it's probably nothing Dad.'

But the nothing turned into a moody temper that neither Joe nor Mary Evans had ever seen from their son. Then when on the night that Annie said that she would come for tea, she arrived two hours late. This made Bill even more upset. 'I can't stay for long,' she told Bill, who was waiting for her at the gate.

This was enough to send Bill into a rage. 'What's going on Annie? I know you want to be a Chemist, but I didn't dream you could want it so much that you have put it before not only me, but now you offend my family. Mum has gone out of her way to cook a nice meal, and you turn up late, and you casually say that you can't stay long. You haven't even met my folks Annie.'

This should have been enough to make Annie realize that the situation was serious. But her mind was so intent on her becoming a Chemist as soon as she could, that nothing else seemed to find its way into her brain. Bill's parents went out of their way to make Bill's fiancée welcome that night, even though they could sense that things were not quite right. Annie stayed longer than she said she would, and it wasn't until a car horn sounded outside the Evans family home that she jumped up and said goodnight. Bill was going to ask her to perhaps stay the night and he would pay for a taxi to take her back in the morning, but Annie said as she quickly kissed him, 'don't come out Bill, I'll try to come back and stay on the weekend.'

Bill, who was now on the verge of losing his temper completely said, 'who's picking you up Annie?'

But she was already out the door when she said, 'don't worry Bill, Professor Blinton had to go this way anyway.'

Bill was very quiet when he came back inside. His mother could sense that things weren't altogether right, so she said, 'care for a coffee my boy?'

The answer came back to her quickly, 'thanks, but no thanks Mum. I think I'll go to bed.'

The weekend came and Bill was just coming back from a long jog, when a car stopped alongside him and Annie got out. 'Keep jogging boyfriend, I can keep up with you, even with my backpack,' she laughed. As they jogged, Bill said 'looks like you're going coming to stay, or am I dreaming?'

Annie was made welcome, and did stay the Saturday night. Bill was much happier and after tea they told Bill's parents many tales of their times in the goldfields. It was quite late when the Evans household went to bed that night.

Annie was the first to arise and as she quietly went to cook breakfast, she whispered to Bill to stay in bed for a while. When he did get out of bed, his mother was already in the kitchen. Bill watched for a moment as the two cooks somehow put together a huge breakfast. 'The way you two were talking and laughing, it's a wonder any cooking got done,' Bill said.

'Don't be cheeky to your mother Bill Evans,' Annie told him.

Just then Joe wheeled himself into the dining room. He was happy to see things might be working out, so he thought he might try to sound happy. He asked, 'what's all the noise then?'

Bill thought, 'this is more like home,' as he tucked into bacon and eggs, followed by his mother's home-made bread with plum jam, and to Bill's delight, there was a bowl of cream on the table. He spread this cream as thick as he could over the jam, and said, 'this is just like the old days in Northcliffe, eh Dad?'

Mary Evans said, 'young Kevin Flanagan dropped by with a big jar of cream, and some cheese while you were out running Bill. He said to say hello, and to tell you that Vince is married and still living in Northcliffe.'

Bill was pleased to hear this news and was about to ask his mother if Kevin had said anything else, when Mary changed the subject rather quickly. 'You are welcome to stay as long as you like, Annie,' she said.

Annie replied, 'well thank you so much Mrs Evans. I would like to stay, but tomorrow there are three lectures, plus a visit to the Fremantle hospital on the agenda.'

Bill and Annie, at her suggestion went for a walk that morning. They had just reached Lake Monger and were admiring all the birdlife, when Annie asked Bill if he could possibly help her with her next year's University fees. 'They have to be paid in advance,' she said.

Bill knew that Annie had over four hundred pounds from their gold sales, so he asked her why she needed more money already. 'Oh I wanted to keep most of my money for when I graduate, so I can start my own business,' she said.

Bill thought for a while, and was a little wary of giving her any more money. He casually said, I've invested most of my money in a fixed deposit account and I can't touch it for about a year.'

Annie got a little upset and said, 'but Bill you know how much I want to succeed.' A strange sensation, like a cold shiver came over Bill. He was feeling uneasy now. Last night had been wonderful and he was hoping that things were going to be like they were before, but it seemed that Annie was more intent than ever to give all her life to her Chemistry dream.

The walk back was in almost silence, and when Annie started packing, Bill sat on the edge of the bed and asked her to stay the rest of the day and sleep the night. 'I'll take you back by taxi in the morning,' he offered. Bill suddenly realized that he didn't, and hadn't been, calling Annie girlfriend, or any other affectionate name for a while.

Also he thought, 'she hasn't called me any of the names that we used to use to each other.'

So Bill was not surprised when his fiancée said, 'I'm sorry Bill, but Professor Blinton is going to pick me up shortly and is going to give me extra tutoring this afternoon.'

Nearly a week went by before they saw each other again. Bill had busied himself by doing odd jobs around his parent's house, and visiting his sister and brother in-law in Mount Hawthorn, which was only a short jog away. Each day he would also take Blackie for a ride and would lead his packhorse as well. 'Gotta keep you fit,' he said to his horses one morning. 'The way things are going with "Gun Woman" we'll be off bush again before long.' Blackie seemed to understand and neighed his agreement and stamped his front foot.

One evening Bill asked his mother if Kevin Flanagan had any more news when he called, and how did he know where to come. Mary Evans told her son that she and Bill's father had given their address to Mr and Mrs Flanagan at Peggy's wedding. 'Yes Son, there was some other news from young Kevin. He said to tell you that the Sparrow family have moved back to Northcliffe, and that Beatrice is continually asking about you.'

Bill then told his mother that Beatrice had gotten engaged a couple of years ago. 'She wrote and told me so,' Bill said.

Then Bill got a real shock when his mother said, 'well she's not married now, and never was according to Kevin.'

Saturday came around, and as it was exactly a week since Annie had come to stay. The Evans household were hoping that she would come again, but when mid-afternoon came around, Bill knew that he would not see her this weekend. 'Give it time Son, things have a way of working out one way or the other,' Bill's father said.

The two of them were sitting on the front porch of Joe and Mary's house. Mary had gone inside to make a cuppa, so Joe had taken this opportunity to try to console his son. 'Annie will make her mind up as to what is most important to her, and then you'll know what to do Bill,' he said.

Bill thought for a while, then he said quietly, 'thanks Dad, but it's not easy. I know one thing though. I wish I could have met someone that has been as good as Mum has been for you.'

Then it was Joe Evan's turn to think for a moment. Then he told his son 'they don't make them like that anymore my boy.'

Bill realizing that his father was in a nostalgic and a rare talkative mood, thought it might be a good time to ask him something that he had always wanted to know, so he said, 'Dad why don't you like me to box?'

It took a long time for Joe to answer, then he said, 'Bill I used to love boxing. I was the school champion two years in a row. I was lucky enough to win the inter college title, and was chosen to represent England when I was only eighteen.' Joe stopped for a while and Bill thought that no more was going to be said about boxing. But then the sad but proud man said, 'Son, one night I was matched against the second in line for the British Middle Weight Title. I thought I was doing well, but my trainer told me before the last round that if I didn't knock my opponent out, then I would probably lose.' Bill's dad took another break from talking, probably to compose himself. Then when he tried to tell Bill the rest of the story, he broke down. Mary had been standing just outside the door, but now she came in and consoled her husband.

Bill said that he was sorry to have upset his father, but Mary Evans said, 'It's alright Son. It's about time you knew the reason why you have been disallowed to enjoy your sport. Now I'll tell you the rest of the story. Your father went into the last round with the instructions to knock out his man. So he did. But the poor fellow stayed knocked out for four weeks and they thought he may die. He recovered but could never box or play sport again.'

Bill's father now spoke again, and he was genuinely sorry for stopping his son from having a bright career in boxing. 'Forgive me please boy. I know now that I was too harsh on you.'

He hugged his father and told him that he understands how he must have felt all those years ago. 'You were right Dad. Anyway if I had of won those Golden Gloves, who knows where I might have finished up?'

Joe Evans nodded, then thanked Bill for his being so understanding. 'One thing is for sure Dad, I wouldn't swap this country for any boxing title. So thank you for bringing us to Australia, you did the right thing.'

After their talk, Bill enjoyed the cuppa that his mother had made, but as soon as he had finished, he felt compelled to go to the University to see Annie.

The taxi had to drop Bill a bit away from the normal parking area, but it didn't bother him as he felt like a walk. As he got to the campus, he saw a group of students sitting at a table, so he asked one of them if they could direct him to Miss Oakley. A silence came over the group, then a girl said, 'Oh do you mean Annie? She's over in room eleven, but I wouldn't interrupt her if I was you.'

This brought a few giggles from the others in the group, so he asked the girl why not? Bill got an answer he did not expect when the girl said, 'she's busy studying with her boyfriend, that's why Mister.'

This brought more giggles, and as Bill stormed off to room eleven, he heard someone say, 'you shouldn't have told the poor chap that Doris, he might just be the fiancée that Annie told us about.'

These words spurred Bill on even more, and by the time he reached what he presumed was Annie's room, he was as wild as he had ever been in his life. His temper and his voice left him when his knock was answered by a tall man dressed only in his underwear, who said 'Yes old chap, what can I do for you then?'

There was no need for Bill to speak, because the next person to come to the door, dressed in only a see through negligee, spoke before he could. 'Who is it darling?' The words were frozen on Annie's lips when she saw Bill standing there.

Bill now found his voice. 'Sorry to interrupt your studies Miss Oakley. I see you're dressed for the occasion. I had no trouble finding you, the whole campus obviously knows that you and your Professor were enjoying your afternoon.' Annie was speechless as Bill continued, 'now Gun Lady if you'll be so kind as to give me back my engagement ring, I'll leave you and your professor to your precious studies.'

The half-dressed man was about to move towards Bill, but then he suddenly realized that this man in front of him was the fiancée of the woman he was not only the tutor of, but was involved with in a romantic way as well. 'Look old man,' the Professor started, but was stopped by Bill who was in no mood to be called "old man".

The now irate Bill said, 'just be quiet, get dressed, then get lost if you know what's good for you old chap.'

Annie who had not moved, now pulled her Negligee tighter, started to say something, but Bill had noticed that she was not even wearing her engagement ring, grabbed her by the hand and pointed to where the ring should have been. 'I'm sorry Bill, I didn't plan for this to happen,' Annie said through tears.

Bill had calmed down enough to notice that there were several onlookers standing near. 'You may keep the ring Miss Oakley. Perhaps you can sell it to help pay for your fees that people like your darling Professor like to accept from you. Forgive me for the pun, but that's not all that he accepts from you.'

He was now talking to a broken woman, and for a moment he almost weakened, but then the Professor came barging out of Annie's room. The now fully dressed, highly credentialed University Professor, who did not want to be made look smaller than he already had been, by this brash and obviously uneducated man, walked up to Bill and almost made the mistake of challenging him. If Annie had not quickly stopped him by saying 'don't be silly Douglas. Bill is a boxer and he will belt you senseless,' then anything could have happened that day.

As it turned out, Bill cooled down enough to tell his now ex fiancée that he hoped she did become a chemist one day. 'But you must be yourself in this world, not try to use people to get something that you badly want. The girl that I thought I knew, and the girl that your wonderful father raised, did not need to change.'

Annie now only had her head visible from behind the door, as she said, 'if the old "Gun Woman" was to return, would you have me back Bill?'

No words came from Bill's mouth for several moments, and Annie thought that he might be going to give her another chance, but finally the young man who had been hurt too many times said, 'I'll keep the rifle that I bought you. I might even give it to The Tall One.'

The few onlookers quickly moved on as Bill walked away from the University, and the girl he had thought was going to be his wife.

Chapter Sixteen
Never Again

The only thing that stopped Bill from packing up and going somewhere, anywhere, away from the city where Annie was living, was Don Travis.

When Bill arrived back from his bust up with Annie, he barely had time to tell his parents that he was no longer engaged, when a young man knocked on the door. Bill had told his parents all about his invitation to Don, and they said that they had no objections to him staying with them for a while. So Bill answered the door, and took the young man in to meet his parents. 'Pleased to meet you Don,' Joe Evans said on behalf of himself and his wife.

Then Mary Evans asked him if he had eaten? 'Well to tell the truth, Mrs Evans, I am kinda hungry. But please don't go to any trouble for me.'

Don was given Peggy's old room, but was told that he must not expect that he was a permanent boarder. 'I'll pay his way for a while,' Bill told his parents. Bill did the right thing and took him to Joe Evans and had a man to man talk. 'Is it alright with you Dad if we train Don for a while?' Bill asked.

Joe told them that this must be fate that has given them the opportunity to help another to perhaps carry on his boxing career. Bill then explained to Don how both he and his father had their chances of becoming a top contender, or even better, cut short by circumstances out of their control. 'I am glad that you have given us the chance to help you Don,' Joe said. 'But you must help yourself. We are going to push you, particularly in the first month or so, and if you can't handle it, then it's over lad. Do you agree Don?'

The young man stood and walked over to Bill's father and held out his hand. As they shook hands, Don said, 'I give you my word that I will do the right thing firstly by your family, and also by your training methods. I will pass any test that you throw at me Sir. Please accept my thanks for allowing me to stay here with your family Mr Evans.' Bill thought this usually quiet youngster was finished, but he continued talking, 'I have not a lot of money Mr Evans, but here is a month's board, and if you are happy for me to stay longer, I will pay you more,' he said.

Bill was not surprised, but was certainly excited that his father had reacted in this way. His knew his father would be a great help, especially when he watches Don box, and sees how good he is.

Having a new interest was a blessing for Bill's father. He would wheel himself out the back and watch every training session, giving his advice. This advice was welcomed by Bill, who was surprised by the knowledge and input his Dad gave. Each morning Bill and Don would jog five mile or so before breakfast, and Bill was happy when Don would sometimes ask if they could go again in the evening. Fitness was not a big problem with the training program, as it was obvious that this youngster had kept himself in good shape. 'I want to succeed so badly,' he told Bill and his father one day. 'I am going to do so for not only myself but for both of you. I dream to hold a championship belt one day. A belt that both of you could have had,' he said.

Time went quickly for the three of them. Mary Evans would smile as she watched them eat every piece of food she served them. Bill and Don were hungry from training so hard, and she could see that her husband was much healthier because of the renewed interest that he now had. One morning Bill got a shock when his father said, 'help me out with this blasted chair son, and I'm coming too.' Eyes from passer byes turned to see an old man in a wheelchair keeping up with these two young men jogging along the streets of Leederville.

Then to Don Travis came what he had been waiting and training for. One evening about a month after Don had started training, Joe Evans said, 'I think you are ready for a bout young man.'

Bill agreed, so that day he took Don to the boxing hall to enter him in the Friday night tournament. The man in charge remembered Bill, and asked him if he wanted to box on Friday night? Bill told him that he had an up and coming boxer who he would like him to give a go. Don was introduced, and told to put on some gloves. Don was matched with a light heavy weight, who gave him a good test, which he passed with flying colours. 'Be here at seven o'clock this Friday Don. You'll be fighting another newcomer,' the promoter said.

Joe was given a front row seat and Bill acted as both trainer and Don's second for his first fight in what he called the big time. The training and advice that Don had received, paid off handsomely as he won a unanimous points decision. The promoter signed the young boxer up for the next Friday night tournament, telling him that if he fought well again then he could become a permanent drawcard. The few pounds that he got from his fight, Don gave to Joe for board, and to pay for his training.

With advice and extra training from both Bill and his father, Don got better and more confident, so much so that within several weeks he did become the main drawcard each Friday. 'Now is the time to step up your training young man,' Joe told him just after he had won his seventh straight fight. The promoter was not happy when he was told that his main draw card would not be fighting for a month or so.

Bill was acting as manager and after the month was up he told the promoter that he thought that Don was ready for a big fight. The promoter agreed, so the two approached the manager of one of the contenders for the middle weight state title. A deal was done and a date was set for six weeks from that day. The promoter worked a deal where the contender would get forty per cent, Don was to get twenty per cent, with the rest to go to the promoter. Bill quickly said, 'I think that we will only fight if our man gets thirty per cent.' To his surprise it was agreed and the fight was organized.

Under his father's guidance, Bill increased Don's training schedule. Instead of a slow jog, Don, with Bill joining in, ran for only half the usual distance, but at a much faster pace. Also the punch bag was done away with, and the speed ball work was increased. Each week the amount and the speed was increased, so much so that Don and Bill were exhausted after each session. Then sometimes Joe would make them do an extra session. If it were not for the sake of helping Don, Bill felt he would have thrown the towel in many times over that gruelling five weeks.

With just four days to go to the fight, Joe Evans called a meeting. 'Today boys, we don't train,' he said.

Both Bill and Don thought that they were going to get the day off, but they got a shock when Joe then told them that instead of training they would be having a bout between themselves. Bill felt a bit like refusing, because the last time they fought he thought that he may have really injured Don. Joe told them that it was not to be a fight as such, but more to improve Dons speed and footwork. So that's what the two boxers did that day. The following day they were instructed to do the same, after which Joe asked Bill to have a talk with Don, and tell him of any mistakes he may have made. Bill had already been conversing with Don every evening, showing him ways to improve, and many ringcraft tricks that would help him.

Joe and Bill had to fill in the boxing associations registration form, and when it came to the part where the name of the trainer had to be included, Bill said that the name Joe Evans must be written. So for the coming fight which would give the winner the right to challenge for the state title, Joe was listed as the official trainer and Bill was listed as Don's second. Both of them were pleased when Joe told them that the last three days were rest days. 'A fresh fighter will have the last say,' he said.

When the big night came Don had a cheer squad in the front row. Bill's whole family was there, including Peggy and Harold. Bill hadn't seen a lot of his sister and Harold since his break up with Annie, as he had been busy training Don. Bill knew that he, himself was probably as fit as he had ever been, so when the promoter told him that a boxer had pulled out of his bout, he asked his father if he had any objections to him taking his place. The bout was to take place straight after the main billing, which was Don's fight. 'I would love to watch you box again son,' said Joe Evans.

The announcer introduced Don first, then his opponent, which brought the crowd to their feet. Frank Buller was the name on most people's lips when the bell started for the first round. The bout was even and Bill was not worried as Don was very fit. It was a ten round fight and after eight had gone, Joe yelled to Bill to step it up. Don did not need much telling. He had been cruising up until now, so when he was told to, he started the ninth with a flurry. After the end of that round, in which Don must have hit his opponent at least fifty times, the fight was over. The towel was thrown in by Frank's trainer, and the referee raised Don Travis's hand and declared him the winner.

Bill jumped into the ring to congratulate him, but before he could, Don had gone over and reached through the ropes and thanked Joe. Then a reporter from The West Australian newspaper started interviewing this young man that had defeated the next in line for the state middle weight title.

Bill was to fight the next bout, so he had to get to the change rooms and put on borrowed shorts and gloves. He just made it in time to start his bout, which he won comfortably on points. He was paid ten pounds, which he gave to his mother and sister to share.

There was excitement that night at the Evans house. Bill noticed that his father had found a new lease of life, mainly because of the interest he had in training Don. Joe even gave a little speech, thanking Bill for his help in getting his boxer this far. Peggy went to make a cuppa, so Bill followed her into the kitchen which was a good spot to talk freely. Bill said that he thinks their father can manage training Don by himself from now on. 'I getting itchy feet again,' he told his sister.

'Well I've told you before Bill, you are not a city man. Go and follow your feelings,' she said.

So after a celebration, during which young Don thanked them all for their help, and split his takings from his fight, fifty-fifty with Bill's parents, Bill announced that he was going to head bush.

Mary Evans told Bill that he needed to get married and settle down. 'I've given that sort of thing a go three times and each time fate has dealt me a blow.' As he hugged her goodbye he said, 'thanks Mum, but as far as romance goes, never again. Not the way I feel now.'

Blackie and his pack horse were happy to be on the road again. 'But which road,' thought Bill?

Chapter Seventeen
Go Blackie Go

It was three weeks since Bill had left to go bush, and he had seen some country that he had not seen before. He had passed through several small towns, with one of the most memorable being the picturesque York. Bill liked this quaint little town and stayed a few days at the boarding house, where he enjoyed good food and met several friendly people with similar interests. One evening he was asked to accompany a couple of fellow travellers to a concert. This concert was held in a magnificent Town Hall, which he read was built in nineteen hundred and eleven. This Hall had many high pillars that supported a big clock tower.

The concert was a local affair, and turned into a sing song, involving many people from the crowd. The Emcee called for volunteers from the audience, and the couple who Bill went with were the first to go up on the stage. The husband, whose name was Roger, dragged a hesitant Bill up with him and his wife, who had introduced herself as Dolly.

The couple chose to sing Bill's favourite song Danny Boy, so he joined in also. Roger later told Bill that he had heard him singing this song when he was in the bathroom, and that was the reason he and his wife chose it. Bill sang quietly for a start, then without realizing, he increased his tempo and volume. Then when the chorus came he found that he was singing the lead, with his new friend's harmonising, Bill sang as though he was releasing all the tension from his body. The entire audience then joined in and the York Town Hall almost shook. The band then played by themselves, until the notes of the chorus were played solo by a young fiddle player. Then the fiddler nodded to Bill who re-sang the chorus with the band, then the whole audience as well. Now the Hall vibrated with the standing ovation, which lasted several minutes.

Then as Bill and his friends were walking back to their seats, the same young fiddler, who was probably only about ten years of age, filled the Hall with the eerie and moving tune of Amazing Grace. Not only did this youngster receive a huge ovation, but many of the audience threw coins onto the stage to show their appreciation. After the concert was over, the Country Women's Association put on supper for everyone.

Another place to impress Bill was the tiny settlement of Toodyay. Here he took a few hours to look around, and learnt how a notorious bushranger had dug his way out of the local gaol with a kitchen fork, then had eluded the Police and trackers. Legend has it that this bushranger whose name was Moondyne Joe, actually escaped on several other occasions from other prisons. Like York, Toodyay was built near the pretty Avon River. This river was so clean it helped make the town one of the prettiest places Bill had ever seen.

Bill now realized he was subconsciously heading towards Corrigin, where his friend that came out to Australia on the same ship as him, had come to be a settler. So a month or so after starting off Bill rode into the wheat belt town of Corrigin.

It was early morning when he rode into this relatively new town, so Bill went to the local store and purchased a few supplies. He then asked if a Dave Thomas lived around this district. 'Oh yes he sure does young fella,' said the storekeeper. 'Matter of fact he's one of my best customers.' The talkative storekeeper then explained the way to the Thomas farm. As Bill was about to leave, the storekeeper said, 'if you wait a couple of hours Dave will be at the hotel. He always comes to town each Friday to bring his wife shopping. Dave downs a few schooners while she shops.'

Bill stabled his horses, then when it was ten o'clock, he walked into an empty barroom. The barman said, 'what will it be stranger?'

He felt at ease knowing that unlike the time in Southern Cross, he could order a lemonade without being challenged, or called names by some troublemaker. But just as he was about to order his drink, a voice from near the door beat him. 'It's my shout Ted, so make it two beers please.'

Bill knew the voice, but before he could turn around, Dave Thomas, his friend from the old days back in England was slapping him on the back. 'Bill bloody Evans. Fancy meeting you here,' he said.

It was a different Dave than what he had expected. Instead of a tall slim fit looking young man, here in front of him was a still tall, but grossly overweight almost middle aged man, who looked anything but fit. 'Good to see you again Dave,' said Bill.

The barman, who obviously knew Dave well, placed two beers in front of Bill and his old friend. Then before Bill could say that he didn't drink, Dave said, 'let's drink to old times eh Bill?'

So more to please Dave than anything, Bill had his first drink since he went on a bender after Jenny died. He thought that he would only have the one beer, but his former school, and shipmate had other ideas. 'Come along Bill, drink up mate, it's your shout,' he said loudly. Thinking that he would lose face if he didn't pay his shout, Bill duly paid for another round. The conversation changed from talking about the good old days, to the hard times on the land, then to things like horseracing.

Without realizing it, Bill had drank about six beers before Dave said, 'I better go mate. My wife will have finished her shopping by now.' He got up to leave, but changed his mind and said, 'what are your plans Bill?' After being told that Bill had no real plans, but was looking for farm work, Dave then offered Bill a job. 'The harvesting starts soon, and we badly need a good worker. Ray Stephens from Boyup Brook told us that you are that. So what about it Bill, do you want to work for us?'

Feeling a bit lightheaded from the drink, Bill told his old friend, 'yes mate, I probably would like to do a harvest season.' So with one more drink to seal the deal, they headed off to Dave's farm.

Bill had been introduced to Dave's wife Edna and their two children, Robert and Glenys. Now with his pack horse in tow, he rode Blackie behind the horse and buggy of the Thomas family. It was about an hour or so to Dave's farm, and as it was midday, Glenys invited Bill to the homestead for lunch.

Bill tried to say that he was right as he had plenty of provisions, but Dave said, 'don't be silly mate, put your horses over in the stables, then come on over to the house. I'll show you your quarters later.'

A light lunch was followed by a hot cup of tea, then Bill was taken over to the original homestead of the Thomas family, who had come out in the year nineteen twenty four. Neither of Dave's parents remembered Bill, so had he had to repeat his surname several times before they finally remembered his mother and father. Then they spoke about the old times for ages, asking Bill many questions about his times in Northcliffe. 'We could have gone to Northcliffe you know,' said Mrs Thomas.

On the way to showing Bill his quarters, Dave Thomas told him how his parents had to battle to make a go of things in the early years. 'We had three bad seasons in a row, then mother-nature must have reckoned that we couldn't possibly take another bad one. Twenty four inches we had the next year Bill. Dad was praying for five bags of wheat to the acre, but we harvested ten bags. The bank manager was stopped from closing us down, and we haven't looked back since.'

Bill was happy to find that his living quarters were completely self-contained, because he preferred to cook for himself. He was surprised to see a new kerosene refrigerator in the kitchen, and inside were a dozen cold bottles of beer. 'I often come over for the odd drink, but if you object to having a beer with an old mate then I won't.'

There was no time for Bill to say anything, because no sooner than he had finished talking, Dave was pulling the top off two bottles. 'Cheers,' he said to Bill, who was in two minds, but gave in and started drinking. When Dave had finished his bottle, he said 'how about another mate?'

Still only half finished his bottle, Bill said, 'fair go Dave, I'm not used to this stuff.' He had heard that some people in the outback liked to drink a lot, especially in the hot weather.

'We'll train you, don't worry,' Dave said between swallows.

After unpacking, then cleaning the quarters, Bill rode Blackie for a couple of hours. He didn't know it, but Dave and his father were watching when he galloped Blackie for a mile or so on the way back. Apparently Ray Stephens had told them about Bill's fast horse, and they were keen to see him gallop. Bill was therefore surprised when Dave came from where he and his father had been watching, and said a little too keenly, 'Ray Stephens said you had a good horse Bill. Ever thought of racing him?'

Bill thought for a moment, then told Dave that Blackie was his special horse and he didn't want him whipped or treated rough. 'Tell you what,' said Dave, 'why don't we enter your horse in what they call the hack's race at the next meeting. That way you can ride him yourself?'

Still not really keen on the idea of racing his horse, Bill said, 'is it worth much if Blackie wins?'

Dave was keen, so to encourage his friend to allow him to enter in this race, he said, 'there's a trophy and twenty quid to the winner, and Dad and I will enter for you and cart Blackie to the race. What do you say Bill?' So it was settled and Blackie was nominated for his first race.

It was still a couple of weeks to the start of harvesting, so most of the days were filled with maintaince work around the farm. Then each afternoon, Dave and his father would watch as Bill worked Blackie around a track in a big paddock. Mr Thomas was very keen on this. Mainly because he had a back problem and couldn't work much. He would time Blackie each day, telling Bill to hold his horse back until the last half a mile or so, then let him go.

Harvesting started, but Bill still found time to ride each day, usually just at daylight. With the extra oats and other foods that Mr Thomas insisted that Bill feed him, Blackie was getting fitter and faster. Then one morning as Bill was hosing his horse down, he noticed dapples appearing in Blackie's coat. He hadn't heard Mr Thomas coming but was pleased that the old man took such an interest. 'Looks as though the big blokes just about ready eh Bill?'

Bill turned and said that he didn't think he could get him much fitter. 'You're right lad, but you can get him a bit faster,' said Mr Thomas. He then explained that if Bill was to gallop Blackie two mornings a week, over only a mile, it would increase his speed. 'We've still got three weeks to the race,' he told Bill.

Race day came and Blackie and all the Thomas family took the day off, as did most of the people in the district. There wasn't a lot of social events where people could meet, so they all looked forward to the race day. The woman folk would put on their good clothes and the men would wear a suit, probably the one that they got married in, and a good time was had by everyone. The children were given a motorized merry go round, and under the guidance of an elderly man dressed as a clown, they would take turns at riding on it.

The Hack race was the first on the card, so Bill was so busy getting Blackie ready that he didn't notice Dave go over to the one bookmaker and put money on Blackie to win.

Well Blackie won that day, and again at the next meeting. Bill liked the good feeling of his special horse seemingly finding another gear when asked to. Bill would only have to say, "let's go Blackie" and go he would. Dave bet on Blackie and gave Bill a handful of one pound notes after each win. The night of Blackie's second win, Bill was counting out these notes, when to his surprise one of them was a Ned Kelly, legal tender one pound note. Bill read the numbers 158888 out loud, because out of the numbers on this well-kept note, were all the numbers of his and his sister's birth dates. He still wore the silver chain that Peggy had given him several years ago.

Bill was now in a nostalgic mood and his mind took him back over parts of his life. He thought of Jenny, then Annie, but somehow his mind kept going back to Beatrice. 'Perhaps she was the one I really liked the most after all,' he thought. Then it came back to him, how his mother had told him that Kevin Flanagan had said that Beatrice was living back at Northcliffe and was asking after him.

Bill woke the next morning, still holding the Ned Kelly one pound note, then he remembered how his mind had kept on returning to Beatrice. Now all the advice of his old friend Charlie Burns flashed into his vision. As clear as crystal he could re-hear Charlie telling him to follow his feelings, no matter how strange or sudden they may happen. Dave picked up on the fact that his friend was quieter than usual that evening when he came for their nightly bottle of beer each at Bill's quarters. 'What's up mate?'

At first Bill didn't say much, but after his beer he told Dave that he might head off to see what life brings. 'But not until after the harvesting is over,' he said.

Dave told him that another couple of weeks would see most of it finished, 'so it's alright by us if you want to take off then,' he said.

The two weeks went by and Bill was invited to Dave's house for dinner on his last night, after which Mr Thomas surprised Bill by asking him if he would sell Blackie? 'I've always wanted a good racehorse,' he said. Bill was thinking and didn't have time to answer before the ageing farmer said, 'I'll pay you a hundred quid for him Bill.'

Now Bill did speak, 'I'm sorry Mr Thomas, but he's not for sale at any price.' The place went quiet, as the family, as well as Bill knew how helping to train Blackie had given the old man a new interest, and as Bill could tell, he loved horses.

Bill broke the silence by saying, 'Mr Thomas, I was going to ask if I could leave both of my horses here, while I take the train to Pemberton, so if you would like to, we can come to some sort of agreement that would let you race Blackie while I'm away.'

Dave drove Bill to the Corrigin train station, then headed off to the hotel. Bill had found that he also had grown used to the beer that Dave had introduced him back into, so as it was another hour before the train was due to pull out, he walked over the road and joined Dave in downing several beers. 'I 'm not sure when I'll be back,' Bill yelled to Dave as his train took him away from Corrigin.

Chapter Eighteen
Not Again

Bill's train stopped at Manjimup and even though he thought it might happen, he was genuinely surprised to see Charlie Burns waiting on the station platform. 'What kept you Bill Evans?' Charlie's smile was a mile wide, as he greeted Bill with his special handshake.

The two talked for a few minutes, then Charlie told Bill that he was welcome to stay for a while with him if he had time before he headed to Northcliffe. 'Charlie Burns, you must tell me a bit more how you seem to know most things that are going to, or will happen,' Bill said.

Shaking his head, this man of many talents simply said, 'maybe its luck, maybe I can see things that even I can't explain. Tell you what Bill, now that you are a drinker, why don't you change your ticket and come for a beer with your mate?'

A beer turned into several, and Bill was glad he did change his ticket to Pemberton, because he was now feeling a little light headed. 'How did you know I was drinking?' Bill asked.

Charlie grinned broadly towards his friend then said, 'reckon anyone could tell Bill. Anyway I'm glad because I now like a drink or two.'

The next day was a total mix up for Bill. Firstly, Charlie told him that what he was looking for, might not be in Northcliffe, but he went there anyway. He managed to get a lift with the mail truck from Pemberton to Northcliffe, as there still wasn't a rail service. Bill felt almost like he was coming home when he arrived in the tiny town.

Firstly he went to the Northcliffe store, where he spoke with several people that he remembered. There were lots of new folk though, as more adventurous settlers had arrived even after the Evans family had left. As he didn't have any transport, Bill stayed out the front of the store, hoping to catch a glimpse of Beatrice.

Finally Vince Flanagan showed up, and after exchanging stories, he told Bill that Beatrice and her family were now living in Pemberton. Vince invited Bill to the club for a beer, and the two of them had a good time, drinking and playing darts, after which Bill slept at the club.

Knowing that he should have listened to Charlie Burns, Bill went back to Pemberton with the mail truck the next day. Pemberton had grown considerably, so Bill had to ask several people before he found out where the Sparrow family were living. Finally a chap that knew Bill, directed him to a small house on the road to the swimming pool.

Bill walked to the address, and as luck would have it, he saw Beatrice on the front veranda. She was talking to a man who was obviously about to leave. Beatrice hugged, then kissed the young man, telling him to come again soon. Bill thought the obvious, and still unnoticed, he walked away.

Not again, he thought. Surely his luck could not be this bad. Pemberton had a workers club that served cold beer, and Bill took a table in a corner and drank at least his share that day, and the next. The world-wide monetary depression had worsened more, and some of the banks were withholding customer's money to ease the pressure put on them by overseas financial institutions. Bill found this out when, after spending most of the money he had allocated himself for a couple of months, he approached the bank in Pemberton. 'There seems to be a holdup in the withdrawal department Sir,' he was told by the clerk.

Bill asked when he could make his withdrawal, but was met with an indifferent reply. 'I'm sorry Sir but you'll have to try again tomorrow,' was his answer.

The bartender at the Pemberton Club refused to give any credit, so Bill went through his pockets and found that he had just enough to purchase a train ticket to Manjimup. So the next day he tried to withdraw money from the Manjimup branch of his bank, but was given the same answer. Being not at all happy, Bill asked to see the Bank Manager. 'I'm very sorry Sir, but he is busy, in fact he has no free appointment times left all this week,' said the young clerk.

Bill sat down and waited until a customer walked out of the manager's office, then promptly marched in himself. The clerk tried to stop him, but it was too late, as Bill had already shut the door behind him and was confronting the manager. 'Now are you going to tell me what's going on with my savings, or do I have to tell all of your customers that you have no money?'

The clearly upset manager asked Bill to please sit down, then he explained that not only his bank, but all the banks in the world are nearly bankrupt, due to failing investments. 'I'm sorry to have to tell you Mr Evans, but we cannot honour your withdrawal now or in the foreseeable future,' he said.

Bill was in no mood to be talked to like a child, so he said, 'does that mean you mongrels are going to keep my money?'

The manager gave Bill a typical answer. 'Let me explain Mr Evans. When a customer places money into an account in any bank, he or she automatically becomes a shareholder in that bank. As a shareholder, you can make money by the way of interest when things are stable and going well, but as we all know the whole world is not going well. Therefore as a shareholder when we lose, or go nearly broke, so to speak, then I'm sorry, but you too suffer the same dire consequences Mr Evans,' he said.

Bill was dumfounded. He had just been told that he was broke, and here was this Bank Manager talking to him like a man with a plumb in his mouth, telling him that that's the way things are, not only here in Australia, but right through the world. 'All countries are going through these tough times Mr Evans, and the Government is not going to help. They are expecting things to worsen more, and there is even talk of a world war.'

Reasoning with Bill when he was in this temper didn't work. 'You rotten thieving swine. How can you just take a man's money like that,' he yelled.

The manager was a little wary of Bill now and he said, 'I have the authority to release to certain hardship cases, some of the savings, I mean shareholder investment. Now in your case, as you are not married, you come under the category section C, so I am going to instruct my clerk to let you have five percent of your balance. Gooday to you Mr Evans.'

Bill was infuriated and wanted to carry things further, but something told him to take the five percent before he lost control of his temper. 'There you are Sir, exactly five percent of eight hundred and forty seven pounds comes to, forty two pounds three and sixpence. Now is there anything else we can do for you today Sir?' asked the clerk.

Bill took his money then said, 'as a matter of fact there is something you can do for me, and all of the other poor sods who your bank has seen fit to take money off. You can go and rot in hell, you thieving mongrels.'

Charlie Burns told Bill that he never put any money in them banks. 'They're crooks, the whole lot of them,' he said when Bill told him what had happened.

Bill nodded and said, 'never again will I trust them either. Also never again will I allow myself to fall for a woman.'

Charlie said, 'you might be making a mistake Bill. That girl in Northcliffe, I think she might be the right one for you.'

Without saying goodbye, Charlie came to the Manjimup station to see his friend off. Bill had no other plans now. It looked like Beatrice had another man in her life. 'Goodness knows,' thought Bill, 'she can't really be blamed. I haven't made any approaches or made any effort to see her for a few years now.' Bill was getting mixed up more and more. 'I did feel she may have been the right one for me, and Charlie is hardly ever wrong,' he thought.

He was so unsure of what to do that he very nearly jumped off the slow moving train to head back to Northcliffe, but then he remembered that his horses and most of his gear was still at the Thomas farm. Something made Bill change his mind and he did grab his bag and jump down from the train. The guard yelled out something, probably a telling off for dismounting a moving train, but that was not as loud as the laugh from Charlie Burns. When he saw his friend jump back onto the station platform, he reckoned that it was about the funniest thing he had seen for a while. 'Change your crazy mind did you mate?' he said to a now laughing Bill. When they both got their breath back, Bill said that he thought he better go and see his family before heading back to Corrigin.

The last letter that he had received from his parents was the normal news, except that young Don Travis had lost his next bout narrowly. The letter explained how straight after the fight Don was made an offer from another trainer, which he accepted. So when Bill surprised his parents when he arrived at their house, it was a quiet place compared to when he and Don were training. His father then had an interest, but now as he looked at him, Bill could not see the same spark that was there before. Mary Evans, as always was excited to see her son, and after a cuppa, and telling him all the news about Peggy, she told Bill that his brother Don had come to Australia. 'Where is he?' Bill said excitedly.

Mary went on to say that their son had only stayed a week with her and Joe. 'He's living over Eastern Australia at a mining town named Newcastle, with his wife's parents,' she said.

Bill's father then told him that his brother was now about six foot four in height and about seventeen stone. The three of them talked for ages about old times, both here and back in England, and Bill wished he had gotten to see his brother. 'He didn't let us know he was on the way,' said Joe.

Bill's mother was wiping the tears from her eyes as she said, 'your brother said he was sorry he missed you Bill. He said to tell you that he hoped one day that you will both meet again.'

Then Bill was happy when his sister and brother in law came for dinner, and was over the moon when after the meal, she told Bill that she was going to have a baby. Mary and Joe already knew the good news, but wanted Peggy to tell Bill herself.

As it was still early, Bill ran to the nearest hotel and bought a bottle of champagne and two bottles of Swan Lager Beer. So there was a celebration in the Evans house that night.

Bill stayed another two weeks with his parents, then boarded the train for Corrigin. He travelled on a Friday, knowing that Dave would be in town. So about midday Bill walked into the hotel, but a few minutes later he wished that he hadn't.

Dave Thomas looked like he had seen a ghost when Bill walked in. As soon as Bill got close to his friend, he could tell that there was something terribly wrong. He shook

Dave's outstretched hand and before he could ask him what the trouble was, Dave said just one word, 'Blackie.'

Bill heard what Dave had said, but nothing seemed to register, yet the way Dave had said "Blackie" it could mean only one thing. 'No, you didn't say that. Tell me you didn't Dave,' Bill was yelling now.

Dave tried to console his friend, but it was no good. Bill stormed outside so he could be alone, because that's how he felt, alone. First he lost Jenny, then Annie. Then he reckoned that Beatrice has another man. But now he had lost his horse. 'No,' he yelled again. Blackie was more than just a horse, he was a friend, but now…

Bill recovered enough to go back and find out what had happened. Dave again said he was so sorry, then he told Bill that he and his father had entered Blackie in a race. 'We both told the jockey not to whip him Bill. Blackie was going to win anyway, but the stupid bloke whipped him with only fifty yards to go and Blackie reared up and crashed into the running rail. He broke his fetlock Bill. The Vet had to put him down. I'm sorry mate.'

Dave was emotional now and Bill could tell he was genuine, so he grabbed his friend by the shoulders and said, 'not your fault Dave, I told your father he could race Blackie, but if I could get hold of that jockey.'

After a few moments Dave said, 'the stewards rubbed him out for a year for excessive use of the whip. The stewards also asked him how he got his black eye, but he was sensible enough not to tell them that I reckoned that's what you would have given him.'

Bill travelled back to the Thomas farm with Dave and his wife, then Mr Thomas showed him Blackie's grave. The old man was crying as he apologized to Bill. 'It's alright,' said Bill, 'but I would like to be alone for a while thanks Mr Thomas.'

The broken old man left Bill to spend a few minutes saying his farewell to his beloved horse, then as Bill started to walk away, he called him into his house. Mr Thomas took Bill into a small room at the rear of his old home, and while his wife put the kettle on, he showed Bill all the trophy's and memorabilia that he collected. 'I trained the winner of the Ascot Derby.' Then he passed Bill a big cup that he was obviously proud of. 'The owner gave me this cup.'

Bill could feel the emotion in the room as the old man then said, 'I'm never going to forgive myself for your horse's tragedy my boy. He was as good a horse as I've ever trained and I hope that one day you can forgive me.'

Forgiveness and understanding go hand in hand, and Bill understood what this old English gentleman was going through, and that he meant every word he said. 'I understand that it was not your fault, and I forgive you, but I also thank you for the decent way you buried Blackie Mr Thomas.'

Mrs Thomas poured the three of them a hot cup of tea and they talked for several minutes. 'Now Bill, I know that Dave has been handling your wages, but my wife and I insist that you take this small bonus.' Bill was going to refuse the envelope that he was given, but Mrs Thomas stopped him, 'please son, take it,' she said.

Dave Thomas told Bill that he could stay on now, or he could come back to work or visit anytime. He too handed Bill an envelope, saying that he appreciated not only his good work, but was happy to have seen him again. 'Remember how we held up the ship in Cape Town Bill,' he said.

Bill remembered how at Cape Town, he and Dave took too long exploring the Table-top Mountain and were late getting back. 'Yeah because you didn't run fast enough mate,' Bill replied.

The two old school friends didn't want this moment to end, but finally Bill flicked the reins, and now riding his packhorse horse, down the laneway, and away they went. Bill looked back and there as a group, were the entire Thomas family waving goodbye to him.

Bill waved to them, then said out loud to himself, 'goodbye Blackie.'

Chapter Nineteen
"Take Me"

As he rode away Bill's mind relived the good times he and his big black horse had been through together. He laughed as he thought back to the day when Blackie was delivered to their farm in Northcliffe and how he, then his father, were thrown like a sack of potatoes when they tried to ride him. Now as he headed into Corrigin, he thought, 'mother-nature always gets her own way. Blackie was gone so it must have been meant to be.'

His mood was broken as he remembered the two envelopes in his pocket. Bill opened Mr Thomas's first and inside was a short note saying how he and his good wife were sorry about Blackie. They also wished him well for his future. Finally they would like to be remembered to Bill's parents. A new twenty pound note was tucked into the neatly folded letter. Then he opened Dave's envelope, to find that he too had written a note. Dave explained that he had bet on Blackie when he won his first two races, so he wanted Bill to have the winnings. Bill counted out forty seven pounds, which he put together with Dave's parents money and the money that the bank had refunded him. He now had over a hundred pounds, so he said to his former pack horse, 'I don't know where to go, but if you were Blackie I would just say take me.' Then like Blackie used to, this horse seemed to understand and headed off.

It took them three weeks to make Kalgoorlie, where Bill posted a letter to his parents. Inside he put the twenty pound note that Mr and Mrs Thomas had given him. Bill then purchased some supplies and headed to where he had befriended the Aborigine tribe over a year ago. That night he slept about a mile from where they had their camp when he was here last. Early the next morning Bill rode to their camp site, but there was no one there.

He scouted the area and soon found a marker in the form of tree sticks. He followed similar markers for about ten mile, then from behind a bush appeared his Aboriginal friend. Bill had learned enough of the tribal language to be able to speak a little to The Tall One.

The news that he got was not good. Apparently a mining company had pegged the area where the natives had lived, including the special cave. The Tall One told Bill that at first there were a group of prospectors with big guns, who chased the tribe away. The proud Aborigine said that two of the bad men shot five of his tribe, including his wife. The Tall One told Bill that there is now a mine on their land near the special cave.

Bill told him how he was sorry about what happened and he would try to get these bad men punished. He then gave The Tall One half of his supplies. Unbeknown to Bill there were six of his friends warriors hidden in the scrub nearby. Suddenly one of them gave a strange animal call, which was a signal to any other Aboriginals around that there was danger. The Tall One told Bill to follow him and them both also hid. After a few minutes two men on horseback appeared and rode into the clearing.

The Tall One whispered to Bill that these were the bad men that had shot his wife and tribesmen. Bill checked both his rifles, then signalling to the warriors to stay hidden, he stepped out and spoke to the men. 'Gooday strangers. Can you help me please? I've been lost for two days.'

The bigger of the two said, 'it's a wonder you are alive then. Those blacks should have speared you by now,' he said. Bill told them that he hadn't seen any Aboriginals and asked the now off guard killers if they had had any trouble with them.

As Bill hoped, the over confident man said, 'we didn't give them a chance to give us any trouble mate. We rode into their camp and shot first.'

The cocky killer was smiling as he then told Bill how he and his friend had shot about half a dozen of them. 'They didn't even know what hit them,' this lowest of low loudmouth said.

Bill had both his trusty Lithgow rifle and the one he had purchased for Annie, then took back when they split up. He had heard enough and he raised both rifles up and would have willingly shot both of these two murderers. 'Get down off your horses, or better still go for your guns and give me an excuse to shoot you,' said a now angry Bill.

For a moment Bill thought he would have to shoot them, but the killer who hadn't yet spoken said nervously, 'I think he means it Col.'

They both did as Bill had ordered them, then were told to lay face down on the ground. The bigger of the two looked as though he might grab his rifle, but stopped and lay down as Bill said, 'please do. Give me the reason I need, and I will shoot you.'

The Tall One and his warriors came when Bill called them. Then he had trouble stopping them from spearing the killers of their families. 'No, my brother, do not kill them. Let me take them to our law, and they will punish them.'

The Aboriginal leader was in two minds and raised his spear as if to kill the two. 'No Tall One,' said Bill as he stepped between them. The two sworn blood brothers stared at each other, until finally at their leaders signal, the warriors stepped back and watched as Bill tied each of the two murderer's hands together. He then told them to stand up so he could tie a rope around their midriff then the other end to the saddles on their horses. Then he put a rope hobble on each of them so they couldn't run.

Satisfied that they were ready to walk back to Kalgoorlie and face the law, Bill turned to The Tall One and held out his hand. It was an emotional farewell, as both men sensed that this would certainly be the last time they would ever see each other.

Bill mounted his horse and led the two murderers away. Then he stopped to look back at his native friends. The Tall One stepped forward and giving Bill a salute, he sang a special warrior's song that Bill could still hear for several minutes as he rode away.

It took the rest of that day and half the next to bring the two to the Kalgoorlie Police station. Bill then had to fill in several pages of paperwork, after which the officer on duty told him that for a committal hearing to take place there needs to be more evidence. 'We really need to view the deceased, and interview the Aboriginals concerned as well,' he said.

Bill, being more than willing to help find a way to have these murderers punished, said, 'then I had better take you out to the site.'

The Police officer then said to come back tomorrow. 'By then the Sergeant will have made a decision as to what action we must take next,' he explained.

The next morning Bill was told that two officers would be going out to investigate the charges, and would appreciate it if he could go with them. So Bill took the two officers to the site of the murders, but there was no sign of The Tall One or his warriors. The officer in charge said, 'unless we have more evidence then there is no case.' Bill fired his rifle into the air and waited, but there was no Aboriginals anywhere. 'I'm terribly sorry Mr Evans, but we must go back now,' said the Policeman.

So the Magistrate granted the two murderers bail and they were free to go. As they left the courtroom, the loudmouth one said to Bill, 'you are nothing but an Abo lover.'

This fired Bill's temper and if it hadn't of been for the Policeman stepping in, then he would have hit this uncouth murderer. Not feeling at all like going prospecting, Bill stayed in Kalgoorlie. He booked into the same boarding house that he had met old Tom, then Annie. He didn't see Tom the first night, so he asked the new owner, a clean cut, well-mannered chap who had introduced himself as Jeff, if he knew where Tom might be. 'Oh he passed on about a year ago. Nice old man he was,' he told Bill.

The urge for a beer was too strong for Bill to resist, so he ventured over to a newly built hotel further along Hannan Street. Inside he noticed Paddy O'Reilly, the Irishman that he had prospected with a couple of years earlier. He saw that Paddy was drinking alone, so he went over and joined him. 'Well if it's not Bill Evans. How have you been mate?'

The two of them relived the moments when they found the Sunshine Nugget, then Bill said, 'did you find much more there Paddy?'

The proud Irishman took another sip of his drink, then told his former prospecting partner that a big mining company did buy his claim. 'They offered me a very high price Bill, so I said yes and signed the documents. But I didn't read the fine print, and the mongrels got my claim for a fraction of what it was worth.'

Bill, thinking back to how Paddy had taken him to his patch, thought that the poor chap must be near broke, so he said, 'here's a few bob if you need it mate.'

Paddy laughed as he refused the five pound note that Bill had offered him. 'Thank you kindly, but I'm not that badly off,' he said.

He lowered his voice now as he told Bill that even though he didn't get the full value of his claim, he still got a thousand quid. 'And you know me lad, I still haven't spent all of the money that we made from your Sunshine nugget. So if you ever get stuck, come and see me.'

Paddy was still laughing as he ordered two more beers. Then he asked Bill how his life had been since they had last seen each other. This got them talking again, then the drinks flowed and before they knew it the Publican was yelling 'last round men.'

As they were leaving the hotel Paddy said, 'don't forget what I said Bill, if you need a few quid at any time, give old Paddy a call.' Bill didn't get a chance to answer his big Irish friend, because from out of the shadows came three rough looking men.

One of them charged straight at Paddy, 'we'll gladly take some of your money,' he said. Even though he was a little drunk, Bill was quick enough to drop one of the other two and front the third attacker. Paddy meanwhile was having a tough time of things with the first bloke who had caught the big Irishman off guard. Bill soon disposed of his man and was about to give Paddy a hand, but Paddy yelled for him to keep away. 'I'm just getting warmed up lad,' he said.

So Bill watched as the Irish temper started to come out, and Paddy got the robber in a bear hug that threatened to break all of his ribs. 'Enough, I'm sorry,' squealed the big man who couldn't breathe because Paddy had put all of his massive strength into squeezing the wind out of him.

Finally, Paddy let him drop next to his two mates who were also in a bad way. 'Do you think we should take them to the Police Station, or give them another hiding?' Paddy asked.

The thought of more punishment was too much for the three robbers who must have been watching Bill and Paddy drinking. Half crawling and half staggering they got away as fast as they could.

Laughter now filled the area as both friends shook hands. 'Thank you Bill,' said Paddy. 'I doubt that I could've beat the three of them on me own lad.' Then he said, 'what do you say about a go at two up? I played last month and I won two quid.'

So around the back of the hotel they went, and to Bill's amazement there were about thirty men in a circle and one in the middle. The chap in the middle would throw two pennies into the air and the men in the circle would bet on how they would land.

Bill watched and soon worked out that a wager on heads, meant that both coins needed to land with two heads showing. The same for tails applied. Most of the betters, Bill noticed would for some reason bet on heads, so his first bet was on tails. This brought lots of sullen looks from the other players. Then when the two pennies landed and both showed tails, several of the other players glared at Bill. 'What did I do wrong?' Bill asked Paddy.

Paddy took over the situation. 'Don't worry,' said the Irishman, making sure he spoke loud enough for everyone to hear. 'It's your first game ever, so how were you to know that to have your first bet and to place it on tails breaks the luck of the rest of the mob.'

Being a bit put off by the way the rest of the players reacted, Bill placed two bob on tails. 'Tails,' called the thrower. The next three throws were odds, which meant that there being one heads and one tails showing, so the man in the middle had to toss the pennies again. Bill had bet on tails and he won again. Paddy said, 'looks like you've taken the luck Bill. I reckon you should leave your money there and if you win again you get double.'

Taking Paddy's advice, Bill did leave his money and he won again and again, until there was over fifty pound in front of him. The thrower waited for Bill to either pull out or continue doubling. Bill looked at the rest of the men, but they all looked away. Then he noticed that they all took a step back and nobody placed a bet. So Bill glanced at Paddy and he too had stepped back and wouldn't look Bill in the eye.

Not sure what was going on, Bill motioned to the thrower that he was leaving his money there. Then to his surprise the rest of the men cheered and barracked for Bills bet. 'Tails, Tails,' they chanted, and sure enough for the tenth consecutive time tails came up.

Now Paddy came over to Bill and explained the unwritten rules that all the players stood by. 'If you have a run of ten or more wins, and you have left your money in to double up, then you the winner take half, and the rest of the players share the other half. So if I was you Bill I would tell the thrower you have finished.'

Bill could sense that the crowd was watching and judging him, so he had a quick count of his winning and was amazed that there was one hundred and three pound and two shillings. With all eyes on him Bill took fifty pounds from the pile, then said, 'thanks for your support men. Please share the rest.'

A loud cheer went up, and Paddy slapped Bill on the back, as the others sorted out their shares. A big bloke handed Paddy his share, then asked Bill his name. 'Three cheers for Bill Evans,' he said to the happy group. The game started again and Bill had a couple more bets, then told the group that he was shouting the bar tomorrow night at seven o'clock. More cheers followed as he headed off to his room.

There were over thirty men waiting at the bar the next night as Bill walked in. He went straight to the bartender and said, 'how much to shout the bar for an hour?'

The eager barman said, 'I reckon this lot would have no trouble downing five quids worth Sir.'

Bill placed a five pound note on the bar and to the delight of the crowd, they drank heartily for an hour, during which the story of ten successive tail was told over and over. Most of the men stood on the stage and started a song, then the crowd would join in the chorus. 'It's your turn mate,' the same big bloke that had spoken to him the night before told Bill.

Having no choice, Bill jumped up on the small stage and as nobody had sung his favourite this night, he sang 'Danny Boy.' Soon the hotel was filled with tenor and baritones alike and as soon as that song was finished another man jumped up and started the crowd off again, this time with Waltzing Matilda. Then a hush came over the now larger crowd, because the bartender had yelled, 'times up gentlemen. No more free beer for you lot.'

Now this happy group were having a great time, and no bartender was going to spoil it for them. Then a voice came to the rescue. 'I'll be buggered there's not,' said the big bloke that had befriended Bill as he slapped a fiver on to the bar.

The party went on, as did the singing. The big bloke who had just said his name was Des, dragged Bill back onto the stage and after asking him what song he would like to have a go at. The pair of new friends sang "Mother McCree." This time the rest of the bar didn't join in, but when Bill and Des had crooned the last note, they cheered and yelled for more. 'Do you know any more?' asked Des.

Bill had been drinking a fair bit, but he still managed to get out the words to "I'll Take You Home Kathleen" and this time the whole mob sang along. Closing time seemed come too soon for the happy lot, but as they were leaving the hotel, someone yelled, 'two up anyone?'

This went on for several nights, except that Bill didn't always win and he never shouted the bar again. Des was at the hotel each night, and Bill and he talked a lot and seemed to have quite a bit in common. Des had elderly parents in Perth also and supported them with any spare money he had. Bill learnt that Des also had done a lot of gold prospecting, but now survives by winning enough at two up and betting on the races. 'Mind you I did have a good bank balance to start with, because my parents sold the family farm and my share was pretty good,' he said.

Their friendship was strengthened one evening, when Des was being hassled by a burley bloke who kept hounding him for money. The menace of words looked like turning violent, until Bill stepped in and told him that enough was enough, and if he continued to pester them anymore, then he would be in more trouble than he could handle. The hassler stared at Bill for a moment, then turned away and the two friends were left alone.

Before he had realized or actually thought about it, Bill had been in Kalgoorlie for over six months. It was only because Des had a copy of a newspaper and had pointed out a story to him that he worked out how long he had been drinking and gambling. Bill took the offered newspaper and after reading the date on the front, he turned to the story that Des reckoned he might be interested in. The headlines read, "Two miners stabbed to death in outback." The report told how these two miners had been surprised by about a dozen Aboriginal warriors, and after a fierce battle in which one native was shot, the miners were speared to death. The names of the speared men were the same as the two that Bill had brought into the Police over six months ago. Bill gave thought to The Tall One, who he had no doubt had taken revenge on these two murderers who had killed his wife. Bill said nothing to Des nor to anyone about this ever again, but he felt that justice may have been done.

Reading this story and realizing the date, Bill said to his friend that he was off to Perth the next day as his sister was due to have a baby about now. 'Mind if I come along mate? I reckon I might go and check on my parents and maybe go to the races,' said Des.

Peggy was proud as punch as she passed her baby to Bill for a nurse. Bill had just missed the birth of his nephew, who he now held. Then as he took a closer look said, 'he looks just like you Harold.'

With a shake of his head Harold said, 'you're the first to say that Bill. Everyone else has said that he is a spitting image of his uncle Bill.'

Joe Evans piped up and said, 'don't wish that upon the poor blighter.' This brought laughter all round and as Bill passed his nephew to Mary Evans, he said, 'congratulations Granny.'

Bill was glad he had come home to be with his family at such an important time. Peggy and Harold asked him if he could stay for the christening. 'I wouldn't miss it for anything,' Bill told them. So a new member of the Morris family was duly christened and given the name John.

Chapter Twenty
Riots

Two weeks later Bill was back in Kalgoorlie, as was Des, and they continued where they left off. Most nights found them drinking, then playing two up. Bill had been shown by his friend to watch the way the pennies dropped. If heads were coming up a lot in the first ten minutes, then Des would bet on tails, doubling up until tails was a winner. This would never make him a fortune, but he nearly always won enough to keep him in food and drink.

Des also showed Bill how he would win two out of three, or even more often, on the races. Des would study the form and pick what he reckoned was a top chance of winning a horserace, then he would back it for a place. 'Some weeks I don't even have a bet and sometimes I may have two bets, but only ever do I bet for a place,' Des said.

So Bill, on a much smaller scale than his friend, became a gambler. He found that if he stuck to the rules that Des had set, then he would win most times. This meant he, like many others, didn't have to work, which was just as well because work was getting harder to find, particularly in the mines.

But the drink started to become more than just a social thing. Now he found that he actually needed to drink to be able to feel like keeping going. On more than one occasion, Bill felt the effects of a hangover and feeling sorry for himself, mainly because of his luckless love life, he would take to drinking out of a bottle first thing in the morning. The alcohol in his blood made him sleep in a half dream like state, asleep one minute, then wide awake and talking to himself the next. He would dream horrible things, like he was being attacked by wild animals. Then one time he dreamt he was surrounded by monsters who were trying to pull him apart, and it was only when he heard a loud voice saying, 'take me, take me,' that he woke up. Bill was shocked to realize that it was his own voice that was shouting.

Des one evening said to Bill, 'how about coming to a meeting tonight? The blasted Italians are working in the mines at lower than the normal rate of pay, so they are doing everyone else out of a job.'

Bill had noticed that there were more and more Italians in town. 'Somethings got to be done about it,' said Des.

So that night, instead of going straight to the hotel after tea, Bill accompanied Des to a shed on the outskirts of town. There were already over two hundred angry miners crammed inside and more were still arriving. The meeting started when a well-dressed middle aged man, who Bill reckoned could be a politician, stood on a fruit box and spoke for several minutes on how the average Aussie workers were getting put off, because a certain group were undercutting their rate of pay. 'You mean the Bloody Ities don't you Steve?' someone yelled.

This started a general growling amongst the rowdy mob, many of who were out of work and could barely support their families. 'I know how you all feel men,' said Steve, who was well known to most of the men. 'We are here to work out a positive course of action to stop the way the mines are employing these scabs, because if we don't do something soon then we will all starve,' he said.

Many different ideas were put forward to the angry mob. Someone suggested that they all go on strike, but this was refused, because as a fellow in the front row pointed out, 'the employers will then give all our jobs to the scabs.'

Another chap who was standing near Bill said, 'maybe we should run these scabs out of town.'

This met with a roar of approval, but Steve said, 'violence should be our last resort. I nominate that we all march, peacefully mind you, to the Department of Mines and voice our case to them.'

This idea was accepted, and it was agreed that everyone bring as many people as they can, and meet at the top of Hannan Street at ten o'clock the next morning. Everyone cheered loudly, then someone said, 'let's drink on it,' and nearly three hundred thirsty men gave the publicans of Kalgoorlie a busy time.

The mob was angry enough already, but near boiling point was reached when a young chap who had not been part of the meeting, rushed into one of the hotels that most of the miners were drinking at and yelled, 'there has been a fight and a group of these scabs have killed one of ours.'

By the time Bill and all the mob got to the bar, which belonged to an Italian man, there were another several hundred other anti-foreign men already there. The scene got uglier by the minute and got worse still when a witness to the incident where the chap got killed said, 'the barman bashed him, and then a group chased and belted him to death.'

The noise that the now several hundred mob were making, attracted even more men, and within an hour there were over two thousand in the mob. The mood got angrier and violent, then someone set fire to the bar. This increased the tension more, then when someone said that it was Ted Jordan that was dead, the mob went crazy. Ted Jordon was a popular figure around Kalgoorlie and the surrounding towns of Boulder and Coolgardie. Hannan Street was brimming with the miners and their sympathisers, and the lighting of the bar, was the start of what turned into a full scale, out of control riot. Any shops or businesses that were known to be foreign owned, or any that had a foreign name, especially Italian, were set upon. The wild mob smashed windows and threw goods into the streets. Then the urge by some to burn the buildings was too much to resist, so dozens of business houses were burnt to the ground.

Revenge for the death of Ted Jordon was on the minds of this mob that had now grown to the thousands. 'Let's chase those scabs out of town,' one of the ringleaders shouted.

So every house that was known to belong to foreigners, was set upon, until the menfolk came out. Them the mob chased them out across the flats that were commonly known as "Fly Flats".

Bill was caught up in all the rioting, even though he may not have agreed with some of the actions that the mob were taking, he found that he had no choice. The number of wild men in the now running mob was too many to try to get out of, even if he wanted too, so he ran with them.

As he ran across "Fly Flats" with the mob, he noticed the chap next to him was carrying a rifle. 'I hope you're not going to use that,' said Bill, pointing to the rifle.

The chap said, 'only if I have to mate.' They had only run another twenty yards or so, when just in front of them, one of the foreigners being chased, jumped out from behind a bush. Bill could do nothing to prevent this man from using the knife that he was carrying. He stabbed one of the chasing mob in the stomach, then he ran as fast as he could.

Bill watched in amazement as the chap with the rifle stopped running then got down on one knee and shot the knife wielding foreigner. 'Keep running mate,' he said to Bill as he got up from his shooting position.

Run Bill did, as fast as he could, and he didn't look back to see if the man with the rifle was near. Bill didn't want to know who the rifleman was, because he reckoned that there would be trouble and he didn't want to be a witness. The noise of the rifle shot shocked most of the rest of the mob and the riot was over, with most men going home.

The next day meetings were held and most of the thousands that attended, wanted to go on strike. A vote was not held though, because the meeting was also attended by representatives of the Australian Workers Union, who advised them that to strike now would be the wrong time for such an action. 'We will support you if you will give us two days to have talks with your employers and the Department of Mines,' said a delegate.

Members of the Communist Party tried to stop the impending strike and caused a lot of worry and concern for the miners. But despite the Communist Party intervention, a strike went ahead on the following Friday.

This was the same day that twelve members of the mob were arrested and charged with causing a riot. Each of those that were charged were sentenced to one month jail. Bill Evans was one of those incarcerated at the Kalgoorlie lock up.

In a letter that he wrote to his parents, Bill told as well as he could about the incidents that lead to his arrest, and his jailing. He apologized to them, saying that all he did was get caught up in the mob, which thousands of others had done. He explained that for some reason he was picked out as a ringleader of the mob.

While he was supposedly in jail, Bill and the other eleven "scapegoats", as the local Police Sergeant said they were, only spent the nights actually locked up. During the day they were allowed to roam the Police Station yards and do gardening, or cleaning which helped pass the time. The time that Bill had to spend away from his lifestyle that he had gotten used too, was a blessing of sorts. He no longer found the urge for alcohol, and he stopped feeling sorry for himself and pondering about his failed love life. One day, with only a week before his release date, Bill wrote to Beatrice and posted it addressed to the Pemberton Post Office, hoping that she would receive the letter.

It was the last day of February nineteen thirty four that Bill walked out of the confines of the Police lockup at Kalgoorlie. He had been given four days remission for good behaviour, and for his previous good record, which showed that on two different occasions, he had apprehended and brought to justice, lawbreakers of his own accord.

Bill made his way to the livery stables to get his horse. But he got a shock when the manager told him that someone had stolen his horse. His gear which he had stored at the hostel was still there, so he gathered it and promptly left Kalgoorlie on the next train.

Chapter Twenty One
Beatrice

After listening to his son explain how he was picked out of a mob, then falsely locked up, Joe Evans told him that he already knew that he wasn't a criminal. 'There is nothing to forgive,' he told Bill.

Mary Evans was so glad to see her son, that it barley registered that he had been locked up for a month. She told Bill that she was proud of him for all the good things he had done, and if it weren't for his constant help, then she doubted that she and her husband could have made it this far. 'Times have been tough here in Perth,' she said. 'Most days we are approached by starving people begging for a feed.'

Peggy was a proud mother of a little terror who would not lay or sit still for anyone except his father. Harold Morris was the proudest father on earth and each day after work he would quickly kiss Peggy then pick up little John. The two would play until Peggy would call Harold for dinner. Bill nearly fell over when he saw how John had grown. 'I reckon he'll play football for West Perth one day.'

On the second day home, Bill asked his mother if she had heard from anyone from Northcliffe or Pemberton lately. Mary looked at him and said with a little grin on her face, 'you mean have I heard from Beatrice don't you son?'

Bill was surprised at his mother's intuition, but nodded to show that she was right. 'Well Bill, as a matter of fact I have some news that might interest you.' Mary was playing out the news about the girl that she had always felt that Bill had a special soft spot for. 'Beatrice is living in Perth and she was here only a few days ago,' she said.

Bill tried not to seem to keen, but he couldn't fool his mother or his father. 'For goodness sake Mary, put the lad out of his misery and tell him that Beatrice Sparrow came here looking for him and left her address, hoping that he will call on her,' said Bill's father, with a big grin all over his face. 'Now be off with you Bill and find her.'

Bill looked at the address again and was sure he was right, so into a café he went and sat down. He didn't have to wait long before he saw the pretty waitress heading towards his table.

Before he realized what he was doing Bill was standing, then running towards Beatrice, who could not believe her eyes. Beatrice put down the menu she was carrying and met Bill in the middle of the café, where they both momentarily stopped and looked deep into each other's eyes. Bill was the first to break the silence. He took both of Beatrice's hands in his, and said, 'you are just as pretty as the first time we danced at Northcliffe.'

Still holding Bill's hands and with tears running down her cheeks, she said, 'did you miss me?'

Bill took a minute to answer, then with a smile said, 'just a little.'

They talked for a while, then Beatrice said she had better get on with serving the other customers. Bill ordered a coffee, then asked her what time she finished work? 'I'll be off duty in about half an hour,' she said.

So Bill made his coffee last and when Beatrice came to him and said, 'what happens now Bill?' He asked her if she would like to go for a walk, to which she replied, 'that would be nice. There's a park not far from here and we can sit and talk.'

Bill said, 'yes I think we need to talk, it's been too long since those wonderful times we had together in Northcliffe.'

Talk they certainly did, and Bill found out that the chap who he had seen Beatrice kissing and inviting back anytime, was in fact her brother Ray Sparrow. 'He had cancer at the time, but I don't blame you for thinking the worst Bill. But I do wish you would have come and talked to me that day.'

Beatrice went on to tell Bill that she had never forgotten him, and she has never loved anyone since they both left Northcliffe. She also told him that her brother had died a few weeks after he had seen him on the veranda that day. 'Then only a week afterwards, my father died. Now only last week my mother also died, so here I am, all alone.'

Bill said that he was sorry about her losing her family, 'and I'm also sorry for jumping to the wrong conclusion Beatrice. Can you forgive me?'

Fighting back tears, Beatrice said, 'I already have forgiven you. Your mother told me all what you have been doing, so I have sort of been keeping up with you.'

Time was moving on and it was nearly dark, so Bill asked Beatrice if he could walk her home. When they arrived back at the café, Bill was confused and said, 'do you live at the same place that you work at?'

Beatrice went on to explain that after her mother died, the old couple that owned the café, let her rent a room out the back of the shop. 'I have nowhere else to go Bill. I have been hoping for so long that you would be my knight in shining armour. What took you so long Bill?'

Beatrice invited him into her room and they talked away for hours. Bill told her all that he had been through over the years since they parted. Beatrice was a good listener and somehow Bill felt better for telling her even the sad things that had happened, like Jenny's accident and how he had lost Blackie. He told her how Peggy had married and was now a mother. Then a strange thing happened to the now happy pair.

Bill was just about to tell Beatrice about Charlie Burns and how it was him that said that the girl from Northcliffe was the one for him, when suddenly Beatrice said, 'I've been having a sort of dream many nights.' Bill listened closer now as she continued. 'I don't know why Bill but an image of an Aboriginal kept telling me to find you.'

It didn't take Bill long to work out that this was some of Charlie's doing, so he told her all about Charlie Burns, and his ability to do extraordinary things like what had been happening to her. Beatrice smiled and said, 'I must meet this man and thank him one day, because many times I felt like giving up finding you, but then I would be told to find you in my next dream.'

Bill told her that she would undoubtabley meet this good friend one day, 'he'll just turn up when we don't expect him to.'

Every day Bill would visit Beatrice at her room, then after a week or so he invited her to have dinner with his parents. 'Peggy and Harold will be there also and of course little John will steal the limelight,' he said.

Beatrice came for dinner and she immediately fitted into the Evan's way of life. Peggy, when she got the chance to catch her brother alone said, 'looks like you two are a match Bill.'

They were a match and after several months, during which Bill had not touched a drop of alcohol, they at Bill's suggestion went out for dinner to a nice restaurant in Subiaco. It was only a short walk from where Beatrice was staying, the weather was good, Bill had some money, so he thought 'surely nothing can spoil my plans tonight.'

When they were half way through their meal, Bill put down his knife and fork and stood up. Beatrice thinking something was wrong, started to speak, but Bill waved her to be silent. Then he walked close to his partner and said, 'Beatrice Sparrow, will you do me the honour of marrying me?'

There were about a dozen other diners in the restaurant that evening and they all waited in silence for this pretty lady to answer her man. Beatrice wiped a tear from her eye then said, 'oh yes, of course I will Bill Evans.'

The management brought out a bottle of champagne, and as Bill fitted an engagement ring on to his new fiancé's finger, several of the other dinners clapped and raised their glasses to them.

The newly engaged couple told Bill's parents that night, then still excited, they called at Peggy and Harold's to tell them the good news. 'Where are you going to live?' This was the first thing that Peggy asked. Then she said, 'when is the big day?'

Bill did not have an answer to either of his sister's questions, but said, 'we haven't sorted that all out yet. I'm just happy that Beatrice accepted my proposal.'

Beatrice then said, 'I thought he would never ask,' to which both Peggy and Harold gave a little laugh.

Peggy then told Beatrice that in case she had forgotten, that it was now over five years since Bill had come home from a dance in Northcliffe and told his family how he had just met the girl he was going to marry. 'Our Bill does take his time making up his mind,' said Peggy.

As he was walking Beatrice home, Bill asked her when she would like to get married and got a surprise when Beatrice said, 'tomorrow would be fine by me.'

Bill laughed and told her that tomorrow is a bit soon. Beatrice stopped walking and said, 'Do you think so? Your son might have something to say about that,'

Then Bill stopped suddenly, as he realized what she had just said. 'Do you mean you're pregnant?'

Bill was caught by surprise and he got another small one when Beatrice said, 'I don't think there is any other way of having a baby my silly fiancée.'

A smile spread over Bill's face as he hugged Beatrice and told her that he loved her. 'Would you have told me if I hadn't of asked you to marry me?'

He got a smile back and Beatrice said, 'maybe I would and maybe I wouldn't have. I did not want you to think that you had to marry me Bill, but I'm so glad that you want too, because I've waited five good years for this day to come. So you asked me when I want to marry you. Well Bill Evans my answer is five years ago.'

The quiet wedding took place two weeks later at a little Church in Leederville West Perth. Harold was Bill's Best Man, and Joe Evans proudly escorted Beatrice down the aisle and gave her away. Bill had turned to watch as his father wheeled his chair easily and proudly, then he smiled as Beatrice thanked his father, then took Bills outstretched hand. Probably only those near the front in the church heard as he whispered to her, 'hello beautiful.'

Chapter Twenty Two
Life Is Good

The newlyweds had chosen a rental house in West Perth, only about a mile from Bill's parent's home. Bill had applied for many jobs since he had asked Beatrice to marry him, but it wasn't until a week after their wedding that he was successful. The State Government had created jobs to help the financial depression, and the job that Bill got was with The Main Roads Department. He graduated from shovelling gravel, digging ditches, and many other of the manual labour tasks involved with road building. Then one day the man whose job was to visually guide the machines that levelled the roads, didn't turn up for work, so Bill was told to have a go at it. 'Just be confident Bill,' said the foreman.

Bill had been watching the chap do this visual levelling and thought he could do the job. After the first day the foreman told him that the other chap was not returning to work, and the job, which paid an extra ten shillings a week was his. 'You've a good eye Bill,' the foreman said.

As soon as the foreman went to another site, a big Greek bloke said to Bill, 'bloody crawler. I wanted that job.' Bill ignored the loudmouth, but the abuse kept coming to the extent that it was now starting to be annoying. The final crunch came when, as the crew sat down on the verge to have lunch, the Greek said, 'look here comes the crawler.'

To make it worse the big man stood up as if to show the rest of the workers that he was a big tough man. Bill knew that he should ignore him, but something snapped, and before he realized what he was doing, the big Greek was lying unconscious. It was not Bills lucky day, because just as he delivered the blow, the foreman had arrived and had seen what happened. Bill had to tell the foreman the reason why he hit a fellow worker, and it did not look too good for him. But help came in the form of a little Irishman named Mick who approached the foreman, and explained how the man that was laying on the ground had been taunting Bill. 'I'm not one for dobbing Sir, but that there fellow has been abusing all of us for too long and it's about time somebody sorted him out,' he said.

Then several of the other men voiced their agreement. The foreman told Bill that he was going to let him off this time, but if it happened again then he would have to dismiss him. When the lunch break was over and Bill was heading back to his job, the foreman said to him, 'this is off the record, but well done Bill.'

After several weeks, the road levelling job finished for a while, and the crew were given the task of making rock walls on any hilly sections of the road. The rocks were a large blue metal type, and were heavy with sharp edges, as Bill found out on the first day. He was lifting one of these rocks to a gap in the wall about six feet above the road level, when it dislodged and before he could move his right hand, the sharp edge severed the top two joints of his forefinger.

The foreman did the necessary paperwork, then got Bill to sign the report. Treatment for such a wound was a lot of stitches, a bandage and back to work, but on light duties. About a month after losing his finger, Bill got a pleasant surprise when the foreman presented him with a cheque for two hundred and sixty pound, being for the loss of his index finger. Losing the finger became a bit of a problem for Bill, because as the depression got even worse, most jobs had to be shared, which meant that he, like most others only got two or three days work each week and of course this meant less pay. This problem became worse when Beatrice left her job to have their first baby. Bill tried to get extra work on these forced days off, but most employers wouldn't take him on because of his missing finger. Then when it looked likely that a war in Europe was going to happen, Bill was refused entry into the ranks of soldiers that could go to war, again because of his missing finger.

So things for Bill and Beatrice were not easy, but they got by, mainly because they used some of the two hundred pounds that he had kept for a rainy day. Then a few weeks before their baby was due, Bill received a notification that the Australian Army was opening a training camp in Western Australia, and were looking for men to be trained as cooks. The letter went on to say, that as he had already done the application and passed the test for everything but being able to shoot properly, because of his injury, he was high on the list.

Bill Evans became Private Evans two days before Beatrice gave birth to a bonny girl, who they called Margaret. Bill was given leave two days after moving to this new Army camp at Northam. They were proud parents, and Bill would take great pleasure in pushing their daughter around in the pram that his parents bought.

Northam was now becoming a big town, particularly as the Army was increasing their numbers all the time. Bill and his wife considered moving to Northam, but housing was difficult to get, as the Army rented any available buildings for their staff. So Beatrice and little Margaret stayed in Perth and Bill lived in the single men's quarters supplied on Army base in Northam. Bill got leave every two weeks and would travel home by train.

Beatrice was much happier when Bill was home, mainly because there were more and more people begging for food all the time. Sometimes she had to chase them away with a broom and one time she threatened to pour a boiling kettle over two tramps that continually pestered her. Beatrice had no way of visiting Bill's parents as it was a fair walk, and she was pregnant again, so they didn't see a lot of each other. Sometimes on Bill's home leave they would take a taxi and visit them and Peggy's family. Peggy now had two sons. John who everyone still said looked like Bill, now had a young brother named Brian.

Luck was on the side of Bill and Beatrice, because their second baby was born on Bill's leave, and he was given another week's special leave. Bill would always wear his Army uniform home, then change into his normal clothes while he was on leave. Beatrice was proud of Bill when one time he arrived home with three stripes on his uniform. 'Hello Sergeant Evans,' she would say when he would walk in the door.

Bill would continue the merriment by saluting her and saying, 'carry on then.' Then they would laugh and Margaret would crawl to her Daddy for a pick up. The rumours of war were now stronger than ever, and it was on Bill's leave that, he walked to the corner shop and bought a copy of The West Australian newspaper and read the headlines.

Chapter Twenty Three
What War Brings

The headlines said it all, "Australia at War". The younger Evans family were shocked but not surprised. Bill organized for a taxi to take his family to visit his parents, as he knew they would be worried. 'It can't be as bad as the last war,' said Bill's father.

But it was, and it lasted until nineteen forty five. Bill wasn't one to read the newspaper every day, but he happened to pick up a copy late in the war years. Inside the cover page was a photo of his old friend Charlie Burns, with a story below. Charlie was dressed in Army uniform, and with so many of local identities being killed in this terrible war, Bill feared the worst. He quickly read on, and was pleased to find that Charlie was alive and well. In fact, this proud true Australian had just been awarded a bravery citation. As Bill read on, he learned that Charlie had saved a badly wounded soldier from drowning at an unnamed beach. The story went on to say how Charlie put himself at risk from heavy enemy fire to swim out and rescue a fellow digger. Bill worked out that his friend must have lowered his age to be accepted into the Army. Then he smiled as he remembered how this fine man had put his age up so he could fight for his country in the First World War.

Beatrice had given birth to two more sons during this time. Keith Desmond was the first to join Margaret and Noel, then Bert came into the world with the war destined to end a year or so later. Bill stayed in the Army for another three years, as the camp at Northam was still training soldiers, and his pay was good.

Then just as he thought he might be a permanent soldier, Sergeant Bill Evans was informed that he was to be promoted and sent to Melbourne to train Army cooks. This was not what he wanted. Melbourne was too far away. The year was nineteen forty eight and there was a Soldiers Settlers Scheme being started by the Government. The idea was to encourage ex-soldiers to open up new farmlands in the South West of Western Australia. Bill approached his Senior Officer at his Army headquarters and in no time at all he was given a block in Pemberton.

Beatrice and the kids were over the moon with happiness at the thought of a new life away from the hustle and bustle of the city life. 'Good on you son. I wish I could be coming too,' Joe Evans told Bill.

Mary Evans said, 'let's hope the Government has learnt from the mistakes it made with the earlier scheme at Northcliffe.'

Bill left the Army with a distinguished record, and a good pay out. He bought a second hand Dodge car, which had a dicky seat at the back and it was a contest between the boys to see which two could sit in it. 'Take it in turns,' said Beatrice.

The Dodge was duly packed, and Bill's parents as well as Peggy and Harold, with their three sons, John, Brian and Peter, waved goodbye to the young Evans family as they headed off to be farmers. Bill was sad to leave his parents, but he knew that Peggy would always look after them.

The poor car was packed with all their clothing and personal possessions, which didn't leave a lot of room for the kids. 'I'm not leaving my cat behind,' said Margaret. So off they went with Bill driving, Margaret and Noel in the back seat, which left Keith and Bert in the Dicky seat. Top speed in this old Dodge was only about forty miles per hour. Bill had hoped to make Pemberton in the same day, but the old car had different ideas. 'Needs a new radiator hose,' the mechanic told Bill.

The car had been leaking water and was getting hot, so Bridgetown was as far as the family got that day. So the Bridgetown hotel had six more people staying the night. Leaving the cat in the family room, they walked the main street of this quaint little town built above the Blackwood River. The newspaper shop was where Bert wanted to go, hoping that his parents would allow him to buy a comic. 'Wow. Look Dad, they still have the number one Superman, and look there's numbers two and three.'

Bert was excited now. He had always wanted these three comics, especially the number one. He looked at the cover, which showed his favourite comic hero holding up a Volkswagen Car. 'Please Dad, could I have it. I promise I'll work hard on our farm, and when we get some cows I'll help milk them.'

Bill looked at this nearly five year old boy, who had a knack of getting things done. Knowing that with the Army payout money, he could afford it. So as they had to battle for many years, he told Bert to choose any three comics he wanted. 'That goes for all of you,' he said to his other children.

Bert already had his three Superman comics, and his sister and two brothers quickly chose their favourites. As a child, Bill had never seen comics as they didn't start printing them until about ten years previous. Beatrice chose a copy of The Women's Weekly and the evening's entertainment problem was solved. Bill already knew what the answer to his question would be, but he asked it anyway. 'Fish and chips anyone?'

Bert thought that this was the best day of his life, as he carried his Superman Comics back to the hotel. Beatrice had bought a loaf of bread and a pound of butter and she smiled as everyone made a chip sandwich with lots of butter. A big bottle of lemonade washed down the family's favourite meal, then Beatrice said, 'bath time you lot.'

Bright and early the next morning, Bill woke his family and they all helped him pack the car. 'Has anyone got Fluffy?' Margaret cried out. The search was on, but after half an hour of looking everywhere around the hotel and surrounding streets, Bill said, 'I'm very sorry, but we have to go.'

Margaret cried for nearly the whole of the journey to their farm. 'Don't be such a sook,' said Noel, who had never liked the cat. 'Leave her alone,' said Bert, which earnt him a punch on the shoulder from his big brother.

Keith laughed as Bert rubbed his arm, 'that'll teach ya,' he said.

The other kids nodded off to sleep, so Bert quietly gathered up their comics to read. There were copies of Batman, Ginger Megs, Donald Duck and Mickey Mouse and even two of Archie. Bert was in his glory as the old car took them slowly closer to what was to be their new life. As they got closer, Bill would have sworn he could hear his sister Peggy's voice, 'look at these Karri trees, aren't they beautiful,' said Margaret.

The giant trees were more numerous the closer they got to their farm. Then to Bill's shock, about sixty per cent of the farm was covered in still growing Karri's. There was a house and a shed already there, so the first job was to unpack the car. 'Hey, where's my comics?' yelled the other kids as they looked straight at Bert.

'I didn't want them to blow away,' he said. Another blow to the shoulder, then another by the other brother to the other shoulder, is what Bert got, 'but it was worth it,' he thought.

Most of the family's furniture and household goods had been sent to Pemberton by rail, and the Pemberton courier delivered it the next morning. Cattle and horses were delivered the following day and it wasn't long before they were milking cows. As was the case in Northcliffe the Karri trees needed to be ringbarked and cleared away, so there was plenty of work for everyone.

The nearest school was in Pemberton, which was six mile away, so the kids had a healthy walk each day. Bert was not old enough to have gone to school in Perth, but as he had turned five during the school holidays, he started school a week after arriving at their farm. Bert's Dad drove them all to school the first day and took them to the office, where a teacher escorted them to their respective rooms.

Bert didn't want to go, so his father walked him to his room, where a nice lady by the name of Mrs Bunn thanked Bill, and told him that all would be alright. Bert had different ideas and as soon as his Dad walked away and Mrs Bunn took him by the arm to lead him into the classroom, he tried to break free to run away. Mrs Bunn then grabbed this unwilling five year old by the shoulders and pushed him towards the classroom. Well, all the kids in the room gasped and stared, because Bert sunk his teeth into the poor teacher's closest arm and wouldn't stop biting her. Two male teachers were called and finally Bert was pulled away and locked behind a big cupboard in the corner of the classroom.

It was a hungry and sorry Bert Evans that was freed from his lockup at lunch time. Mrs Bunn made him stand in front of the class and say he was sorry, then she sat him down next to a boy named Henry. Bert was a different lad from then on, and he got to like Mrs Bunn. Beatrice had taught Bert to write a bit and how to add up. Then one day, not long after starting school, Mrs Bunn asked the class if anyone could count up to ten, so Bert put his hand up. 'I can count even higher,' he told her.

Not really believing the boy, the teacher told him to come out to the front and count as high as he could. 'Speak up Bert,' said Mrs Bunn. So he shouted as loud as he could and when he got to one hundred and fifty, he was told to sit down.

'But I can count to one thousand Mrs Bunn,' said Bert.

So the teacher promptly sent for the headmaster and when he arrived, Mrs Bunn asked Bert to count as high as he could. 'Just in your normal voice please lad,' said the teacher.

When Bert counted to one thousand without a mistake, the headmaster told him well done and the class clapped him. When he got back to his seat, Henry told him he was too clever and was the teacher's pet. Mrs Bunn heard Henry and for punishment he was made to sit down the front at a single desk. This meant that the girl that was sitting there had to go and sit next to Bert. Her name was Mary Thomson, and as soon as she sat down she whispered to Bert, 'you smell Bert Evans.'

At playtime that day Mary Thomson came over to Bert and said she was sorry for saying that he smells, then she told him that her father owned the butcher shop and sold very good meat. 'You should tell your parents to buy meat at our shop Bert.'

Then as Bert started to walk away, she must have wanted to keep talking, so she said, 'I have a sister and her name is Margaret.' Bert then told her that he also had a sister named Margaret.

'My Father's place is the big place on the hill,' she told him. After a week Mrs Bunn shifted all the kids around, so Mary no longer sat next to Bert.

About a fortnight after starting school, Mrs Bunn told the class that she would like them to all draw a picture. 'This picture can be about, or of anything you want it to be,' she said.

Bert didn't stop to think, but picked up just the one crayon from the packet. He drew everything in his picture, which was of the countryside, in brown. Mrs Bunn was walking around the classroom, looking as the children were drawing. When she got to Bert's desk she stopped and saw that the trees and the logs and all the ground was just this brown colour. When she asked Bert to explain his picture, he said that this is what he pictured the world would be like in the future. 'Why do you think that Bert,' she asked. The five year old then told her that he could see that the people on earth would not always look after it like they should, and it would die and turn to dust.

Almost every night Bill sat with Bert and told him stories and sometimes his youngest son would tell his father things that had happened to him. One night Bert told him how sometimes he would get teased a bit at school and felt that he might have to fight one day. 'Dad you used to be a boxer. Could you teach me please?' Bert asked. So at least once a day young Bert would get his father to teach him how to box.

Bill didn't find a lot of spare time as he had to work hard to get his farm producing milk. The Soldiers Settlers Scheme allocated the necessary farm equipment and the cows and two horses. Having had the experience before, Bill soon got enough land cleared and grass growing. Bert kept his promise and helped with the milking, mainly on weekends.

It was now two months since the night the family had lost their cat in Bridgetown. Margaret still went outside most days and called out to her Fluffy. The two elder boys would laugh and tell her that no cat could ever find its way to a new home, especially as it is about eighty mile to Bridgetown and Fluffy has never been to their farm. Still Margaret would go out and call her cat.

Then to everyone's amazement and disbelief, Bert opened the back door early one morning and saw Fluffy hobbling towards their house. He quickly picked up the skinny pet and gave it a plate of milk. As quick as he could, he ran in and woke his sister. 'Quick Marg, come and look in the kitchen,' he said.

Well Margaret Evans could not believe her eyes, as there, mewing for more milk, was her Fluffy who must have walked for two months to get to the farm. Margaret said, 'Look at your poor feet, they're all blistered.'

Fluffy became the heroine of the district, and as the news spread, people would come to the Evans farm just to get a glimpse at the wonder cat. The local newspaper, then the Perth papers, told the story to everyone.

Bill was milking one morning, when to his surprise both Keith and Bert came over to the dairy. He was mainly surprised because it was a school day and as it was a six mile walk, the boys never usually had enough time to help. 'Well bless my soul if it isn't Squeaker and Possum. What brings the pair of you here then?'

Keith, or Squeaker, as his father had nicknamed him, said in a tired voice, 'Possum, I mean Bert woke me up and told me that we have to help you today.'

Bill picked up his bucket of milk and after letting that cow out, was about to start milking the next one, but Bert stopped him. 'It's your Birthday Dad, so we came to help,' said Bert as he sat on the stool and started milking.

Then the two boys both said, 'Happy Birthday Dad.'

Bill had forgotten that it was in fact his birthday, and when he worked out that he was now forty, he said to his sons, 'I don't suppose I can let you walk to school today then, eh boys?'

Bert looked up from his milking and said, 'not going to school today. Gonna help you all day.'

Well Bill didn't know which way to turn. Here was his five and seven year olds telling him what they're going to do. It got better as Keith then told his father to go up to the house because he and Bert were going to finish the milking. As he walked into the kitchen he could smell bacon cooking, then Margaret told him, 'Happy Birthday,' and made him sit down to his favourite breakfast. 'More toast Daddy?' Margaret asked him.

It was still only six o'clock and he knew that neither his wife nor his eldest son would be out of bed for a while yet, but he got another surprise when Beatrice came into the kitchen and after hugging him and wishing him Happy Birthday, she gave him a parcel. Presents were a rare thing, not only in the Evans household, because money was still a problem with most of the country. A simple hug and a good day wish was more important than a present in these hard times.

Some food and things were still rationed because of the recent war. Petrol was rationed, and ration tickets were handed out to families. This was because of the short supply left for the public, after the defence forces had taken their supplies. This rationing was prolonged because of the probability of a war in Korea. The war had made Bill a soldier and because of this, he was entitled to have this farm under the Soldiers Settlers Scheme. 'That's what war brings,' he thought to himself.

Bill was brought back from his thoughts by his daughter, 'come on Daddy, unwrap it please.'

Bill got a nice surprise to see a rabbit trap as his present. 'Thank you,' he said as he kissed his wife and daughter. Then as he had finished his second cup of tea, Noel came out into the kitchen and still rubbing his eyes, said, 'it's too early to get up yet.' He had started to go back to bed, but was called back to tell his father Happy Birthday.

That evening, just before dark, Bill said, 'who wants to come and help me set my new rabbit trap?'

Both Keith and Bert ran to the old Dodge and off they went to a spot where Bill had seen a big rabbit warren. Bill showed his two sons how to set the trap, making sure to put some paper over the metal plate, then cover it lightly with soil. He then gathered some rabbit droppings and spread them around where he had left any scent.

The next morning before milking, the boys again joined their father to go and check the trap. 'Stay in the car and I'll call you if we've caught one,' he told them.

Sure enough, when Bill got close he could see the trap had caught that night's meal. 'It's alright,' he called, then Keith and Bert watched as he took out the rabbit, and reset the trap.

The next morning the boys went with Bill to check the trap again. They were glad they stayed in the car, because their father could be seen picking up a piece of wood and swinging it at something in the trap. Then they saw a big native cat spring at their father. They had hardly ever heard their Dad swear, but swear he did now as he ran at top speed to the car. 'Open the door,' he yelled.

Keith opened the door just in time, because just as Bill jumped in, the biggest cat that they had ever seen sprung at the spot where their Father had been. 'What was that?' asked Keith.

Bill was still a bit jumpy. 'That was a native cat and the thing nearly got me. Thanks for opening the door Squeaker,'

Beatrice laughed when later that day, Bill told her the story and how he was still pretty fast for a forty year old. 'You Bill Evans are forty one, not forty. Even Bert can count better than you,' she said.

Bill looked at his youngest son and said, 'how high can you count Possum?'

Bert quickly said, 'I can count to one thousand, then two thousand, but not now Dad, I'm busy reading the new Phantom comic you gave me.'

Chapter Twenty Four
Goodbye Farm

Life was enjoyable on the ninety eight acre farm that Bill and his family had worked so hard to try to make a success of. If success could be measured by the amount of work done, or by the good healthy lifestyle that this farm had given the family, then the farm would have been classed as a huge success. But unfortunately nothing is judged by the simple things, but by the amount of income that can be produced. It seemed to Bill that things might get better, so he used some of his savings to enable the farm to continue working. The kids didn't know anything about finances, so they thought that things were all rosy and they enjoyed the wide open spaces of the farm. Each day they would pick up the bread from a roadside bin and carry it home, but all of it never seemed to get all the way home. One of them would peel a little piece off the edge of the loaf, then the other kids would feel left out, so each of them would peel a bit off the loaf and by the time they reached home nearly half a loaf had been eaten. Their mother of course, didn't believe their story that the baker must have made the loaf that way, so she ordered two loaves a day.

The Evan's farm was up Pump Hill Road and straight on for another five mile. Just after Pump Hill Road started to rise, there was an old house and if the kids made any noise when going past this house, then a big black and white dog would bark at them. Of course Noel pretended that he wasn't scared of this dog and would yell and throw stones at it. This would enrage the owner of the dog and she would then tell the dog to chase them. The kids were so scared of this seemingly vicious animal, that Margaret told her father that she wasn't going to school if she had to walk past that house. Noel, fearing he may be in trouble for teasing the poor dog, told his father that the woman always got the wild thing to chase them. 'She started it Dad. We just walked quietly past and she always tells her dog to bite us.'

That afternoon, Bill decided to pay this woman a visit. As he knocked on her front door, the dog came running and barking at him, so Bill got the impression that the animal was vicious. 'I'm Bill Evans from up at farm number ninety six,' he told the woman, 'and if your dog ever chases my kids again, then I'll have to tell the dog catcher.

Also I'll probably have to report you to the police Lady,' he told her. This done the trick and no more problems were had with the Lady or her dog.

The family got a pleasant surprise when one day a car pulled into their driveway and out came Bill's parents. Also with them were Peggy and Harold with their three boys. Bert soon made friends with his young cousin Peter, as he was about the same age. Peter would get up early and help with the milking, and he also liked comics. They stayed two days and Bill was so happy that he could talk to his father about farming. He wheeled his Dad proudly all over the farm and would still talk late into the night, until his mother would come and say, 'time for bed you two farmers.' Bill would hug his mother, then say, 'goodnight Dad, thanks for your advice.'

When it was time for Harold to drive them back to Perth in his Morris Minor, Joe hung back for a minute or so extra, then reached up and hugged firstly the children and Beatrice, then with just the sign of a tear starting in his eye, he grasped his son with both hands and said, 'goodbye my son. I am so proud of you.'

Bill held his father for a moment longer than usual, then with a breaking voice said, 'it's never goodbye Dad. It's see you later. I've missed you and it's been so good to see you. We think of you all the time, and I've probably never told you, but I could not have had a better father. If I am any good, then it has been because of you and Mum.'

Bill started to wheel his father to the car, then he smiled as his sons ran over and helped push the wheelchair to the car. Bill never forgot the look on his father's face as the car drove off. It was as if the old man was telling him something with his eyes.

That night as Bill was telling Bert his stories, he noticed that his son was wiping tears from his eyes. He stopped his story telling and said, 'what's wrong Possum?' It took a while for Bill to work out that Bert was already missing his grandparents. 'They'll be back again soon, don't worry,' he said.

All went quiet for a moment, then Bert said, 'Dad, where do you go when you die?'

Bill was not sure how to answer his son, so he asked him why he was wondering about such a sad thing? Bert said, 'I'm not really sure, but the look Grandad gave you when he left made me think he might be going to die soon.'

An eerie feeling came over Bill, but he didn't want to scare his son, so he told him that even though grandad was old, he was very strong and would probably live for a long time yet. Bert just nodded and said, 'could you tell me again how grandad brought you all out from England?'

Beatrice gave birth to another daughter about a year after they had moved to their farm. After a little thought, the pretty, dark haired baby was named Lorraine. While Beatrice was in hospital, the kids were billeted out to friends. It had been Beatrice's idea for this to happen, but Bill was against the idea, saying that he could look after his own kids as well as anyone.

This was the first time the Evans children had ever heard their parents arguing. Bill raised his voice when a week or so before she was due, Beatrice said that she wanted Margaret to stay at her friend's place. 'You mean at the hunter's place, don't you Beatrice. Neither Margaret or any of our kids are staying at the Hunters.'

Bill won that argument, but as soon as she got the first labour pains, Beatrice organized for the kids to be picked up and billeted out at other of her friends. Margaret didn't stay with the Hunters and no more was said, so everyone seemed happy. Bill picked up three of his children the day before Beatrice was due to come home with her new baby. He didn't have to pick up his youngest son, because Bert had come home on his own accord within a few hours of arriving at his place of billeting.

Bill had been drenching the calves, and as it was a Saturday, he was about to go to town and buy some supplies. As he was walking to his car he couldn't believe his eyes, because running up the road as fast as his little legs would go, was Bert. 'What's the matter Son?' Bill asked.

Bert said in an urgent voice, 'it's Dennis's Dad. He's going to kill me.'

Bill told his youngest boy to slow down and explain what had happened. Bert told him that Dennis, the boy whose family he was made to stay with, was teasing him. 'Then he pushed me Dad, so I stretched the lackey band that held his hat on, then I let it go. He's a sook, and he cried and ran to his father.'

Bill was having trouble stopping himself from laughing, but he managed to ask his son what Dennis's father did next? 'He grabbed me and hit me under the ear and was going to kick me up the backside, but as soon as he let go of me I took off.' Bert was still puffing from his two mile run.

There was no more time for talking now though, because into the driveway came Dennis's father driving his new Morris Ute. Bill met this big man, who was in charge of the Forestry Department and was used to getting his own way. Before Bill could say a word, Dennis's father, ran at Bert and it was obvious that he intended to strike the five year old. Dennis had also got out of the car and Bill could see that this spoilt lad was twice the size of his son. 'Hit him Daddy,' screamed Dennis.

Bill stepped in front of this angry man and said, 'stop right there Godfrey. You have already struck my son, and if you so much as raise your hand to him ever again, I'll not be responsible for what I might do. Now get back in your shiny new car and take your spoilt brat with you.'

Godfrey was almost going to challenge Bill, but had heard of his boxing skills and had seen him deal with a big out of town wrestler at a dance years ago, so he did what Bill told him to and drove away.

Trying his best not to laugh, Bill said, 'let's go to town Son.' It was a happy Bert Evans that not only had a chocolate coated ice cream, but got a new Superman Comic as well that morning. 'What are we going to do with you boy?' asked Bill on the way home.

Bert looked up from his new comic and said in his most confident voice, 'I'm staying with you Dad.'

So father and son had a good time for a week. Bert didn't have to walk to school, because each morning after he had helped his father milk the fifty cows, he was driven there, and picked up after school as well.

The youngest Evans boy thought, 'this is the best week of my whole life,' particularly as he was allowed to have his favourite foods. Bert would start the day off with a huge plate of bread and milk for breakfast. His father would pretend he wasn't watching as Bert would put an extra spoonful of sugar on his breakfast. Then when Bert was sure his Dad wasn't watching, he would put another heaped spoonful of sunshine milk into his bowl. Bill would watch as his son would pack his own school lunch. Usually it would be bread and plum jam sandwiches, or Wheat Bix with butter and Vegemite half an inch thick on them. All this would be wrapped in the greasy wrapping that came from the Wheat Bix packets.

Each afternoon as he was picking up Bert from school, Bill's other children would run to his car and beg to be taken back home with him. Bill nearly gave in and took them home, but he knew that Beatrice would chew his ear off.

Bert would ask his father to tell him stories each night during that week, and Bill would relive most of his earlier life. This was the start of him telling stories to Bert every night and these stories were to stay in Bert's memory bank for a long time. The youngster really enjoyed the stories about when Bill went gold hunting and would ask many questions about what happened. 'Did you really know Annie Oakley Dad,' he asked one time. Bill had to tell Bert that she was not the one in the comic books.

It was indeed an eventful week for Bert Evans. On the fifth day of his time at home with his father, a young Pemberton boy was reported lost, and a call was put out for volunteers to search for him. As the lad was not found by the second day of his being lost, Bill left Bert at home to join the search, and when he reported to the search controller, there were already hundreds of other volunteers. People had come from surrounding towns as well as most of the Pemberton residents. The controller placed Bill in charge of twenty other volunteers and told him to search the area north of the forestry settlement, which was just south of Bill's farm.

It was a Saturday, so as there was no school that day. Bert was allowed to cook chips on top of their wood stove and he had just piled his hot chips onto a plate and was about to pour his favourite tomato sauce all over them, when he heard a knock on the door. There on the doorstep, looking tired and hungry, was a boy about the same age as Bert. 'Could I have something to eat please, I'm lost,' said the lad.

Bert showed him inside and shared his hot chips with him. 'Would you like some bread and jam?' Bert asked him.

The two of them were happy eating away for quite a while, then the boy was so tired that he fell asleep in his chair. Bert covered him with a blanket, then read some comics until his father came home to start the afternoon milking. 'The lost boy is here Dad,' said Bert.

There were celebrations in Pemberton that day. The youngster had been lost for two days and his parents were so happy that they bought Bert a toy truck for finding their son. Bert said, 'but he found me and now he is my friend.'

Beatrice came home with baby Lorraine a few days later. Now there were seven members of the Evans family and as fate would have it, the old saying of "The Young Replace the Old," came to fruition. Within a week of Lorraine settling in at the farm, Bill received a telegram saying that his father had collapsed and was in a critical state in the Royal Perth Hospital. Please come quickly, was the message from Bill's sister.

Bill arrived at the hospital that same day and was shown straight into the ward where his father was surrounded by his wife, Peggy and Harold, with their children, John, Brian and Peter. Bill hugged his mother and sister, shook hands with his brother in law, then went to his father's bedside.

Not sure what to say, Bill simply said, 'hello Dad.'

Old Joe Evans opened his eyes and his face lit up as he saw his son. 'Bill my boy. Come close son,' he whispered. Bill fell into his father's outstretched arms, and as they held each other, he heard the last breath of life leave his father.

Bill reached over and pulled his mother and sister into the embrace, and they all said their last goodbye. Harold took his children outside to let the others have some time alone. It was a sad few days that followed. Bill organized and paid for the funeral, which was attended by not only the family, but several of the early settlers, including some that still lived in Northcliffe. Peggy was upset, but gave a lot of attention to her broken hearted mother over this sad time.

Bill arrived back at the farm with his mother a week later. Mary Evans didn't hesitate to accept her son's offer to come and stay at the farm. Her grandchildren all made her welcome and Beatrice did her best to make her feel at home, but for some reason she felt that Bill's mother didn't like her.

The boys had done all the milking and farm work while Bill was away and he thanked them all individually when he got the chance. Mary Evans never got over losing her beloved husband and her and Bill would talk for ages about the good old days that they had had together. Then after school she would find young Bert bringing her a cup of tea. 'Please tell me a story Granny,' he would say.

Then this proud Granny would relive all the past and put it into words for her eager young Grandson. Bert felt a special closeness towards his "Granny" and was sad and very quiet when she left to go back to Perth. He was worried about who would take care of her, and it wasn't until his father told him that Aunty Peggy would be taking good care of his Granny, that Bert relaxed a little.

That night Bill had to tell Bert stories about Granny Evans. Then when he thought he had talked the young boy to sleep, a voice would ask a question that would need an answer. 'I think you love your grandmother, don't you Bert?'

Then back came an answer that sounded familiar, 'just a little,' said Bert.

The hard work never stopped on the Evans family farm, but as with the hundred or so Soldier Settler Farms around Pemberton, it was getting harder to make ends meet. The final straw came about two years after Bill and his family took the challenge and "had a go." The representative from the now almost defunct scheme, paid farmers the usual monthly visit in early nineteen fifty. The news that he was instructed to bring to the battlers who were clinging to some hope, was not good. Bill, like these other battlers, was told that because he was not making any financial gain, which meant that he wasn't paying the necessary monthly payments to the Western Australian Land Settlement Scheme, his property was to be put on the market. Bill was devastated. He like the other former Soldiers, many that had fought bravely for their country, was now being told, 'you have one month to pay off your debt on this property.'

That night Bill Evans had to tell his family that they were moving off their farm. Silence was his answer. A deathly kind of silence. Beatrice had been through this all before with her parents in Northcliffe, but now she felt that she could not take what life was dealing out anymore. She looked at the disbelief on the faces of her children. Margaret was not a farm lover as such, Noel was more into anything mechanical. Then as she looked at Keith and Bert, she broke down. These two boys loved this farm and many times she had heard them talking about how they were going to run this place when they were grown up. Beatrice picked up Lorraine and headed to her favourite chair by the fire and cried like a baby for about an hour.

Bill made her a cup of tea, then sat next to her. 'Why Bill?' she asked. 'I know nobody could have worked harder, or gone without more than us. This was supposed to be a land of opportunity, but it seems to me that it is a land run by a bunch of inconsiderate nincompoops.' Beatrice had stopped crying now and her temper had taken control of her, 'what are we supposed to do? Where do we go now? I'll bet our last dollar that the Soldier Settler bosses won't help us.'

Bill was at a loss at what to say, because he also felt let down and disappointed at this scheme that appeared to be more interested in getting more money out of the farmers, than helping them. 'We came back strong last time, and we'll do it again,' he said.

Chapter Twenty Five
Life Goes On

In the last month of what Bill knew was going to be his last days on the farm that he and his family had set their hearts on, as being the chance to make a go of life, nothing changed. No bolt of lightning was sent to change things. No act of Government changed the fact that they were going to have to find somewhere to live. Bill had used up all but five pounds of his reserve savings trying in vain to turn their farm into a paying proposition, so the future didn't look good.

Then with just two days to go before they were to have to walk off and go to goodness knows where, a Good Samaritan in the form of a schoolteacher knocked on their door. It was Mrs Bunn, and after a cup of tea, she told The Evans family that they could move into her small farmhouse for as long as it takes for them to sort out things. 'Now while your parents are considering my offer Bert, would you kindly show me around this farm that you have been telling me so much about,' she said.

The house that Bert's favourite teacher had let them have, was half way between the Evans farm and Pemberton, so things didn't change all that much for the kids. They still went to the same school, but they now only had to walk three mile each way. They still had fun on the new property, because the old house was on a twenty acre paddock, so it was almost like still living on a farm. The boys were happy to see a big dam not far from the house and Bill knew that they would be hard to keep out of it on hot days.

Beatrice nearly fell over backwards the first time she walked inside the house. It obviously had not been lived in for many years. There were no floor coverings, in fact there were no floorboards even. The ground though, had been worn hard and smooth and could be swept without disturbing any dust. There was no electricity, and hot water had to be carted from an outside wood fire heated copper. Still it was somewhere to live and within a few days, with Bill's help, Beatrice had cleaned and furnished the quaint old house to a liveable state. The spirit of country people was still alive and well in Pemberton. Many neighbours helped them over the next few months, some dropping in with food and others offering fresh fruit and vegetables.

One close neighbour gave them fresh milk each day. The boys would enjoy going to collect this milk from the neighbour's dairy, as there was always something extra, like fruit or cream for them. The milk was poured into their own billycan, and even when it was full to the top with milk, they could swing it round and round in a full circle without spilling any of the milk.

Amongst the neighbours who came to offer their help, was one young chap who was working at the Pemberton Timber Mill and he told Bill that he thought there could be a job going there. So the next day Bill applied for and got the job. Beatrice had heard through her friends that work was very hard to find and she was surprised that Bill got this job so easily.

The first day was enough to tell Bill why nobody wanted this job. Bill had to clear any bark or branches off and away from the landing. The actual task of moving this debris, was not all that hard, but the risk of joining a list of other men who had been injured doing this job was very high.

The landing is where the big logs, which are released from carriages, are rolled down a steep slope to a pile at the bottom of this slope. The logs roll down on evenly spaced logs which were half buried into the ground. These rolling logs continually drop bark and branches onto the ground and onto the logs that are used as rollers. This causes the rolling logs to change course, therefore instead of a neat pile at the bottom, there was often just an unmanageable heap.

The danger came when the man in charge of releasing the logs at the top of the landing let them go while the man trying to clear away the debris was still on the landing. Bill found out that two men had been injured recently and only a few months previous, a man had been killed by rolling logs. Bill was told many times to make sure that it was clear before clearing this debris, then after a few days the foreman said, 'you're not keeping the landing clean enough. It only takes a piece of bark and a rolling log can change direction.'

So Bill started actually running out in between the release of the logs. All went well until one day, which happened to be school holidays, when the boys had just brought Bill's lunch to him, a near disaster happened. Because the trains that towed the logs to the landing had trouble keeping up with the demand for logs, the unloading did not stop for lunch. The boys had been told where to stay out of harm's way and Bill darted out to clear away a big pile of bark that had been dropped by the previous logs. Normally it only took about three minutes to clear the usual amount or debris, but this time Bill was still trying to clear the landing after four minutes.

The man at the top looked down just as Bill was bending down to pick up some bark, so did not see him. He should have made sure that the landing was clear, but being under pressure to keep the supply of logs up, he took another bite of his sandwich and released the next load of logs.

Young Bert had been watching closely because he was interested in how things worked. When he worked out that his father had taken longer than usual to do his job, he felt a sort of premonition and just before the logs were released, Bert jumped from his safe spot and ran closer to his father. He yelled at the top of his voice to warn him.

Bill hearing his son's screams looked up and saw about forty ton of huge karri logs hurtling down at him. Bill had been told that the worker that had been killed had tried to out run the logs and had been crushed. Bert watched as his father quickly cleared an armload of bark from between the landing logs, then just as it looked as though he was certain to be crushed, Bill lay down in the small hollow he had created.

The dozen huge logs made a lot of dust, and as they crashed into the pile at the bottom of the landing, it was impossible to see any sign of Bill. 'There he is,' yelled Bert. 'Good on you Dad, I knew you wouldn't get squashed.'

Bill stood up and shaking dust off himself walked over to his son and picked him up and threw him in the air. As he caught him, as he had done many times at home, he said, 'thank you my boy. If you hadn't warned me I reckon I'd have been well and truly squashed.'

The mill boss was called and a quick inquiry was held, after which the worker releasing the logs was reprimanded. The boss then called Bill aside and said, 'good thinking Bill. Most men either run or try to jump the logs. Now are you happy to continue in this job?'

Bill firstly told the Mill Boss how it was his son that had warned him, then he also told him that the young boy would like to talk to him. 'Well bring him in then. I'd like to meet him,' said the boss.

Bert was a bit shy at first, but then he said, 'Sir I didn't like seeing my Dad almost get killed and I think I have worked out a way to make sure it doesn't happen again.'

The Mill Boss looked at what Bert had drawn on a sheet of paper and said, 'you know young man, I think it will work.'

The next day the new system was put in place, and the landing became known as one of the safest places in the mill to work. Bert could not understand why nobody had thought of the simple safety idea before. What now happened was the instillation of two lights, one at the top of the landing and the other at the bottom of the landing where Bill worked. The top light was a flashing red globe about ten feet above the ground. It was operated by the worker, who must turn the switch on to make the light work. This gave warning to the worker below that the logs were about to be released. To give the worker below time to move out of harm's way, the worker at the top had to wait one full minute after turning on his light before he was allowed to let the logs go. The light at the bottom had two globes, one red and one green. The worker below must turn on the red light whenever he is on the landing, then when he has finished clearing the debris, he simply turns off the red and turns on the green light, telling the above worker that he may release the logs. The Mill Boss watched as the new system was started and wrote out a citation of safety awareness certificate with Bert Evans's name as the recipient.

At the School Assembly, the first day that the holidays had concluded, the Headmaster called out Bert's name. It was a nervous boy that had to walk out in front of all the teachers and schoolchildren that day. Bert didn't know what he had done wrong, or why he had been called out to the front. Then the Headmaster said to the assembly, 'we have a special award. This award will be presented by the Manager of our towns Timber Mill. This award is for the invention of a life- saving safety feature which is now not only in operation at our towns Timber Mill, but is in the process of being used throughout the entire South West. This award goes to Bert Evans.'

Then the Mill Manager shook Bert's hand and presented him with the certificate. Mrs Bunn then came over and said, 'well done Bert, you may go back to the line now.' Some of the boys patted him on the back as he made his way to where his class was standing.

Later that day the school had sports as there was to be an interschool competition against Manjimup. Usually Bert didn't enter in any of the events, mainly because he was a bit shy. So as the rest of his classmates ran and jumped to try to make the team, Bert either watched or helped some of the teachers with the sporting equipment.

Bert was just about to go and watch his friend Allan run his race. Allan was a good runner and always won his races. As he got close to the starting line, he said, 'good luck Allan.'

His friend then said, 'hey Bert. What about joining in? We've only got five runners and we need six.'

So not wanting to disappoint his friend, Bert joined the line and waited for the teacher to say go. Bert looked towards the finish line and saw that it was only about fifty yards away. He was used to running for miles around the paddocks and knew he wouldn't even get a puff up only running this far. Suddenly he was snapped out of his daydreaming by someone yelling, ''go.''

The other runners who Bert noticed had been bent over in a starters crouch, were off even as Bert started to move his legs. Bert was tall for his age and it took him a few strides to get going. Then he saw Allan a few yards ahead, so he went a bit faster and ran alongside his friend. He could have ran past him, but he didn't want to upset him, because everyone knew that Allan was the fastest runner and Bert didn't have many friends, so he just ran alongside him. Allan was puffing after the race, but he came over to Bert and said, 'I didn't know you could run Bert.'

Not sure what to say or do next, Bert simply said, 'everyone can run Allan.'

The next day the list was put on the notice board to show the athletes selected to compete against Manjimup the following week. The list for the boy's fifty yard sprint had both Allan's and Bert's names on it as the Pemberton representatives. That night Bert showed his Dad the certificate, and instead of having to tell his son a story that night, he listened as Bert told him all about his day. 'Well done Son. I'll buy you a Cherry Ripe if you win your race,' said Bill.

Bert didn't want to beat Allan, so he said to his father, 'do I still get a Cherry Ripe if I come second?'

Bert Evans got his Cherry Ripe the next week, and a ribbon to show that he came second in his race. Mrs Bunn was delighted with Bert for going in the race, 'you helped our school get enough points to beat Manjimup,' she told him.

That night the youngster had to relive the race for his Dad. 'Did you nearly win?'

Bert shrugged his shoulders and said, 'I dunno. I just ran alongside my friend, because he likes to win.' The Cherry Ripe was shared with his family after tea, as it was a rare treat to be able to have any luxuries in these hard times.

Bill was approached by his shift boss after having been working at the mill for several months, 'Bill there's a position going at the boiler room if you're interested,' he said.

So Bill got a pay rise and took home some good news to his family after work. 'We've been given a nice mill house in town, and I've got a pay rise.'

Beatrice cried with joy that night and the very next day the Evans family moved into their new home. 'It's not really ours, we are just renting it,' a very grown up sounding Margaret said.

Little Lorraine was nearly three now and would follow Bill everywhere. Because of the extra income from his new job, Bill bought some cool drink and lollies for Lorraine's birthday and the family had their first party for years.

Some weeks later, the mill workers were all told that the mill would be shutting down for repairs, and all mill workers had to take a week's leave. So as it was school holidays, the Evans family went on their first holiday.

The spot they had chosen to go to was a coastal hide-way called Windy Harbour, which was the other side of Northcliffe. Most Pemberton residents used this quaint little beach as their holiday destination. Some even owned small cottages, and it was in one of these that the Evans family stayed for the week. Bill had seen a notice in the shop window advertising this cottage for rent.

They had a great time at Windy Harbour, all of the kids except Little Lorraine managed to catch some fish, and Bill was offered a fishing trip on a boat. He caught several big fish, so the family ate well.

The fuel pump in the Dodge car stopped working on the way back home, so Bill improvised by fixing a gallon tin of petrol above the carburettor with the idea being that the fuel should gravity feed the motor through a small piece of hose. The trouble was, more fuel than the motor could use left the tin. So some petrol would spill onto the hot motor and catch on fire. Bill would have to quickly stop the car and everyone had to jump out while he threw sand over the flames. Once the fire was put out, off they would go again and all was well until the same thing happened again. This routine happened about every ten mile, so it was a slow trip home. Then to make things worse, Bert got car sick and they had to stop several times while he heaved his heart up.

The job at the boiler room meant that Bill had to work shift work and sometimes the boys would be allowed to go to work at night with him. This was only allowed on weekends or holidays. They could sleep there on top of the boilers where it was nice and warm, but to get up there you needed to climb a steep ladder. The family dog, a little brown Kelpie named Sandy, would always follow the boys, but she would howl at the bottom.

Then one night Sandy must have worked out how to climb this ladder, and after a few tries up she went, and after that she could climb up and down at will. It was a funny sight to behold, and other workers would come and watch as Sandy would follow the boys up and down the ladder.

Bill sometimes felt like a drink and occasionally after a night shift, he would drop by the single men's quarters where he knew some of the Italians would sell him home made wine. One morning as Bill was leaving this single man's area, a wild looking Italian must have mistaken him for someone else and he called out for Bill to stop. 'You not pay me for wine from last time Mister,' he said.

Bill knew that he always paid cash for his wine and he had never seen this man before, so he told him that he must be mistaken. The irate fellow then pulled a knife and slashed Bill across the chest. Seeing what happened, the usual Italian that Bill dealt with, rushed over and stopped the knife wielding man. Bill had to get twenty seven stitches in his chest and was off work for a week. The Police were called when Bill was taken to the hospital, but he told them he had slipped and cut himself on a piece of metal.

After he returned to work, Bill never went near that area again, but he was stopped by a group of Italians that he knew, and they apologized for their countryman's action and thanked him for not telling the Police. 'Don't worry,' one of them said, 'we have punished this man.' Bill never did see the punished man again.

The mill gave Bill a pay rise and promoted him to head boiler attendant that year. They also painted the mill house that they were living in. The children were doing well at school, and they went again to Windy Harbour for a holiday. Bill took the boys to Salmon Beach while they were there and each of them caught at least one Salmon. On the rocks at this holiday place, were thousands of little shell like creatures called periwinkles. When boiled they were delicious, but they had to be hooked out of their shells, usually with a safety pin.

Then one day Bill had a bad accident at work. A pressure release valve got stuck, and try as they did, nobody could make this valve open. The mill manager was called and he was about to evacuate the area, because without releasing pressure, the boiler would surely blow up. If this happened it would be like a bomb going off, and many lives would be at risk. 'What do you reckon Bill,' the manager asked.

Bill was the head boiler attendant and he knew that to risk releasing the valve with a spanner was dangerous, because the whole valve could blow to pieces. The time for thinking was over, because the pressure inside the boiler was that high that the needle was not only showing dangerous, but was past the last mark on the gauge. 'Everybody out now,' ordered Bill. 'Sorry boss, but that means you too,' he told the manager.

Picking up a twelve inch crescent spanner, Bill started turning the gauge to hopefully loosen it enough to allow steam to escape, which would reduce the pressure. The difficult part would be not turning it too far or the gauge would be blown out of the boiler altogether.

This is exactly what happened that day. Bill though he had plenty of thread left on the stem of the gauge, so as he reckoned that not enough steam was being let out, he gave the spanner one more turn. The mill manager had not completely left the area, and as he watched from behind a wall, he saw Bill be knocked backwards as the gauge blew out of the boiler. The problem though, was solved as there was plenty of steam now escaping and the danger of the boiler was over. But Bill Evans was not in a good way. He was knocked unconscious as he was blown against a steel girder. The manager ran to help, but as he got close the noise from the escaping steam was so loud he had to plug his ears with rag. He dragged Bill out of harm's way, then organized for him to be taken to the hospital.

Bill recovered well over the next couple of weeks, but his hearing was reduced by about sixty per cent and it was several weeks before he was cleared to return to work. The Doctor filled in a form and with the mill manager's help and support, and Bill received a lump sum payment for his permanent injury. Bill did not know that he was going to receive this money, and was surprised when the pay clerk added an extra two hundred pounds to his pay packet one Friday. Having had to battle for years the money was a welcome surprise.

Learning to read lips helped Bill to overcome his hearing disability and before too long he could carry on a conversation. Bill received a bravery citation from the mill, and the pressure release valves were replaced every six months after that. The only thing that was wrong after this accident, besides his hearing, was that he would sometimes fell a bit lightheaded. Once or twice he thought he was going to pass out. Bill never mentioned this to anyone, thinking that it would go away.

Life was easier and better for them all and both Noel and Keith got new bikes. 'I want a racing bike please,' said Keith. Each first Sunday of the month, the Pemberton Club would hold cycle races, starting and finishing at the top of the big hill. The first Sunday morning that Keith got his new racer, he entered in the race. There were about fifty starters in the event, and this day the course was a straight ten mile towards Manjimup and, after turning at a checkpoint near Moltonie's farm, it was another ten mile race back.

The organizers had, when accepting applications, overlooked the fact that Keith Evans was only twelve years old, so they weren't sure what to do when this lad lined up at the start line with his shiny brand new "Malvern Star" bike.

After a discussion, Keith was given a ten minute start and the race was on. Bill and the rest of the family did a bit of window shopping, and had a drink of tea and cool drink at the shop belonging to Mrs Varnevedies. Then they waited at the finish line to see how Keith had performed in his race.

The family weren't the only ones to get a shock, when Keith came around the corner about a mile from the finish line. They could see a group of about ten senior riders not far behind Keith, so they yelled loudly for him to go faster. The group never did catch that shiny bike that day and Keith was presented with a nice trophy. He was re-handicapped the next time the cycle club met, and although he led the field for much of the race, he found it difficult to win again. This new handicap meant that he had to ride harder and faster each race, so his fitness improved quickly.

Then about six months after Keith had started entering these races, the club championships were held. Keith was still given his five minute start for the open event. He had done extra training and he told his father that he was going to go as fast as he could in this race, especially for a start. Bill told his son that he thought he could beat them. The big day came and as soon as the starter said "go", Keith rode as though he was only going for a mile sprint. 'He can't keep up that pace for twenty mile,' said most of the onlookers.

As they were every time Keith raced, his family were there to cheer him on. When they saw him come around the bend still leading, they and the crowd cheered extra loudly, because only ten yards behind, was the club champion. With twenty yards to go the other rider drew almost level and it looked as though the young Evans boy was going to be beaten. But everyone got a surprise when he stood up on his pedals and gave it everything he had. 'It's a draw,' someone yelled.

The final decision was made by the officials, and Keith was announced as Pemberton's new club champion. 'Well done lad,' said the club President. 'You only won by the width of your tyre.'

Keith's interest was rekindled one Easter weekend, when the Evans family was paid a surprise visit by four cyclists who had ridden all the way from Perth. One of the keen cyclists was John Morris, Peggy's son. Another was the children's uncle Neil. The other two were friends of John and Neil. All four were made welcome, and Beatrice fed them well. Bill cleaned the back shed out, and the weary cyclists slept the night. They stayed until just after lunch the next day, then Neil said that they had to head back because he had to be back in Perth for work in two days. Keith rode with them for about ten mile. He was amazed that the group had ridden so far, and after only a half a day's rest, here they were riding the two hundred or so miles back already. 'Gee you must be fit,' he said to them as they cycled towards Manjimup.

The Evan's boys, like most of the other town children would go to the pictures most Saturdays. The picture hall was up on the hill, behind the main shopping area. Bert would tell his Dad about each picture, or film as some people called them. Samson and Delilah was one of Bert's favourites. Mostly there would be cowboy pictures on a Saturday afternoon and some of the boys would dress in cowboy outfits and get involved in the action of the film.

This started a sort of club of boys that were interested in Cowboys and Indians, and as most boys were keen, it wasn't long before the club had about forty members. They needed a place to meet, so they built a big fort, like the one in the film, "The Yellow Rose of Texas". Each Saturday morning they would get together at this fort, then usually they would play real life Cowboys and Indians. One of the older boys would take the part of the fort commander, mostly pretending he was John Wayne and another older boy would pretend he was Cochise, or Chief Crazy Horse. He was of course the leader of the Indians. It was good fun for these lads, and no harm was done.

That is until one day the boy who was in charge of the Indians, got his warriors to tie pine needles around the ends of their arrows. He then produced a box of matches and lit these arrows. 'Now fire into the fort,' he said.

So the Indians did just that and burnt the fort to the ground. The problem was it was a hot summer's day and this fire spread quickly. Never before have so many boys raced home so fast. The fire was soon out of control and the Forrest Department took two days to put it out. A lot of boys got punishment from both their parents and the School Headmaster, and the fort was never re-built.

These same boys, like most boys anywhere enjoyed watermelon, especially when this delicious fruit was free, as a result of a watermelon raid. This meant that it was pinched or stolen. Usually two or three of the boys would draw the attention of the grower by openly showing themselves at one end of the melon patch. Then whilst the grower was chasing these boys, the rest of the group would sneak in to the other end of the melon patch and grab a big ripe melon each.

This trick worked well until the growers got together and purchased a small bore shotgun. They would remove the lead pellets from the cartridges, and replace them with saltpetre. This saltpetre, when shot into bare skin, would bite into the flesh and sting for days. So not only were any of the boys who were unlucky enough to be shot, sore for days, but they were left with big red marks, usually on their legs. These marks were a giveaway to both the grower, and to the headmaster, and his schoolteachers. Still the boys would pinch watermelons on a regular basis, so eventually the growers decided that it would be easier to just plant some extra melons and let the boys have them. This was a good idea, because as soon as they knew that they no longer could enjoy the experience of pinching the melons, the fun was gone, the boys stopped taking them.

One evening Keith and Bert, whilst on their way to the pictures, noticed that the apples on a tree that was well inside a neighbour's yard, were ripe and ready for the picking. So on the way home they picked some. This was not to be their lucky night though, because the neighbours also had gone to the pictures, and just as the two brothers were sneaking out through the front gate with their stolen apples stuffed inside their shirts, the family arrived home and caught them in the act. Well the boys dropped their bounty, and apples went everywhere as they made a run for home.

The next day Keith said to Bert, 'we'll cop it from the headmaster today.' ''Copping it'', usually meant getting ''the sixers'', which was the cane six times. This was regarded by some of the kids as a very painful experience, but some of the boys reckoned it was a form of bravery to be able to get such a thing. Especially if one could not yell or cry out as the headmaster whacked his bamboo cane either across the back of ones legs, or across the palm of the hand. Mostly the headmaster would give a choice as to where one would prefer to be whacked. Most of the boys took it as a challenge to their manhood to be able to not cry out or move at all while receiving this punishment. 'I'm going to pull my hand away just as he whacks me,' said Keith.

But both Keith and Bert got a surprise that day, because they were not called up to the office. This would usually mean that the father of the family from where the fruit was stolen from, would come around that night and tell the boy's father. So the two brothers were watching for this man to come and tell their father, who would have to punish them. Sure enough, about six o'clock that evening, the man came trudging up to, then into the Evan's yard. The two guilty boys were watching through the front room window as their father went to answer the door. Then came the call they were dreading, 'come here you two,'

To the open front door and onto the veranda the boys shuffled slowly. 'Our nice neighbour has a bucket of apples for us. Take them inside, but first thank the kind man,' said Bill to his surprised sons.

Bert was so surprised that he was lost for words, so it was up to his older brother to somehow stammer out, 'thank you very much Sir.'

The man smiled at the obviously relieved boys and said, 'that's alright boys. These apples were on the ground and would have gone to waste. There must have been a strong wind last night I reckon.'

Then the man told them that if they ever wanted any more apples, then all they had to do was ask. Both Keith and Bert learnt a valuable lesson that day, and hardly ever stole fruit again. They certainly never took any more apples from that friendly neighbour ever again. That night after tea, Bill said to the two apple grabbers, 'now let that be a lesson to the both of you. But just to make sure you have got the message, you both leave your sweets on the table and go to bed now.'

Neither of the two brothers ever knew how their father knew that they were responsible for those apples being on the ground.

Bill and his family received a welcome visitor one afternoon. It was a much older looking, but still a healthy, and happy Charlie Burns that knocked on their door. The two old mates relived old times and had a few beers that day. Bill didn't query Charlie about his times in the war. He remembered how his friend didn't like wars, but did his duty for his country. Charlie couldn't stay too long as he had to meet someone to go catching marron that night. 'Good luck mate. If you get too many, just leave a few in our back wash-trough will you,' Bill said as they shook hands.

The next morning Beatrice got a fright when she went to do the washing. There in the trough were about thirty big marron. Bill laughed when she screamed at him to take them away. They were taken away, but only as far as the cooking pot, and the family had a feast that lunch time. Bert liked to make marron sandwiches with vinegar and pepper tipped over the tasty white flesh. The claws contained a lot of meat, and the kids would break them open with a pair of pliers to get it out.

Entertainment was self-made those days, and one of the things the Evans boys would do is go fishing. There were plenty of trout in the creeks which ran into the Warren River and they would dig for earthworms on the banks to catch these fish. Marron those days were easily caught, and on more than one occasion the bathtub was used to hold big black marron, while others were cooked in the wood heated copper in the wash house out the back.

Alongside this wash house was the outside toilet. The toilet pan was a big galvanised bucket with handles on either side, so the "Dunny Man" could pick it up and cart it away once a week, replacing it with another clean one. To enable this man to be able to get the bucket out of the toilet, there was a hinged door at the rear.

The three Evans boys, for entertainment, one time, and it was only one time, because the hiding that they copped stopped them from ever doing it again, with some left over firecrackers, thought they would have a bit if fun. They waited until their father went to the toilet, and when it was obvious that he was going to be there for a few minutes, they carefully opened the door at the rear of the toilet and placed a "Penny Bomb" cracker just inside the door. They had only managed to run a few yards when the cracker went off with a loud bang. This was followed by an even louder roar from their father. Bill could not catch his sons that day, so he waited until after tea, when he gave each son six welts across the backside with his belt.

Most boys had a "Ging", which was forked stick with rubber strips attached on either side, and a leather pouch joined to these rubbers. Usually a stone was placed into this pouch, then the operator would pull back to stretch these bands, then let go. The rock was shot forward with quite a bit of force. The usual target was a fruit robbing parrot, or a little green-eye bird that also used to spoil a lot of fruit. But some of the boys, around cracker time, would load a lighted penny bomb cracker into the pouch, and shoot it into the air. Most times this was a harmless game, as the cracker would almost always go off fairly high up, and not cause any problem. This practise was put to an end though, after a youngster got injured, when the fired cracker exploded near his face.

There were still several of these "Penny Bombs" left over at the Evans household and the boys didn't know what to do with them. Their little problem was soon solved for them though. Behind the row of mill houses there was a lane. This lane was used by the "Dunny Pan Collector". He would go from house to house to grab these Pans and heave them, one at a time onto his shoulder and carry them back to his old truck.

Well the house next door to the Evan's, had a boy living there who used to have fits. Whenever any of the other boys would see him having a fit, they used to run to this boy's house and tell his mother. She would come running to help her son through these epileptic fits and to stop him from swallowing his tongue. Then she would thank them and take her son home and they wouldn't see him for the rest of the day. This unfortunate lad couldn't go to school for fear of having an attack or fit, so his mother used to educate him at home. He would be so happy when the other kids came home from school and he could go out and play with them.

The man who collected the "Dunny Cans", used to laugh and tease this young boy. This poor young lad was popular with the Evans boys, and used to play with them.

So when the collector pulled his truck up at the house next door and they heard him tease this boy, whose name was Frankie, they all got the same idea at the same time.

They knew that they had a few minutes before their pan was going to be picked up, so they tied six of these crackers together. Then they lengthened the wick so it would take about a half a minute to burn down and explode these crackers. Then they placed this bundle of penny bombs in the can that the collector was about to pick up. When the man was close one of the boys lit the fuse, then hid behind the shed with the other boys. Frankie watched as his tormentor got his own back that day. As he was walking back to his truck with the Evan's pan on his shoulder, the firecrackers exploded, and a lot of the contents of the "Dunny Can" were splashed all over the poor chap. There was not a boy in sight, but that night there was a visitor to the Evan's house.

It was the "Dunny Man" and it was lucky that the boys had told their father what they had done and why, because this man wanted to have a piece of Bill's sons. Bill was in no mood for nonsense, so when the chap tried to kick his sons, there was only one thing to do. Young Frankie was never teased after that, and the black eye that the "Dunny Man" received, didn't take too long to heal up.

The reason that the boys had these firecrackers was because those days, each November the fifth was Guy Fowlkes night, and everyone would buy a box of crackers and attend a bonfire which was held near the sports oval. This bonfire was a huge pile of old timber and branches which was lit just before it got dark. At the centre and on top of this huge bonfire was a scarecrow type of effigy, made out of old clothes and stuffed with old rags or hay. It was tied to a pole and everyone would watch as it would catch fire and burn. Then to everyone's delight the firecrackers were let off.

There were many different types of these firecrackers, including Catherine Wheels, which needed to be pinned to a post. When lit they would spin around and light up in many colours. There were Tom Thumbs, which some people called Jumping Jacks, because when lit and thrown onto the ground, they would jump all over the place. Sky Rockets were a favourite of most people. These had to be put into a bottle with the cracker part pointed up, and when lit would shoot about fifty yards into the sky, then explode, throwing coloured sparks all over the sky

Most families would take sausages and grill them in the hot coals as the fire burnt down. Potatoes would also be cooked in their jackets this way, and this all made for a good family and community outing. Probably all the town would turn up at this spectacular annual event, which was always held on November the Fifth.

Bill took his sons to a fire lookout tree one time, and after much deliberation, they all climbed to the top. The Evans boys, and most of the other town boys would often ride their bikes the two miles to this tree, which was named "The Gloucester Tree". Many would become so good at climbing up the steel pegs that they could almost run up it. There was a wooden cabin at the tree top, which was used by a fire officer to spot bushfires. The Evans boys and their friends would sometimes take lunch up to this cabin, and if the fire officer was there he would tell them stories about his job, especially the bushfires he had fought. On one occasion a big fire was spotted while Keith and Bert were sharing lunch with the fire officer, and they listened as he radioed his forestry headquarters to report it. Bert read the sign at the bottom of the tree, which said that this Gloucester Tree was one of eight fire lookout trees in the district. It was approximately two hundred and twenty feet tall, and was the second tallest fire lookout tree in the world. Bert wrote down all the information, and this later helped when the school class did a project on this tree. Bert received his first and only "A" mark from the teacher for his project, which he titled, "I climbed this tree".

During the hot summer months, most of the youngsters around Pemberton would spend a fair bit of time at the town swimming pool. It was at this pool that most of them learnt to swim. There was a fenced off area where the water was only about three feet deep, so this was classed as the learners pool. Bert was doing his best to learn, and it wasn't too long before he progressed from splashing along, doing "dog paddle", to doing the more conventional overarm. He was still swimming in the learner's pool one day, when a couple of the bigger boys yelled out that he was a "sook" for still swimming in the small pool.

Bert watched as these bigger boys started climbing the high tower in the deep water area. This tower was about forty feet high, and only the brave kids climbed it, then jumped off into the pool below. Still smarting for being teased about swimming in the small pool, Bert followed these bigger boys up the tower. When he got to the top though, he looked down and nearly died with fright. It looked a mighty long way down to this ten year old, so he reckoned that he would turn around and go back down again. But there were several other big boys coming up, so he had to stay on the small landing. The trouble was that there wasn't enough room for everyone to stay on the landing, and each boy was expected to jump when it was his turn. Bert was now at the front of the line, on the edge of the landing, and had nowhere to go but down. So he closed his eyes and jumped. It seemed like an eternity as he went hurtling the forty feet down to the water, so he opened his eyes just as he hit the pool. Never before had he been under water for so long, and when he finally struggled his way to the surface, he could hear all the big boys up on the tower cheering him. That night Bert had a story to tell his dad, but when he finished saying how he had jumped, his father said that there was a sign at the bottom saying that no child under the age of fourteen was allowed to climb the tower. 'I am proud of you for being brave Bert, but I don't think you better do it again boy,' said Bill.

Also at this swimming pool was a narrow railway line, which was supplied with a trolley. This was on the far side of the pool, and down a steep hill. The bigger boys would ride this trolley down the line and by the time it hit the water it was going fast enough to skim across the top of the water and sometimes nearly make the other side of the pool. The same bigger boys that cheered Bert for jumping off the tower, dared him to ride the trolley. So up the hill went young Bert, with about a dozen big boys. They told him that no one had yet made the other side, but as he was small and quite light he might just make it. They sat him in the trolley, then several of them gave a hefty push, and off went Bert, hanging on for his life. Well the trolley hit the water flat out from this big push, but the trouble was Bert wasn't told to lean back a bit as the trolley hit the water. This would raise the front of the trolley momentarily, then away it would skim across the pool. But because Bert didn't raise the front, the trolley did a nose dive, at top speed, into the water, and down went the trolley with young Bert still hanging on.

It was a full two minutes before the big boys brought Bert to the surface, and it looked as if he may have drowned. Then one of the boys tipped him upside down and out came a pile of water. Then to everyone's surprise, Bert Evans opened his eyes and said, 'wow. Can we do that again?'

Football was a special outing for most of the townsfolk and most Sunday afternoons, Bill would take the family and watch the Pemberton side play against the other nearby towns. One afternoon as they were sitting on the grass watching a close game against Manjimup, the football was inadvertently kicked right where the Evans family were sitting. The ball bounced off a seat then hit Lorraine on the head. She was dazed, but not badly injured.

After the game, a few of the senior players came over to see if she was alright. One of the players introduced himself as Tom Hawkes, and another was Tom Davis. Bill shook hands with these tall men, then he said to Tom Hawkes, 'I think I met your father once, was as he a boxer?'

Bill was answered by this man who had a football in his hands. 'Yes Bill, my Dad Bob, was the Western Australian Heavyweight Champion.' With that he handed the football to Bill and said, 'here you go. We hope your sons can get some fun out of kicking it around.'

The boys did get plenty of fun out of the football, and many of their friends would often join them at the oval after school and on weekends. The two footballers that had taken the time to talk to the Evans family and to give the boys their first football, both finished up playing league football in Perth, as they were very good players.

They organized for The Perth Football Club to come to Pemberton to play a social game against a combined district side. Most of the town turned out to watch this game and were treated to some good football. Tom Davis and Tom Hawkes played for the district side, and they helped make it a close game. Tom Davis kicked four goals and his friend Tom Hawkes played well in the ruck. This game created a lot of interest, and encouraged many boys to play football. After the game the visiting club donated a set of jumpers to the local team, and donated six footballs to the schools in the district.

Another bit of fun was had by riding their bikes to different places on weekends. It was on one of these adventures that Bert and his friend, a Polish boy named Joseph stopped at what they thought was an unlived in old farmhouse. They were surprised when a very old man came out and spoke to them and told them that they could play on his farm. He told them if they could catch his horse they could ride it round. The two boys had no trouble catching this tame old horse and each weekend for ages they would ride it bareback. The old man said that if he died then the horse was theirs to keep.

Well the poor old hermit did die a few months later, so Bert and Joseph went out and brought the horse back to a yard they built behind Joseph's parent's place which was up behind the timber mill.

All went well for several weeks, but then one day after school, when the two lads went to go for a ride, the horse went missing. They looked everywhere for their horse and finally they found it in the yards of the butchers slaughter house. 'They are going to kill our horse,' said Joseph.

The two boys rode their bikes to the Police Station and told the Constable what had happened. It was lucky that this Constable had seen them riding the horse and believed them when they told him that the old man had given them the animal. The butcher was not happy, but on the orders of the Policeman, he let the horse go back to Joseph and Bert. The two friends rode this horse for a long time after that.

Bert's friendship towards Joseph was tested one time when two older and much bigger boys started teasing Joseph, saying that he was Polish and that it was his fault that Australia had to go to war. When they started pushing his friend, Bert said, 'leave him alone, he hasn't done you any harm.'

The bigger of the two bullies said, 'what will do to stop us then little boy?'

Then he moved to push Bert in the chest, but as quick as a flash Bert punched him on the nose. After wiping the blood from his nose, he said, 'why you little rat,' and he rushed at Bert.

Then both of the bigger boys hammered into first Bert, then Joseph. By the time they had finished, the two young friends both had blood noses and cuts over their faces. Both Bert and Joseph were twelve years old, but the other boys were about three years older, so the two friends had little hope.

When Bill got home from work and seen Bert, he asked him what had happened. 'I fell over,' said Bert. Bill looked at his son and said, 'well you better watch where you walking lad. If you need me to help sort out the place where you tripped, then let me know.'

The two bullies were known as such by most of the school, and the next day at playtime, most of the school children watched as they were taken to task by several of the decent bigger boys. Bert and Joseph were never teased again by these two bullies, who both had black eyes for several days. Allan's big brother told Bert to tell him if they had any more trouble with them. Allan's brother was the School Prefect and he did his job well.

Bert got rheumatic fever that year and missed a few months of school, as he was hospitalised for a period of time. When he did recover, the he was not allowed to play sport for several months. Whilst he was in the Pemberton hospital, he was visited by one of his uncles, who was also an inpatient. This uncle had been infected with the mumps, and should have realized that he should not have visited any other patients, because of the high risk of passing on the highly infectious disease. Fortunately the hospital Matron was doing the rounds, and saw Bert's uncle just as he was entering the ward. The Matron told him in no uncertain way to go back to his ward and stay there. 'You could have infected this boy who already has a serious disease,' she said.

Luckily for Bert, even though he had missed a lot of schooling that year, he still passed at the end of the year. Bert later found out that it was Mrs Bunn that had convinced the headmaster that he should not be kept down.

A lot of the kids were comic readers and would take a few comics and swap them outside the picture hall. Bert made the mistake of swapping his numbers one, two and three Superman Comics. 'I don't think you should have let them go,' said his father. 'They will be worth good money one day,' he said.

The next week Bert tried to swap back, but the other boy would not do it. At the time Bill's Mother, or Granny, as the kids called her, was staying with them for a few weeks. Granny was very popular with all the children, and any uneasy feelings that may have been between her and Beatrice, was no longer there. Both of them could be talking and laughing away the hours, especially around meal preparation times. 'You are so lucky to have electric fridges and things,' Granny often told Beatrice.

This would usually start Granny off telling all of them how hard things used to be. She would growl at the kids if they asked for an ice cream, or lollies, 'don't waste money on these things,' she would say.

Then she would tell them about the days of no fridges or electric lights. Usually one of the children would ask her to tell them a story about life in England. On more than one occasion Granny told them about the hard times when the great first world war was being fought. 'Food was hard to buy, because mostly the Army would get the supplies, and what was left was rationed out to the people. Clothing was hard to get for the same reason,' she would tell them.

One time Margaret asked Granny if she had worked in England. 'Oh yes,' said Granny as she sipped her cup of tea. 'I most certainly had to work my dear. I left school when I was thirteen to start work as a kitchen hand in the house of a Lord and Lady, who were rich landowners. Eight servants they employed. My first job was to collect, and wash up all the dishes, as well as help the cook prepare the meals.'

Granny was reliving her old days now, and Lorraine came and sat down to listen as well. 'Then after a year or so I was transferred to the cleaning duties and had to make beds and wash clothes for hours on end. No electric irons those days,' she continued on. 'We had to heat up heavy metal irons on the stove top, and woe be tied if the Mistress found any crinkles in any of your ironing. Sunday was the only day off that was allowed, and sometimes if somebody was sick, I would have to take their place on my Sunday off. Work did you ask me child? To get a shilling a week was all I could expect. I did eat well though, because the cook was a lovely woman, who used to let me into the kitchen at all hours.' Granny could talk for hours, and the girls loved to hear the tales she would tell them.

Bert asked her one day if the Lord and Lady treated them well and looked after them. Granny soon let him know the hard truths of those days when the rich aristocrats ruled the roost. 'Look after us you ask me Bert? The only people they ever thought of was themselves. The servants were looked down upon and were treated like part of the furniture,' she said. 'No,' said Granny, 'I wouldn't swap this country or its people for all the tea in China. Oh that reminds me Bert. Could you make your old Granny a nice cup of tea?'

Then while she was drinking her tea, one of the children would prompt her to start another story. Granny told them how their father when he was about ten years old, would stand by the farm gate when the rich people went fox hunting. 'As these hunters, who were of course on horseback and all dressed up if fine red riding uniforms came to a gate, your Dad would open it, hoping to get a tip for doing so,' she said.

Bert said 'Did he get a tip Granny?'

Granny told him 'sometimes one of these aristocrats would throw a farthing, or a halfpenny in the mud for the boys to fight over,' she said.

One of the sayings that Granny became famous for was, "look after the pennies my child and the pounds will look after themselves." The children would sometimes ask her to tell them this saying, because each time that Granny quoted it she would give each child a penny. Bill would smile, but afterwards would tell them not to annoy their Grandmother too often. Mostly the boys would save their pennies and when they had threepence, they would ride their bikes to the corner shop and buy a chocolate coated ice cream in a cone. Granny would just smile, knowing that the boys would not save their pennies, but she noticed that the girls were never eating an ice cream. 'Now Margaret and Lorraine, come here and tell your old Granny why you never buy an ice cream like your brothers,' she asked.

Both girls said the same thing, 'we're saving our pennies so they'll turn into pounds.'

It was always a sad day when Granny had to go back to Perth. The whole Evans family would take her to the station to wave her off. Bill knew that his sister Peggy would look after their mother. As he gave her a kiss goodbye, Bill would hand his mother an envelope, which had a few pounds in it. The children would still be waving to Granny's train as it was going further out of sight, and she would wave her handkerchief out of the train window.

After Granny had gone, the children would be off, either kicking the footy, shooting the "ging", or swimming or fishing. They would always ride their bikes to get to wherever they wanted to go, except on picture night, when they, like all the other kids would walk up the hill to the old tin shed. All these things helped pass the time for not only the Evans family, but for all the kids of those days. Mostly all the fun was harmless, and all the kids were friends, and played happily together. This went on for several years, and Granny would visit at least once a year. Then on her last visit she said to Bill, 'I'm not one to molly coddle, or try to tell you how to look after yourself son, but you don't look too well. Maybe you should go for a check-up.'

Bill told her that he was alright, and she shouldn't worry about him. So he didn't go to the Doctors, as his worried mother wanted him to.

Bert would still pester his father to spar most days, still with tea towels wrapped around their hands. Then finally Bill purchased a set of much wanted boxing gloves. The Police and Citizens Youth Club had advertised that they were having a clearance sale, so Bill took Bert along and as there were no other bidders for a set of quite good lightweight gloves, they were happy to let them go for four shillings.

While father and son were in the hall, Bert noticed the boxing ring in one corner. Without thinking, he followed an urge to go closer to this rope ring. Next thing Bill watched as his son climbed into the ring and started shadow boxing.

As Bill stood and looked, he heard a voice he knew, 'I should've known you'd be here Bill Evans.'

Even before he turned to look, Bill knew that the voice belonged to his old friend Charlie Burns. The two shook hands in the special way that Charlie had taught Bill to do all those years ago in Northcliffe. Bill said, 'how come you didn't know I was here earlier, like you would have all those years ago?'

Charlie told him that the years of hard work taken a lot out of him and he was not the same man he used to be when he met Bill on their farm in nineteen twenty four. 'Might be a good time to go a few rounds with you then mate,' said Bill.

Then as quick as a flash Charlie said, 'I often wondered who would win if we did have a serious bout Bill.'

All was quiet, then Bill said, 'I reckon you are the best I've boxed against, even though we were only training.'

Charlie smiled and said, 'even as good as that world champ mate?'

Bill was going to say more, but a voice from behind his friend stopped him, 'Mr Burns, don't forget you promised me a training session today sir.'

Charlie had to drag a young boy, of about Bert's age from behind him. 'This is a youngster I've been training to box. Les come and meet Mr Evans.'

The young boy nodded and put out his left hand. Bill shook his hand and felt strength there. 'I'm very pleased to meet you Mr Evans. Mr Burns has told me all about you. Did you really knock out the World Champ?' said the now at ease youngster.

Bill didn't get the chance to explain that he had fought the former champion when he was forty two years old, and past his prime. Charlie had quickly cut him short by saying, 'I knick-named this lad after the great Les Darcy, and he is already boxing like him.'

Then Bill said, 'except this Les is a southpaw.'

With a laugh Charlie said, 'so you noticed that did you Bill. Looks like I might have taught my friend something at least.'

A serious tone came into Bill's voice now, 'yes my friend, my best friend, you did teach me a lot and I thank you for that and your friendship. Now come and meet my Son.'

With a glance towards the boxing ring, Charlie said, 'you mean that boy punching the hell out of the air is your son?'

The two old friends laughed out loud, and then Bill called his Son to come out of the ring. 'Bert this is the man named Charlie, you know, my friend I told you about,' he said. Bert shook hands with his Dad's friend, remembering to use all his strength in the handshake.

Charlie told Bert that he was pleased to meet him, then said, 'now Bert, tell me what your Dad has told you about me.'

Without having to think, Bert said, 'Dad talks about you all the time Mr Burns. He told me how you helped him do fencing on his first farm, and he said you know when things are going to happen before they do. Also he told me that you might be the only boxer who he may not be able to beat. Did you really beat twenty three men in one night Sir?'

Tears appeared in the now past middle aged Charlie Burns. 'Let me tell you something Bert,' Charlie said. 'If all the men in this country were as hard a worker as your father and treated others as equals, like he has done, then our country would be better. Oh, one more thing young man. Don't ever tell your father, but he would have beaten me if we had ever met in a ring. Now Bert shake hands with a good young boxer that is keen to learn.'

The two old friends looked on proudly as the boys, one black and one white, seemed to become friends immediately. They wandered around the P.C.Y.C. hall for a while, then finished up back at the boxing ring. 'Dad could I please have my new gloves for a while?' Bert asked.

Both Bill and Charlie helped the youngsters put on these boxing gloves, then they went and sat down to watch. This was Bert's first ever spar with anyone except his father, and the first time he had ever worn proper gloves.

He and his father had always wrapped old rags around their hands and it felt good to have real boxing gloves on thought Bert. There was something about boxing that he couldn't understand. Whenever he would spar with his Dad, or think about it, he would get a strange feeling. Like when he had seen the boxing ring a little while ago and he just had to climb inside it. He remembered having this feeling when he saw a boxing film at the tin shed on the hill recently. He had looked at the poster every day for a week before he watched it. Each night before and again after, he could see the poster in his mind. The film was called "Iron Man" starring Jeff Chandler, who played the part of a champion boxer named Coke Mason. Bert would feel that he was this boxer as he watched him take on all comers, including Kirk Douglas who played the part of a bad boy boxer named Mider.

Bert was still daydreaming as he stood outside the ring, but as soon as he climbed in, then held the ropes up for his new friend to get in, he came wide awake and the feeling came over him.

Young Darcy had been doing boxing lessons for a few years now. His instructor at the Manjimup P.C.Y.C. was Charlie Burns, who had seen something special in this young boxer, so he had gone out of his way to train him as best as he could. Young Darcy, as Charlie had called him, shaped up quickly and started sparring. A trained boxer could hold back his punches when just sparring, like these two young boys were doing, so it was not a serious bout as such. They sparred for several minutes, then shook hands. 'You're pretty good Bert,' said Darcy.

Bert thanked him and said, 'so are you mate.'

Bill and Charlie were talking about old times, and pretended they hadn't been watching the two boys, so when they reported back to have their gloves removed,

Charlie winked at Bill as he said, 'what have you finished already? We didn't even know you had started.'

Both men didn't want the boys to think that they had to box, or be pressured into thinking that they were expected to do so. That is why Bill and Charlie pretended they weren't even watching the two lads while they were in the ring.

With their gloves off the two boys went off again to play, and the two now almost elderly men kept on talking. 'Where are you working?' was one of the questions they asked each other. Bill told Charlie all about the failed farm venture, then how he was now, like most men in Pemberton, working at the mill. Charlie told Bill how he had started working at the Railway in Manjimup, and had done a lot of fencing around the district. 'I brought young Darcy to this sale to get some equipment for our P.C.Y.C. centre at Manjimup.'

Then Charlie told his friend something that he usually didn't tell others, 'I can only just remember this Bill. Mr Brockman was visiting where I was living up in the Kimberley, and he found out that I was an orphan, so he adopted me.' Charlie was thinking back now. 'I only wish my adopters were as ready to accept us dark skinned people as you are Bill. I don't think they thought I was good enough for their lifestyle.'

Time seemed to fly for these two mates and it wasn't until the two boys came back and told them that they were hungry, that sadly, they realised the day was over. 'Been good seeing you Bill,' said Charlie.

Bill had a thought, 'why don't you and Darcy come around home for lunch Charlie,' he said.

Beatrice was a good host and she soon had a meal for them all. Charlie stayed for a while, then said that he had better get young "Darcy" home. 'His parents are my cousins, but they are pretty strict, and we said we would only be a few hours.'

Then just before he left, Charlie said something to Bill that he didn't understand, and then like many times before, when the two friends had been together, he was gone.

After they had left, Bert asked his Father why Mr Burns called the young boy that he was training to box, "Darcy"? Bill then told his son the story of the famous Les Darcy, who was the Australian champion boxer who had gone to America, but got sick and died. 'He was probably the best boxer ever produced in Australia,' Bill said.

The day had been a good one for Bill. He had seen his old friend again, and his youngest son had become friends with a lad who had similar interests. A lot of other people might not have made friends so easily with an Aboriginal, but Bill was proud that his son did not have any stupid racial feelings. These thoughts were making Bill feel a bit nostalgic and weary, so when his children asked him to play a board game with them, he said that he might give it a miss, 'but I'll play a bit later.'

Then what Charlie had said to him came back into his mind. 'Where you are soon to go my friend, we all must go. I will see you there and I will think of you until we meet again.'

Bill still didn't understand what his old friend had meant. He was for some reason feeling too tired to try to work it all out. His wife noticed this and asked him if he was alright, and he just nodded to her. Beatrice made him a cup of tea and told him to go and read the paper. Bill patted his kids on the head as he walked past them. They were all playing monopoly and he was glad that they were happy. Then for some unknown reason he turned back and kissed Beatrice then looked again at his children. Bert looked up and smiled at his father, and Bill smiled back at him.

Bill sat in his lounge chair, supposedly to read his newspaper, but his mind would not relax. Thoughts of past years kept coming back to him. Memories of coming to this country, and all the things that had happened since, seemed to be cluttering up his head.

It was only early afternoon and he never had a nap or rested at this time of the day. Then he saw visions of his father and mother, then these would be taken over by images of other things that had happened in his life. Memories seemed to get mixed up with the present, and he wasn't sure if he was awake or dreaming.

Bill knew something was wrong when his son Bert was standing in front of him shouting, but he couldn't hear him. Then he could see two of Bert, or was it all the kids? What did Beatrice mean? She told me to rest, now she's yelling for me to wake up. Then slowly things started to go blurry.

Bill could feel his son shaking him, and faintly, ever so faintly, he heard a distant voice say, 'are you feeling sick Dad?'

Then somehow Bill Evans could see nothing, but heard his own voice whisper back, 'just a little, son. Just a litt..'

Song Reference

Page 13. Waltzing Matilda, a bush ballad by Banjo Patterson.
Page 30. Keep The Home Fires Burning. John McCormack, 1914.
Page 30. I'll take you Home Kathleen.
Written by Thomas P Westerndorf 1875.
Page 30. You Are My Sunshine. Jimmie Davis and Charles Mucher.
Page 103. Ave Maria. Franz Schubert.
Page 173. Danny Boy.
Written by the English Songster, Frederic Weathery.
Page 190. Amazing Grace. Author John Newton.
Page 191. Mother McCree. By John McDermott

Epilogue

THE town chosen by the organizers of the "Land Settlement Scheme", Northcliffe, is now a quaint little town, and many of the descendants of the early pioneers still live there. There are a few of the old settlers who were children when they arrived in nineteen twenty four and afterwards, still living, so the spirit of the early settles still lives on in this town.

An example of this was proven, when the recent bushfires threatened to destroy the town. Many of these townsfolk refused to leave their houses, even when the flames were visible. One couple who were children when they arrived in nineteen twenty five, Mr and Mrs Kevin Flanagan, got ready to protect their home and were prepared for the worst. Some of the residents who stayed were told that the fire would be impossible to stop unless the wind changed. But it was forecast to continue blowing the fire towards the town. Still the stalwarts, including the storekeeper refused to leave. Kevin Flanagan said, 'the wind changed as if it was meant to be, and the bushfire turned away from us at the last moment and headed towards Windy Harbour.'

Almost all the information about the early settlers can be found in Northcliffe's wonderful Pioneer Museum, which is situated in the middle of town. Many visitors come to Northcliffe for the reason of looking up the history of the early settlers. There are old school photographs and details available for these tourists and relatives of the early settlers, who come not only from Australia, but from England, Scotland and Ireland.

The road to Windy Harbour is now fully sealed and has a nice caravan park, which is kept busy by tourists and fisher people alike. Salmon Beach, near Windy Harbour is a Mecca for Salmon fishers and around Easter time, the beach is usually full of keen anglers.

Pemberton and Manjimup are still thriving towns, and many descendants of these settlers have made these towns their homes. The old tin shed used to show films in, is still standing in Pemberton today. If this shed could talk, it would tell of the countless times that the townsfolk sat and enjoyed an evening of film watching. Perhaps if one was to listen closely, it may be possible to hear the echoes from long ago. Echoes of children like, the Bradbury boys, and Ruth and Anne, and Margaret Thomson, clapping and cheering the cartoons and the funny films like Jerry Lewis, and Ma and Pa Kettle. Then this old tin shed might echo the screams of frightened people that watched some of the scary films like "Physcho", or "The Hunchback of Notre Dame". One might hear also the echoes of Willie and Tommy Love, howling out loud like a dingo, whenever a spooky film was shown.

The stones that somehow fell through walls and rooves, is a well-documented fact, and books have been written about this strange paranormal happening. The Australian Broadcasting Commission did a television documentary entirely about these stones and is well worth watching. In this documentary, several Indigenous Australians gave in depth interviews about these paranormal happenings, and their factual recollections are from having seen them.

> *"We came to this land with great expectations*
> *With hopes of a new and better life out here*
> *But the hardships far exceeded our invitations*
> *We didn't all give in, but most came very near*
> *Still the memories of those days are very dear"*

A poem written by Granny in 1955.

Other Titles by Bert O'Flannagan

The Spirit of Ned

If in my writing of this book my words appear to be telling the life of Ned Kelly in a different way to other books, or if some may believe that some of what my pen has been guided to write, may not be the actual facts, then I cannot apologise. I can only say that how do we or anyone write anything with the knowledge that what they write are the actual happenings? Remembering that the supposed actual facts were first written by somebody, then in our minds it will always come back to what we believe or is believable.

The Indigenous Australians have the ability to through their minds, pass on history and folklore from generation to generation. The human mind is a marvellous piece of machinery.

I ask you to open your mind and take in these writings that I somehow have been guided to scribble out. I named this book as such, because each time I picked up a pen my arm was in fact directed what to write, and I found it almost impossible to stop.